TABLE OF CONTENTS

Secret Key #1 – Time is Your Greatest Enemy

To succeed on the GACE, you must use your time wisely. Many students do not finish at least one section. The time constraints are brutal. To succeed, you must ration your time properly.

Pace Yourself

Wear a watch. At the beginning of the test, check the time (or start a chronometer on your watch to count the minutes), and check the time after every few questions to make sure you are "on schedule."

If you are forced to speed up, do it efficiently. Usually one or more answer choices can be eliminated without too much difficulty. Above all, don't panic. Don't speed up and just begin guessing at random choices. By pacing yourself, and continually monitoring your progress against your watch, you will always know exactly how far ahead or behind you are with your available time. If you find that you are one minute behind on the test, don't skip one question without spending any time on it, just to catch back up. Take 15 fewer seconds on the next four questions, and after four questions you'll have caught back up. Once you catch back up, you can continue working each problem at your normal pace.

Furthermore, don't dwell on the problems that you were rushed on. If a problem was taking up too much time and you made a hurried guess, it must be difficult. The difficult questions are the ones you are most likely to miss anyway, so it isn't a big loss. It is better to end with more time than you need than to run out of time.

Lastly, sometimes it is beneficial to slow down if you are constantly getting ahead of time. You are always more likely to catch a careless mistake by working more slowly than quickly, and among very high-scoring test takers (those who are likely to have lots of time left over), careless errors affect the score more than mastery of material.

Secret Key #2 - Guessing is not Guesswork

You probably know that guessing is a good idea - unlike other standardized tests, there is no penalty for getting a wrong answer. Even if you have no idea about a question, you still have a 20-25% chance of getting it right.

Most test takers do not understand the impact that proper guessing can have on their score. Unless you score extremely high, guessing will significantly contribute to your final score.

Monkeys Take the Test

What most test takers don't realize is that to insure that 20-25% chance, you have to guess randomly. If you put 20 monkeys in a room to take this test, assuming they answered once per question and behaved themselves, on average they would get 20-25% of the questions correct. Put 20 test takers in the room, and the average will be much lower among guessed questions. Why?

1. The test writers intentionally writes deceptive answer choices that "look" right. A test taker has no idea about a question, so picks the "best looking" answer, which is often wrong. The monkey has no idea what looks good and what doesn't, so will consistently be lucky about 20-25% of the time.
2. Test takers will eliminate answer choices from the guessing pool based on a hunch or intuition. Simple but correct answers often get excluded, leaving a 0% chance of being correct.

The monkey has no clue, and often gets lucky with the best choice.

This is why the process of elimination endorsed by most test courses is flawed and detrimental to your performance- test takers don't guess, they make an ignorant stab in the dark that is usually worse than random.

$5 Challenge

Let me introduce one of the most valuable ideas of this course- the $5 challenge:

You only mark your "best guess" if you are willing to bet $5 on it.
You only eliminate choices from guessing if you are willing to bet $5 on it.

Why $5? Five dollars is an amount of money that is small yet not insignificant, and can really add up fast (20 questions could cost you $100). Likewise, each answer choice on one question of the test will have a small impact on your overall score, but it can really add up to a lot of points in the end.

The process of elimination IS valuable. The following shows your chance of guessing it right:

If you eliminate wrong answer choices until only this many answer choices remain:	Chance of getting it correct:
1	100%
2	50%
3	33%

However, if you accidentally eliminate the right answer or go on a hunch for an incorrect answer, your chances drop dramatically: to 0%. By guessing among all the answer choices, you are GUARANTEED to have a shot at the right answer.

That's why the $5 test is so valuable- if you give up the advantage and safety of a pure guess, it had better be worth the risk.

What we still haven't covered is how to be sure that whatever guess you make is truly random. Here's the easiest way:

Always pick the first answer choice among those remaining.

Such a technique means that you have decided, before you see a single test question, exactly how you are going to guess- and since the order of choices tells you nothing about which one is correct, this guessing technique is perfectly random.

This section is not meant to scare you away from making educated guesses or eliminating choices- you just need to define when a choice is worth eliminating. The $5 test, along with a pre-defined random guessing strategy, is the best way to make sure you reap all of the benefits of guessing.

Secret Key #3 - Practice Smarter, Not Harder

Many test takers delay the test preparation process because they dread the awful amounts of practice time they think necessary to succeed on the test. We have refined an effective method that will take you only a fraction of the time.

There are a number of "obstacles" in your way to succeed. Among these are answering questions, finishing in time, and mastering test-taking strategies. All must be executed on the day of the test at peak performance, or your score will suffer. The test is a mental marathon that has a large impact on your future.

Just like a marathon runner, it is important to work your way up to the full challenge. So first you just worry about questions, and then time, and finally strategy:

Success Strategy

1. Find a good source for practice tests.
2. If you are willing to make a larger time investment, consider using more than one study guide- often the different approaches of multiple authors will help you "get" difficult concepts.
3. Take a practice test with no time constraints, with all study helps "open book." Take your time with questions and focus on applying strategies.
4. Take a practice test with time constraints, with all guides "open book."
5. Take a final practice test with no open material and time limits

If you have time to take more practice tests, just repeat step 5. By gradually exposing yourself to the full rigors of the test environment, you will condition your mind to the stress of test day and maximize your success.

Secret Key #4 - Prepare, Don't Procrastinate

Let me state an obvious fact: if you take the test three times, you will get three different scores. This is due to the way you feel on test day, the level of preparedness you have, and, despite the test writers' claims to the contrary, some tests WILL be easier for you than others.

Since your future depends so much on your score, you should maximize your chances of success. In order to maximize the likelihood of success, you've got to prepare in advance. This means taking practice tests and spending time learning the information and test taking strategies you will need to succeed.

Never take the test as a "practice" test, expecting that you can just take it again if you need to. Feel free to take sample tests on your own, but when you go to take the official test, be prepared, be focused, and do your best the first time!

Secret Key #5 - Test Yourself

Everyone knows that time is money. There is no need to spend too much of your time or too little of your time preparing for the test. You should only spend as much of your precious time preparing as is necessary for you to get the score you need.

Once you have taken a practice test under real conditions of time constraints, then you will know if you are ready for the test or not.

If you have scored extremely high the first time that you take the practice test, then there is not much point in spending countless hours studying. You are already there.

Benchmark your abilities by retaking practice tests and seeing how much you have improved. Once you score high enough to guarantee success, then you are ready.

If you have scored well below where you need, then knuckle down and begin studying in earnest. Check your improvement regularly through the use of practice tests under real conditions. Above all, don't worry, panic, or give up. The key is perseverance!

Then, when you go to take the test, remain confident and remember how well you did on the practice tests. If you can score high enough on a practice test, then you can do the same on the real thing.

General Strategies

The most important thing you can do is to ignore your fears and jump into the test immediately- do not be overwhelmed by any strange-sounding terms. You have to jump into the test like jumping into a pool- all at once is the easiest way.

Make Predictions

As you read and understand the question, try to guess what the answer will be. Remember that several of the answer choices are wrong, and once you begin reading them, your mind will immediately become cluttered with answer choices designed to throw you off. Your mind is typically the most focused immediately after you have read the question and digested its contents. If you can, try to predict what the correct answer will be. You may be surprised at what you can predict.

Quickly scan the choices and see if your prediction is in the listed answer choices. If it is, then you can be quite confident that you have the right answer. It still won't hurt to check the other answer choices, but most of the time, you've got it!

Answer the Question

It may seem obvious to only pick answer choices that answer the question, but the test writers can create some excellent answer choices that are wrong. Don't pick an answer just because it sounds right, or you believe it to be true. It MUST answer the question. Once you've made your selection, always go back and check it against the question and make sure that you didn't misread the question, and the answer choice does answer the question posed.

Benchmark

After you read the first answer choice, decide if you think it sounds correct or not. If it doesn't, move on to the next answer choice. If it does, mentally mark that answer choice.

This doesn't mean that you've definitely selected it as your answer choice, it just means that it's the best you've seen thus far. Go ahead and read the next choice. If the next choice is worse than the one you've already selected, keep going to the next answer choice. If the next choice is better than the choice you've already selected, mentally mark the new answer choice as your best guess.

The first answer choice that you select becomes your standard. Every other answer choice must be benchmarked against that standard. That choice is correct until proven otherwise by another answer choice beating it out. Once you've decided that no other answer choice seems as good, do one final check to ensure that your answer choice answers the question posed.

Valid Information

Don't discount any of the information provided in the question. Every piece of information may be necessary to determine the correct answer. None of the information in the question is there to throw you off (while the answer choices will certainly have information to throw you off). If two seemingly unrelated topics are discussed, don't ignore either. You can be confident there is a relationship, or it wouldn't be included in the question, and you are probably going to have to determine what is that relationship to find the answer.

Avoid "Fact Traps"

Don't get distracted by a choice that is factually true. Your search is for the answer that answers the question. Stay focused and don't fall for an answer that is true but incorrect. Always go back to the question and make sure you're choosing an answer that actually answers the question and is not just a true statement. An answer can be factually correct, but it MUST answer the question asked. Additionally, two answers can both be seemingly correct, so be sure to read all of the answer choices, and make sure that you get the one that BEST answers the question.

Milk the Question

Some of the questions may throw you completely off. They might deal with a subject you have not been exposed to, or one that you haven't reviewed in years. While your lack of knowledge about the subject will be a hindrance, the question itself can give you many clues that will help you find the correct answer. Read the question carefully and look for clues. Watch particularly for adjectives and nouns describing difficult terms or words that you don't recognize. Regardless of if you completely understand a word or not, replacing it with a synonym either provided or one you more familiar with may help you to understand what the questions are asking. Rather than wracking your mind about specific detailed information concerning a difficult term or word, try to use mental substitutes that are easier to understand.

The Trap of Familiarity

Don't just choose a word because you recognize it. On difficult questions, you may not recognize a number of words in the answer choices. The test writers don't put "make-believe" words on the test; so don't think that just because you only recognize all the words in one answer choice means that answer choice must be correct. If you only recognize words in one answer choice, then focus on that one. Is it correct? Try your best to determine if it is correct. If it is, that is great, but if it doesn't, eliminate it. Each word and answer choice you eliminate increases your chances of getting the question correct, even if you then have to guess among the unfamiliar choices.

Eliminate Answers

Eliminate choices as soon as you realize they are wrong. But be careful! Make sure you consider all of the possible answer choices. Just because one appears right, doesn't mean that the next one won't be even better! The test writers will usually put more than one good answer choice for every question, so read all of them. Don't worry if you are stuck between two that seem right. By getting down to just two remaining possible choices, your odds are now 50/50. Rather than wasting too much time, play the odds. You are guessing, but guessing wisely, because you've been able to knock out some of the answer choices that you know are wrong. If you are eliminating choices and realize that the last answer choice you are left with is also obviously wrong, don't panic. Start over and consider each choice again. There may easily be something that you missed the first time and will realize on the second pass.

Tough Questions

If you are stumped on a problem or it appears too hard or too difficult, don't waste time. Move on! Remember though, if you can quickly check for obviously incorrect answer choices, your chances of guessing correctly are greatly improved. Before you completely give up, at least try to knock out a couple of possible answers. Eliminate what you can and then guess at the remaining answer choices before moving on.

Brainstorm

If you get stuck on a difficult question, spend a few seconds quickly brainstorming. Run through the complete list of possible answer choices. Look at each choice and ask yourself, "Could this answer the question satisfactorily?" Go through each answer choice and consider it independently of the other. By systematically going through all possibilities, you may find something that you would otherwise overlook. Remember that when you get stuck, it's important to try to keep moving.

Read Carefully

Understand the problem. Read the question and answer choices carefully. Don't miss the question because you misread the terms. You have plenty of time to read each question thoroughly and make sure you understand what is being asked. Yet a happy medium must be attained, so don't waste too much time. You must read carefully, but efficiently.

Face Value

When in doubt, use common sense. Always accept the situation in the problem at face value. Don't read too much into it. These problems will not require you to make huge leaps of logic. The test writers aren't trying to throw you off with a cheap trick. If you have to go beyond creativity and make a leap of logic in order to have an answer choice answer the question, then you should look at the other answer choices. Don't overcomplicate the problem by creating theoretical relationships or explanations that will warp time or space. These are normal problems rooted in reality. It's just that the applicable relationship or explanation may not be readily apparent and you have to figure things out. Use your common sense to interpret anything that isn't clear.

Prefixes

If you're having trouble with a word in the question or answer choices, try dissecting it. Take advantage of every clue that the word might include. Prefixes and suffixes can be a huge help. Usually they allow you to determine a basic meaning. Pre- means before, post- means after, pro - is positive, de- is negative. From these prefixes and suffixes, you can get an idea of the general meaning of the word and try to put it into context. Beware though of any traps. Just because con is the opposite of pro, doesn't necessarily mean congress is the opposite of progress!

Hedge Phrases

Watch out for critical "hedge" phrases, such as likely, may, can, will often, sometimes, often, almost, mostly, usually, generally, rarely, sometimes. Question writers insert these hedge phrases to cover every possibility. Often an answer choice will be wrong simply because it leaves no room for exception. Avoid answer choices that have definitive words like "exactly," and "always".

Switchback Words

Stay alert for "switchbacks". These are the words and phrases frequently used to alert you to shifts in thought. The most common switchback word is "but". Others include although, however, nevertheless, on the other hand, even though, while, in spite of, despite, regardless of.

New Information

Correct answer choices will rarely have completely new information included. Answer choices typically are straightforward reflections of the material asked about and will directly relate to the question. If a new piece of information is included in an answer choice that doesn't even seem to relate to the topic being asked about, then that answer choice is likely incorrect. All of the information needed to answer the question is usually provided for you, and so you should not have to make guesses that are unsupported or choose answer choices that require unknown information that cannot be reasoned on its own.

Time Management

On technical questions, don't get lost on the technical terms. Don't spend too much time on any one question. If you don't know what a term means, then since you don't have a dictionary, odds are you aren't going to get much further. You should immediately recognize terms as whether or not you know them. If you don't, work with the other clues that you have, the other answer choices and terms provided, but don't waste too much time trying to figure out a difficult term.

Contextual Clues

Look for contextual clues. An answer can be right but not correct. The contextual clues will help you find the answer that is most right and is correct. Understand the context in which a phrase or statement is made. This will help you make important distinctions.

Don't Panic

Panicking will not answer any questions for you. Therefore, it isn't helpful. When you first see the question, if your mind goes blank, take a deep breath. Force yourself to mechanically go through the steps of solving the problem and using the strategies you've learned.

Pace Yourself

Don't get clock fever. It's easy to be overwhelmed when you're looking at a page full of questions, your mind is full of random thoughts and feeling confused, and the clock is ticking down faster than you would like. Calm down and maintain the pace that you have set for yourself. As long as you are on track by monitoring your pace, you are guaranteed to have enough time for yourself. When you get to the last few minutes of the test, it may seem like you won't have enough time left, but if you only have as many questions as you should have left at that point, then you're right on track!

Answer Selection

The best way to pick an answer choice is to eliminate all of those that are wrong, until only one is left and confirm that is the correct answer. Sometimes though, an answer choice may immediately look right. Be careful! Take a second to make sure that the other choices are not equally obvious. Don't make a hasty mistake. There are only two times that you should stop before checking other answers. First is when you are positive that the answer choice you have selected is correct. Second is when time is almost out and you have to make a quick guess!

Check Your Work

Since you will probably not know every term listed and the answer to every question, it is important that you get credit for the ones that you do know. Don't miss any questions through careless mistakes. If at all possible, try to take a second to look back over your answer selection and make sure you've selected the correct answer choice and haven't made a costly careless mistake (such as marking an answer choice that you didn't mean to mark). This quick double check

should more than pay for itself in caught mistakes for the time it costs.

Beware of Directly Quoted Answers

Sometimes an answer choice will repeat word for word a portion of the question or reference section. However, beware of such exact duplication – it may be a trap! More than likely, the correct choice will paraphrase or summarize a point, rather than being exactly the same wording.

Slang

Scientific sounding answers are better than slang ones. An answer choice that begins "To compare the outcomes..." is much more likely to be correct than one that begins "Because some people insisted..."

Extreme Statements

Avoid wild answers that throw out highly controversial ideas that are proclaimed as established fact. An answer choice that states the "process should used in certain situations, if..." is much more likely to be correct than one that states the "process should be discontinued completely." The first is a calm rational statement and doesn't even make a definitive, uncompromising stance, using a hedge word "if" to provide wiggle room, whereas the second choice is a radical idea and far more extreme.

Answer Choice Families

When you have two or more answer choices that are direct opposites or parallels, one of them is usually the correct answer. For instance, if one answer choice states "x increases" and another answer choice states "x decreases" or "y increases," then those two or three answer choices are very similar in construction and fall into the same family of answer choices. A family of answer choices is when two or three answer choices are very similar in construction, and yet often have a directly opposite meaning. Usually the correct answer choice will be in that family of answer choices. The "odd man out" or answer choice that doesn't seem to fit the parallel construction of the other answer choices is more likely to be incorrect.

Top 20 Test Taking Tips

1. Carefully follow all the test registration procedures
2. Know the test directions, duration, topics, question types, how many questions
3. Setup a flexible study schedule at least 3-4 weeks before test day
4. Study during the time of day you are most alert, relaxed, and stress free
5. Maximize your learning style; visual learner use visual study aids, auditory learner use auditory study aids
6. Focus on your weakest knowledge base
7. Find a study partner to review with and help clarify questions
8. Practice, practice, practice
9. Get a good night's sleep; don't try to cram the night before the test
10. Eat a well balanced meal
11. Know the exact physical location of the testing site; drive the route to the site prior to test day
12. Bring a set of ear plugs; the testing center could be noisy
13. Wear comfortable, loose fitting, layered clothing to the testing center; prepare for it to be either cold or hot during the test
14. Bring at least 2 current forms of ID to the testing center
15. Arrive to the test early; be prepared to wait and be patient
16. Eliminate the obviously wrong answer choices, then guess the first remaining choice
17. Pace yourself; don't rush, but keep working and move on if you get stuck
18. Maintain a positive attitude even if the test is going poorly
19. Keep your first answer unless you are positive it is wrong
20. Check your work, don't make a careless mistake

Integrated Language Arts

History of the English language

English is a language that may have said to be differentiated in the 7th century. Old English, Anglo-Saxon was modified by the Norman conquest in the 11th century. After the conquest, Middle English was heavily influenced by French, most notably in the large and central areas of vocabulary. A standard form, based on eastern dialects spoken in London, developed increasingly from the end of the Middle Ages.

The expansion of English to other continents began in the 17th century with the successful colonization of the eastern seaboard of America. Subsequently spread from colonization from England and America across North America, Australia, New Zealand, southern Africa and elsewhere. Promoted as a second language throughout the British Empire and in countries similarly occupied by the United States, it became an official language of countries such as India. English has become dominant as an international language, based on American English, since the mid-20th century.

Children's literature

Children's literature is designed to be read and enjoyed primarily by young readers. Early children's literature was written exclusively for educational purposes. Beginning in the middle of the 18th century, children's books were written to entertain as well as edify. Adventure stories for boys became popular in the 19th century, as did fiction designed for girls, such as Louisa May Alcott's "Little Women" (1868), and Johanna Spyri's " Heidi" (1880). Mark Twain and Robert Louis Stevenson became important writers of children's fiction during this time.

Recent years have emphasized more realism in children's literature. Opposed to the traditional view of shielding children from the realities of life, many now advocate books not only realistic but tragic, providing an opportunity for catharsis for young readers. An example of this type of fiction is William Armstrong's "Sounder" (1969), a novel of the evils of a segregated society written for young readers.

Phonetics

Phonetics seeks to provide a descriptive terminology for the sounds of spoken language. This includes the physiology for the production of speech sounds, the classification of speech sounds including vowels and consonants, the dynamic features of speech production, and the study of instrumental phonetics, the investigation of human speech by laboratory techniques. The dynamic aspects of phonetics include voice quality, stress, rhythm, and speech melody.

Instrumental phonetics underlines both the complexity of speech production, and the subtlety of the human brain in interpreting a constantly changing flow of acoustic data as recognizable speech-sounds. The correlation between acoustic quality, auditory perception, and articulatory position is a complex and not yet fully understood process. It represents a fertile area of research for phoneticians, psychologists, and perhaps philosophers.

General phonetics classifies the speech sounds of all languages. Any one language uses only possibilities of the selections available. Sounds and how they are used in a language is the phonology of a language. Dynamic features of phonology include speech melody, stress, rhythmic organization, length and syllabicity. The central unit of phonology is the phoneme, the smallest distinct sound in a given language. Two words are composed of different phonemes only if they differ phonetically in ways that are found to make a difference in meaning.

Phonemic transcription of a word or phrase is its representation as a sequence or other combinations of phonemes.

Phonology

Phonology is a controversial and enigmatic part of linguistics. It is widely studied and defined but there is no agreement on the definition of a phoneme or phonology theory. There may be as many theories as there are phonologies in linguistics.

Linguistics

Linguistics is the branch of knowledge that deals with language. Grammar, an integral part of linguistics, in its widest sense, includes the study of the structure of words and syntactic constructions, and that of sound systems. Linguistics is concerned with the lexical and grammatical categories of individual languages, and the differences between languages and the historical relations between families of languages. Each lexical entry informs us about the linguistic properties of the word. It will indicate a word's phonological, grammatical, and somatic properties.

- Grammar may be said to generate a set of phrases and sentences, so linguistics is also the study of generative grammar. Grammar must also contain a phonological component, since this determines the phonetic form of words in speech.
- Phonology, the study of sound systems and processes affecting the way words are pronounced, is another aspect of linguistics.

Psysholinguistics

Psycholinguistics is concerned with how linguistic competence is employed in the production and comprehension of speech.

- The first step in language comprehension is to use the phonological processor to identify sounds.

- Then the lexical processor identifies the component words.
- Finally the syntactic processor provides a syntactic representation of the sentence.
- The last step is for the semantic processor to compute a meaning representation for the sentence, on the basis of syntactical and lexical information supplied by previous steps in the process.

The relevant meaning of the words serves as the end-product of the process, and once this has been computed the sentence is understood. All stages of the psycholinguistic process take place in real time, so that measurements of each specific part of the process may be compared to the level of complexity of the grammar itself. Such is the experimental study of psycholinguistics applied.

Developmental linguistics

Neurolinguistics is concerned with the physical representations of linguistic processes in the brain. The most effective way to study this is to observe the effects on language capacity in brain-injured individuals. The frontal lobe of the brain appears to be the area responsible for controlling the production of speech. As research has become more refined over the years, it is evident that language functions are located in different parts of the brain. As improved diagnostic and sophisticated imaging techniques are developed, it is anticipated that the mysteries of language capacity and competence corresponding to specific parts of the brain will become clearer. For now, our knowledge in this field is imperfect, and the process of mapping the brain for linguistic capacity and performance is limited. Neurolinguistics is closely tied to neurology and neuro-physiology.

Sociolinguistics

Sociolinguistics is the study of the relationship between language and the structure of society. It takes into account the social backgrounds of both the speaker and the addressee, the relationship between the speaker and the addressee, and the context and manner of the interaction. Because the emphasis in sociolinguistics is on language use, the analysis of language in this field is typically based on taped recordings of everyday interactions. The sociolinguists seek to discover universal properties of languages, attempting to analyze questions such as "do all languages change in the same ways"? Answers are sought to the larger questions about universals in society in which language plays a major role. The multifaceted nature of language and its broad impact on many areas of society make this field an exciting and cutting edge part of linguistics.

Meaning
Meaning is traditionally something said to be expressed by a sentence. Modern theories in linguistics often elaborate on this. The four major theories are:
1. The meaning of a sentence is different depending on the context of the utterance.
2. Sentence meanings are part of the language system and form a level of semantic representation independent of other levels.
3. Representations are derivable from the level of syntax, given a lexicon which specifies the meaning of words and a set of semantic rules.
4. The meaning of utterances follows from separate principles that are in the domain of context or pragmatics.

Other theories assert that neither words or sentences can be assigned meanings independently of situations in which they are uttered. These theories all seek to establish a standard understanding of meaning so that linguists can refine and extend their research.

Etmology
Etymology is the study of the historical relation between a word and earlier form or forms from which it has developed.

Etymology can be loosely defined as the study of the origins of words. This study may occur on different levels of linguistic approach. Word meanings and their historical antecedents are often a complicated and controversial source of study. Tracing the meaning of words often includes understanding the social, political, and cultural time that the definition existed. The evolution of words from earlier forms suggests a cross-fertilization of social contexts and common usage that is a fascinating field of study.

An etymological fallacy is that the notion that a true meaning of a word can be derived from it etymology. Modern linguistic theory provides a substantial body of knowledge that compares and evaluates etymology and provides numerous avenues for new research.

Lexicology
Lexicon is the aspect of a language that is centered on individual words or similar units. Its scope varies widely from one theory to another. In some systems, lexicon is a simple component of generative grammar. In others it is the basis for all grammatical patterns. some view a lexicon as an unstructured list, while others see it as an elaborate network of entries governed by lexical rules and shared features. Lexicon in linguistics is to be distinguished as a theory from a dictionary or part of a practical description.

Lexicology is the branch of linguistics concerned with the semantic structure of the lexicon. Lexical diffusion is the gradual spread of a phonetic or other change across the vocabulary of a language or across a speech community? The term may also refer to the diffusion of individual lexical units within a lexicon.

Lexical decomposition is the analysis of word meanings into smaller units.

Grammar

Grammar may be practically defined as the study of how words are put together or the study of sentences. There are multiple approaches to grammar in modern linguistics. Any systematic account of the structure of a language and the patterns it describes is grammar. Modern definitions of grammar state grammar is the knowledge of a language developed in the minds of the speakers.

A grammar in the broadest sense is a set of rules internalized by members of a speech community, and an account, by a linguist, of such a grammar. This internalized grammar is what is commonly called a language. Grammar is often restricted to units that have meaning. The expanded scope of grammar includes morphology and syntax, and a lexicon. Grammatical meaning is described as part of the syntax and morphology of a language as distinct from its lexicon.

The ability to learn language is determined by a biologically determined innate language facility. This widely accepted theory is known as the innateness hypothesis. The knowledge of adult grammar appears to go far beyond anything supplied by the child's linguistic experience, implying an innate ability to learn language. A language facility must incorporate a set of Universal Grammar principles which enable a child to form and interpret sentences in any natural language. Children have the ability to acquire any natural language so it follows that the contents of the innate language facility must not be specific to any one human language. Developmental linguistics is concerned with examining children's grammar and the conditions under which they emerge. The language faculty is species-specific and the ability to develop a grammar of a language is unique to human beings. The study of non-human communication forms a different field of study.

Structuralized grammar

Structuralize grammar tends to be formal in nature as it is concerned with grammatical and phonological considerations, rather than semantics. The chief goal is to uncover the structure of a language. There are valid criticisms of the structural approach to grammar. problems exist in the available descriptive frameworks to manage, difficulties with definitions, and inconsistency and contradiction between theory and practice. These concerns have not invalidated the study of structural grammar, but have been utilized by linguists to perfect the analysis.

Transformational grammar

Transformational grammar is any grammar in which different syntactic structures are related by transformations. The main role of transformations was to relate the sentences of a language as a whole to a small set of kernel sentences. A base component of a grammar generated a deep structure for each sentence. these structures were an input to a transformational component, which was an ordered structure of transformational rules. Its output was a set of surface structures, which combined with the deep structures, formed its syntactic description. Further rules supplied its semantic representation and phonetic representation.

Transformational grammar was invented and promulgated by Noam Chomsky, a revolutionary figure in linguistics. Much of Chomsky's work has been directed to the development of a universal grammar, conceived as an account of what is inherited by the individual. Chomsky remains the dominant figure of the 20th century in linguistics.

Sentences

The largest structural unit normally recognized by grammar is the sentence. Any attempt to accurately define the sentence is in error. Any such definition will not bear up under Linguistic Analysis. In every language, there are a limited number of favorite sentence-types to which most others can be related. They vary from language to language. Certain utterances, while not immediately conforming to favorite sentence types, can be expanded in their context to become one sentence of a particular type. These can be called referable sentences. Other utterances that do not conform to favorite sentence types may reveal obsolete sentence types; these are proverbial sayings and are called gnomic or fossilized sentences. A very small number of utterances not conforming to the favorite sentence-types are found in prescribed social situations, such as "Hello" or "Bye".

Sentence patterns
Sentence patterns fall into five common modes with some exceptions. They are:
1. Subject / linking verb / subject complement
2. Subject / transitive verb / direct object
3. Subject / transitive verb / indirect object / direct object
4. Subject / transitive verb / direct object / object complement
5. Subject / intransitive verb

Common exceptions to these patterns are questions and commands, sentences with delayed subjects, and passive transformations. Writers sometimes use the passive voice when the active voice would be more appropriate.

Sentence classification
Sentences are classified in two ways:
• according to their structure
• according to their purpose

Writers use declarative sentences to make statements, imperative sentences to issue requests or commands, interrogative sentences to ask questions, and exclamatory sentences to make exclamations.

Depending on the number and types of clauses they contain, sentences may be classified as simple, compound, complex, or compound-complex.

Clauses come in two varieties: Independent and subordinate.
• An independent clause is a full sentence pattern that does not function within another sentence pattern; it contains a subject and modifiers plus a verb and any objects, complements, and modifiers of that verb. It either stands alone or could stand alone.
• A subordinate clause is a full sentence pattern that functions within a sentence as an adjective, an adverb, or a noun but that cannot stand alone as a complete sentence.

Sentence structures
The four major types of sentence structure are:
1. Simple sentences - Simple sentences have one independent clause with no subordinate clauses. a simple sentence may contain compound elements,- a compound subject, verb, or object for example, but does not contain more than one full sentence pattern.
2. Compound sentences - Compound sentences are composed of two or more independent clauses with no subordinate clauses. The independent clauses are usually joined with a comma and a coordinating conjunction, or with a semicolon.
3. Complex sentences - A complex sentence is composed of one independent clause with one or more dependent clauses.
4. Compound-complex sentences - A compound-complex sentence contains at least two independent clauses and at least one subordinate clause. sometimes they contain two full

sentence patters that can stand alone. When each independent clause contains a subordinate clause, this makes the sentence both compound and complex.

Chomsky's sentence structure
Deep structure is a representation of the syntax of a sentence distinguished by various criteria from its surface structure. Initially defined by Noam Chomsky as the part of the syntactic description of a of a sentence that determines its semantic interpretation by the base component of a generative grammar.

Surface sentence structure is a representation of the syntax of a sentence seen as deriving by one ore more transformations, from a an underlying deep structure. Such a sentence is in the order in which the corresponding phonetic forms are spoken. Surface structure was later broadened by Chomsky to include semantic structure. Chomsky's later minimalist program no longer takes this for granted. Minimalist theory assumes no more than a minimum of types of statements and levels of representation.

The technical analysis outlined by Chomsky over three decades forms an integral part of transformational grammar.

Language investigation

The investigation of a language by classification is the goal of the modern linguist. When the observer has determined the phonemic structure of a language, and has classified all its constructions, both morphological and syntactic, the resulting description will be an accurate and usable grammar of the language, accounting in the simplest way for all the utterances of the speech community.

Language families

A language family is a group of languages that have been developed from a single ancestor. An example would be Indo-European, of which English is one of many members. Language families are identified whenever a common origin can be accepted as certain. When a family origin in speculative or uncertain, it may be called a projected family, a proposed family, or a probable family. Some linguists have tried to apply a biological method of classification of language families, following the genus, order, species model. They have classed languages as beginning with "superficies", "macro families", "stocks", "super stocks", or "phyla" at the top. Below those will be "subfamilies", "branches", and "groups". This attempt has proved faulty as the classifications imply more than is known about family origins. It has been difficult and largely unaccepted to class language families in these descending modes of importance.

Language descriptions

The levels of language descriptions represent a distinct phase in the description of a language at which specific types of elements and the relations between them are studied or investigated.
- At the level of phonology, one studies the sound structure of a language, words or larger units that are specific to that level.
- At the level of syntax, sentences are represented as the configuration of words or morphemes standing in specific construction in relationship to one another.

Levels of language are an important part of structural linguistics, whether they focus on formal analyses or representation. Some give an order of procedures which govern the formal structural analysis of language. Others propose a hierarchy of greater or lesser degrees of abstraction, ranging from phonetics as the highest and semantics as the lowest. In many of these levels are defined by the different components of an integrated structural grammar.

Morphology

Morphology is the grammatical structure of words and their categories. The morphological process includes any of the formal processes or operations by which the forms of words are derived from stems or roots. Types of morphological processes include affix, any element in the structure of a word other than a root; reduplication, where all or part of a form is duplicated; subtraction, where part of a form is deleted; supple ton, where one part of the morphological process replaces another; compound, where two parts of the morphological process are joined; and modification, where one part of a form is modified.

Forms of morphological classification distinguished isolating, in which each grammatical classification is represented by a single word, agglutinating, where words are easily divided into separate sections, and inflectional, concerned with inflections in languages.

Functions of language

1. Language is a means of social control making human society possible. The communication of thoughts is but a small part of this.
2. Language acts as an index to various things about the speaker - age, sex, physical and mental wellbeing, and personality characteristics.
3. Language acts to limit classes within a society, either by accent, dialect, choice of words and grammatical features.
4. Language brings human beings into relationship with the external world. It mediates between man and his environment.
5. Language is the material of artistic creation, including not only literary works but poetic and oral traditions.

Any list of languages functions is arbitrary. There are dozens of other possible classifications of language functions in the literature of linguistics. The classification given above includes the basic elements of language and their societal effect.

Semantics

Semantics studies the meaning of utterances and why particular utterances have the meanings they do. Semantics originally covered grammar, the account of meaningful forms, and the lexicon or body of words contained in a language. When the study of forms was separated from that of meanings, the field of generative grammar became associated with semantics. Currently, the scope of semantics will cover word meanings or lexical semantics, and the meaning of utterances studied in pragmatics, the meaning of language in everyday life.

Some narrow definitions of semantics understand the term to mean the study of problems encounted in formal semantics, excluding lexical meaning completely. This last definition is an extreme one, and is included to illustrate the broad vistas that are opened when we discuss semantics. What can be asserted is that semantics in its broadest and most common usage is the field of study in linguistics that deals with meaning in all its forms.

Spoken and written language

The relationship of spoken language and written form has been the subject of differences of attitudes among linguists. The spoken form is historically prior, both for the language community and the individual. It is also more complicated. For these reasons, emphasis is placed on the sound systems of languages which has led some linguists to describe the spoken form as language, and the written form as written language. Both are equal examples of language. The relationship is not a straightforward case of deriving the written from the spoken form. When a written form evolves, it tends to take on a life of its own and acquires usages different from the spoken.

Linguists are concerned with the analysis and development of language as a whole, both written and spoken. Much of the controversy in linguistic theory is concerned with both forms of languages. Linguistics is in a sense a search for the universals in language, which includes both spoken and written forms.

Parts of speech

Nouns

Nouns are the name of a person, place, or thing, and are usually signaled by an article (a, an, the). Nouns sometimes function as adjectives modifying other nouns. Nouns used in this manner are called noun/adjectives. Nouns are classified for a number of purposes: capitalization, word choice, count/no count nouns, and collective nouns are examples.

Pronouns

Pronouns is a word used in place of a noun. Usually the pronoun substitutes for the specific noun, called the antecedent. Although most pronouns function as substitutes for nouns, some can function as adjectives modifying nouns. pronouns may be classed as personal, possessive, intensive, relative, interrogative, demonstrative, indefinite, and reciprocal. pronouns can cause a number of problems for writers including pronoun-antecedent agreement, distinguishing between who and whom, and differentiating pronouns such as I and me.

Problems with pronouns:
Pronouns are words that substitute for nouns: he, it, them, her, me, and so on. Four frequently encountered problems with pronouns include:
1. Pronoun - antecedent agreement - The antecedent of a pronoun is the word the pronoun refers to. A pronoun and its antecedent agree when they are both singular or plural.
2. Pronoun reference - A pronoun should refer clearly to its antecedent. A pronoun's reference will be unclear if it id ambiguous, implied, vague, or indefinite.
3. Personal pronouns - Some pronouns change their case form according to their grammatical structure in a sentence. Pronouns functioning as subjects appear in the subjective case, those functioning as objects appear in the objective case, and those functioning as possessives appear in the possessive case.
4. Who or whom - Who, a subjective-case pronoun, can only be used subjects and subject complements. Whom, an objective case pronoun, can only be used for objects. The words who and whom appear primarily in subordinate clauses or in questions.

Verbs

The verb of a sentence usually expresses action or being. It is composed of a main verb and sometimes supporting verbs. These helping verbs are forms of have, do, and be, and nine modals. The modals are "can, could, may, might, shall, should, will, would, and ought". Some verbs are followed by words that look like prepositions, but are so closely associated with the verb to be part of its meaning. These words are known as particles, and examples include "call off", "look up", and "drop off".

The main verb of a sentence is always one that would change form from base form to past tense, past participle, present participle and, -s forms. When both the past-tense and past-participle forms of a verb end in "ed", the verb is regular. In all other cases the verb is irregular. The verb "be" is highly irregular, having eight forms instead of the usual five.
- Linking verbs link the subject to a subject complement, a word or word group that completes the meaning of the subject by renaming or describing it.
- A transitive verb takes a direct object, a word or word group that names a receiver of the action. The direct

object of a transitive verb is sometimes preceded by an indirect object. Transitive verbs usually appear in the active voice, with a subject doing the action and a direct object receiving the action. The direct object of a transitive verb is sometimes followed by an object complement, a word or word group that completes the direct object's meaning by renaming or describing it.

- Intransitive verbs take no objects or complements. Their pattern is subject verb.

A dictionary will disclose whether a verb is transitive or intransitive. Some verbs have both transitive and intransitive functions.

Verb phrases

A verbal phrase is a verb form that does not function as the verb of a clause. There are three major types of verbal phrases:

1. Participial phrases - These always function as adjectives. Their verbals are always present participles, always ending in "ing", or past participles frequently ending in "-d,-ed,-n.-en,or -t". Participial phrases frequently appear immediately following the noun or pronoun they modify.
2. Gerund phrases - Gerund phrases are built around present participles and they always function as nouns. : usually as subjects subject complements, direct objects, or objects of a preposition.
3. Infinitive phrases are usually structured around "to" plus the base form of the verb. they can function as nouns, as adjectives, or as adverbs. When functioning as a noun, an infinitive phrase may appear in almost any noun slot in a sentence, usually as a subject, subject complement, or direct object. Infinitive phrases functioning as adjectives usually appear immediately following the noun or pronoun they

modify. adverbial phrases usually qualify the meaning of the verb.

Problems with verbs:

The verb is the heart of the sentence. Verbs have several potential problems including:

1. Irregular verbs - Verbs that do not follow usual grammatical rules.
2. Tense - Tenses indicate the time of an action in relation to the time of speaking or writing about the action.
3. Mood - There are three moods in English: the indicative, used for facts, opinions, and questions; the imperative, used for orders or advice, and the subjunctive, used for wishes. The subjective mood is the most likely to cause problems. The subjective mood is used for wishes, and in "if"clauses expressing conditions contrary to facts. The subjective in such cases is the past tense form of the verb; in the case of "be", it is always "were", even if the subject is singular. The subjective mood is also used in "that' clauses following verbs such as "ask, insist, recommend, and request. The subjunctive in such cases is the base or dictionary form of the verb.

Adjectives

An adjective is a word use to modify or describe a noun or pronoun. An adjective usually answers one of these question: "Which one?, What kind of?, and How many?" Adjectives usually precede the words they modify, although they sometimes follow linking verbs, in which case they describe the subject. Most adjectives have three forms: the positive, the comparative, and the superlative. The comparative should be used to compare two things, the superlative to compare three or more things.

Articles

Articles, sometimes classed as nouns, are used to mark nouns. There are only three: the definite article "the," and the indefinite articles "a", and "and".

- 21 -

Adverbs

An adverb is a word used to modify or qualify a verb, adjective, or another adverb. It usually answers one of these questions: "When?, where?, how?, and why?" Adverbs modifying adjectives or other adverbs usually intensify or limit the intensity of words they modify. The negators "not" and "never" are classified as adverbs. Writers sometimes misuse adverbs, and multilingual speakers have trouble placing them correctly. Most adverbs also have three forms: the positive, the comparative, and the superlative. The comparative should be used to compare two things, the superlative to compare three or more things.

Prepositions

A preposition is a word placed before a noun or pronoun to form a phrase modifying another word in the sentence. The prepositional phrase usually functions as an adjective or adverb. There are a limited number of prepositions in English, perhaps around 80. Some prepositions are more than one word long. "Along with", "listen to", and "next to" are some examples.

Conjunctions

Conjunctions join words, phrases, or clauses, and they indicate the relationship between the elements that are joined. There are coordinating conjunctions that connect grammatically equal element, correlative conjunctions that connect pairs, subordinating conjunctions that introduces a subordinate clause, and conjunctive adverbs which may be used with a semicolon to connect independent clauses. The most common conjunctive adverbs include "then, thus, and however". Using adverbs correctly helps avoid sentence fragments and run-on sentences.

Subjects

The subject of a sentence names who or what the sentence is about. The complete subject is composed of the simple subject and all of its modifiers.

To find the complete subject, ask "Who" or "What", and insert the verb to complete the question. The answer is the complete subject. To find the simple subject, strip away all the modifiers in the complete subject.

In imperative sentences, the verb's subject is understood but not actually present in the sentence. Although the subject ordinarily comes before the verb, sentences that begin with "There are" or "There was", the subject follows the verb.

The ability to recognize the subject of a sentence helps in editing a variety of problems such as sentence fragments and subject-verb agreement, as well as the choice of pronouns.

Subordinate word groups

Subordinate word groups cannot stand alone. They function only within sentences, as adjectives, adverbs, or nouns.

- Prepositional phrases begins with a preposition and ends with a noun or noun equivalent called its object. Prepositional phrases function as adjectives or adverbs.
- Subordinate clauses are patterned like sentences, having subject, verbs, and objects or complements. They function within sentences as adverbs, adjectives, or nouns.
- Adjective clauses modify nouns or pronouns and begin with a relative pronoun or relative adverb.
- Adverb clauses modify verbs, adjectives, and other adverbs.
- Noun clauses function as subjects, objects, or complements. In both adjective and noun clauses words may appear out of their normal order. The parts of a noun clause may also appear in their normal order.

Appositive and absolute phrases

Strictly speaking, appositive phrases are not subordinate word groups. Appositive phrases function somewhat as adjectives do, to describe nouns or pronouns. Instead of modifying nouns or pronouns however, appositive phrases rename them. In form they are nouns or nouns equivalents. Appositives are said to be in " in apposition" to the nouns or pronouns they rename. For example, in the sentence "Terriers, hunters at heart, have been dandled up to look like lap dogs", "hunters at heart" is apposition to the noun "terriers".

An absolute phrase modifies a whole clause or sentence, not just one word, and it may appear nearly anywhere in the sentence. It consists of a noun or noun equivalent usually followed by a participial phrase. Both appositive and absolute phrases can cause confusion in their usage in grammatical structures. They are particularly difficult for a person whose first language is not English.

Common problems with sentences

Subject-verb agreement
In the present tense, verbs agree with their subjects in number, (singular or plural), and in person, (first ,second, or third). The present tense ending -s is used on a verb if its subject is third person singular; otherwise the verb takes no ending. The verb "be" varies from this pattern, and alone among verbs it has special forms in both the present and past tense.

Problems with subject-verb agreement tend to arise in certain contexts:
1. Words between subject and verbs.
2. Subjects joined by "and".
3. Subjects joined by "or" or "nor".
4. Indefinite pronouns such as "someone".
5. Collective nouns.
6. Subject after verb.
7. Who, which, and that.
8. Plural form, singular meaning.
9. Titles, company names, and words mentioned as words.

Sentence fragments
As a rule a part of a sentence should not be treated as a complete sentence. A sentence must be composed of at least one full independent clause. An independent clause has a subject, a verb, and can stand alone as a sentence. Some fragments are clauses that contain a subject and a verb, but begin with a subordinating word. Other fragments lack a subject, verb, or both.

A sentence fragment can be repaired by combining the fragment with a nearby sentence, punctuating the new sentence correctly, or turn the fragment into a sentence by adding the missing elements. Some sentence fragments are used by writers for emphasis. Although sentence fragments are sometimes acceptable, readers and writers do not always agree on when they are appropriate. A conservative approach is to write in complete sentences only unless a special circumstance dictates otherwise.

Run-on sentences
Run-on sentences are independent clauses that have not been joined correctly. An independent clause is a word group that does or could stand alone in a sentence. When two or more independent clauses appear in one sentence, they must be joined in one of these ways:
1. Revision with a comma and a coordinating conjunction.
2. Revision with a semicolon, a colon, or a dash. Used when independent clauses are closely related and their relationship is clear without a coordinating conjunction.
3. Revision by separating sentences. This approach may be used when both independent clauses are long,
1. or if one is a question and one is not. Separate sentences may be the best option in this case.
4. Revision by restructuring the sentence. For sentence variety, consider restructuring the sentence, perhaps by turning one of the independent clauses into a subordinate phrase or clause.

Usually one of these choices will be an obvious solution to the run-on sentence. The fourth technique above is often the most effective solution, but requires the most revision.

Double negatives

Standard English allows two negatives only if a positive meaning is intended. "The team was not displeased with their performance" is an example. Double negatives used to emphasize negation are nonstandard.

Negative modifiers such as "never, no, and not" should not be paired with other negative modifiers or negative words such as " none, nobody, nothing, or neither". The modifiers "hardly, barely, and scarcely" are also considered negatives in standard English, so they should not be used with other negatives such as "not, no one, or never".

Double superlatives

Do not use double superlatives or comparatives. When "er" or "est" has been added to an adjective or adverb, avoid using "more" or "most". Avoid expressions such as "more perfect", and "very round". Either something is or is not. It is not logical to suggest that absolute concepts come in degrees. Use the comparative to compare two things, and the superlative to compare three or more things.

Punctuation

Commas

The comma was invented to help readers. Without it, sentence parts can run together, making meanings unclear. Various rules for comma use include:
1. Use a comma between a coordinating conjunction joining independent clauses.
2. Use a comma after an introductory clause or phrase.
3. Use a comma between items in a series.
4. Use a comma between coordinate adjectives not joined with "and". Do

not use a comma between cumulative adjectives.
5. Use commas to set off nonrestrictive elements. Do not use commas to set off restrictive elements.
6. Use commas to set off transitional and parenthetical expressions, absolute phrases, and elements expressing contrast.
7. Use commas to set off nouns of direct address, the words yes and no, interrogative tags, and interjections.
8. Use commas with dates, addresses, titles, and numbers.

Some situations where commas are unnecessary include:
1. Do not use a comma between compound elements that are not independent clauses.
2. Do not use a comma after a phrase that begins with an inverted sentence.
3. Do not use a comma between the first or after the last item in a series or before the word "although".
4. Do not use a comma between cumulative adjectives, between an adjective and a noun, or between an adverb and an adjective.
5. Do not use commas to set off restrictive or mildly parenthetical elements or to set off an indirect quotation.
6. Do not use a comma to set off a concluding adverb clause that is essential to the meaning of the sentence or after the word "although".
7. Do not use a comma to separate a verb from its subject or object. Do not use a comma after a coordinating conjunction or before a parenthesis.
8. Do not use a comma with a question mark or an exclamation point.
9. Use commas to prevent confusion.
10. Use commas to set off direct quotations.

Semicolons

The semicolon is used to connect major sentence elements of equal grammatical rank. Some rules regarding semicolons include:

1. Use a semicolon between closely related independent clauses not joined with a coordinating conjunction.
2. Use a semicolon between independent clauses linked with a transitional expression.
3. Use a semicolon between items in a series containing internal punctuation.
4. Avoid using a semicolon between a subordinate clause and the rest of the sentence.
5. Avoid using a semicolon between an appositive word and the word it refers to.
6. Avoid using a semicolon to introduce a list.
7. Avoid using a semicolon between independent clauses joined by "and, but, or, nor, for, so, or yet".

Colons

The colon is used primarily to call attention to the words that follow it. In addition the colon has some other conventional uses:

1. Use a colon after an independent clause to direct attention to a list, an appositive, or a quotation.
2. Use a colon between independent clauses if the second summarizes or explains the first.
3. Use a colon after the salutation in a formal letter, to indicate hours and minutes, to show proportions between a title and subtitle, and between city and publisher in bibliographic entries.

A colon must be preceded by a full independent clause. Avoid using colons in the following situations:

1. Avoid using a colon between a verb and its object or complement.
2. Avoid using a colon between a preposition and its object.

3. Avoid using a colon after "such as, including, or for example"

Apostrophes

An apostrophe is used to indicate that a noun is possessive. Possessive nouns usually indicate ownership, as in Bill's coat or the dog's biscuit. Sometimes ownership is only loosely implied, as in the dog's coat or the forest's trees. If it is unclear whether a noun is possessive, turning into phrase may clarify it.

If the noun is plural and ends in-s, add only an apostrophe. To show joint possession, use -'s with the last noun only. To show individual possession, make all nouns possessive.

An apostrophe is often optional in plural numbers, letters, abbreviations, and words mentioned as words.

Common errors in using apostrophes include:

- Do not use an apostrophe with nouns that are not possessive.
- Do not use an apostrophe in the possessive pronouns "its, whose, his, hers, ours, yours, and theirs".

Quotation marks

Use quotation marks to enclose direct quotations of a person's words, spoken or written. Do not use quotation marks around indirect quotations. An indirect quotation reports someone's ideas without using that person's exact words.

Set off long quotations of prose or poetry by indenting. Use single quotation marks to enclose a quotation within a quotation. Quotation marks should be used around the titles of short works: newspaper and magazine articles, poems, short stories, songs, episodes of television and radio programs, and subdivisions of books or web sites.

Quotation marks may be used to set off words used as words. Punctuation is used with quotation marks according to convention.

Periods and commas are placed inside quotation marks, while colons and semicolons are placed outside quotation marks. Question marks and exclamation points are placed inside quotation marks. Do not use quotation marks around the title of your own essay.

Dashes

When typing, use two hyphens to form a dash. Do not put spaces before or after the dash. Dashes are used for the following purposes:

1. To set off parenthetical material that deserves emphasis.
2. To set off appositives that contain commas.
3. To prepare for a list, a restatement, an amplification, or a dramatic shift in tone or thought.

Unless there is a specific reason for using the dash, omit it. It can give text a choppy effect.

Parentheses

Parentheses are used to enclose supplemental material, minor digressions, and afterthoughts. They are also used to enclose letters or numbers labeling them items in a series. Parentheses should be used sparingly, as they break up text in a distracting manner when overused.

Brackets

Brackets are used to enclose any words or phrases that have been inserted into an otherwise word-for-word quotation.

Ellipsis marks

The ellipsis mark consists of three spaced periods (...), and is used to indicate when certain words have been deleted from an otherwise word-for-word quotation. If a full sentence or more is deleted in the middle of quoted passage, a person should be inserted before the ellipsis dots. The ellipsis mark should not be used at the beginning of a quotation. It should also not be used at the end of a quotation unless some words have been deleted from the end of the final sentence.

Slashes

The slash, (/), may be used to separate two or three lines of poetry that have been run into a text. If there are more than three lines of poetry they should be handled as an indented quotation. The slash may occasionally be used to separate paired terms such as passed/failed or either/or. In this case, apace is not placed before or after the slash. The slash should be used sparingly, only when it is clearly appropriate.

End punctuations

- Use a period to end all sentences except direct questions or genuine exclamations. Periods should be used in abbreviations according to convention. Problems can arise when there is a choice between a period and a question mark or exclamation point. If a sentence reports a question rather than asking it directly, it should end with a period, not a question mark.
- Question marks should be used following a direct question. If a polite request is written in the form of a question, it may be followed by a period. Questions in a series may be followed by question marks even when they are not in complete sentences.
- Exclamation marks are used after a word group or sentence that expresses exceptional feeling or deserves special emphasis. Exclamation marks should not be overused, being reserved for appropriate exclamatory interjections.

Genres

Literary genres refer to the basic generic types of poetry, drama, fiction, and nonfiction. Literary genre is a method of classifying and analyzing literature. There are numerous subdivisions within genre, including such categories as novels, novellas, and short stories in fiction. Drama may also be subdivided into comedy, tragedy, and many other categories. Poetry and nonfiction have there own distinct divisions.

Genres are often overlapping and the distinctions blurred, such as the nonfiction novel, and docudramas as well as many others. However, the use of genres is helpful to the reader as a set of understandings that guide our responses to a work. The generic norm sets expectations and forms the framework within which we read and evaluate a work. This framework will guide both our understanding and interpretation of the work. It is a useful tool for both literary criticism and analysis.

Fiction

Fiction is a general term for any form of literary narrative that is invented or imagined rather than being factual. For those individuals who equate fact with truth, the imagined or invented character of fiction tends to male fiction relatively unimportant or trivial among the genres. Defenders of fiction are quick to point out that the fictional mode is an essential part of being. The ability to imagine or discuss "what if" plots, characters, and events is clearly part of the human experience.

Fiction is much wider than simply prose fiction. Songs, ballads, epics, and narrative poems are examples of non-prose fiction. A full definition of fiction must include not only the work itself, but also the framework in which it is read. Literary fiction seems matter of not-true, rather than non-existent, as many works of historical fiction refer to real people, places and events which are treated imaginatively as if it were true. These imaginary elements enrich and broaden literary expression.

Prose Fiction
Prose is derived from the Latin and means 'straightforward discourse". Prose fiction, while having many categories, may be divided into three main groups:

1. Short stories - a fictional narrative, the length of which varies, usually under 20,000 words. Short stories usually have only a few characters, and generally describe one major event or insight. The short story began in magazines in the late 1800's and have flourished ever since.
2. Novels - a longer work of fiction, often containing a large cast of characters, and extensive plotting. The emphasis may be on an event, action, social problems or any experience. There is now a genre of non-fiction novels pioneered by Truman Capote's "In Cold Blood" in the 1960's. Novels may also be written in verse.
3. Novellas - a work of narrative fiction longer than a short story but shorter than a novel. Novellas may also be called short novels or novelettes. They originated from the German tradition, and have become common forms in all of the world's literature.

There are many elements that influence a work of prose fiction. Some important ones include:
1. Speech and dialogue - characters may speak for themselves or through the narrator. Dialogue may be realistic or fantastic, depending on the authors aim.
2. Thoughts and mental processes - there may be internal dialogue used as a device for plot development or character understanding.
3. Dramatic Involvement - some narrators encourage readers to become involved in the events of the story, while others attempt to distance readers through literary devices.
4. Action - Any information that advances the plot, or involves new interactions between the characters.
5. Duration - the time frame of the work may be long or short and the relationship between described time and narrative time may vary.

6. Setting and description - is the setting critical to the plot or characters and how are the action scenes described?
7. Themes - any point of view or topic given sustained attention.
8. Symbolism - authors often veil meanings through imagery and other literary constructions.

Characterization

A character is a person intimately involved with the plot and development of the novel. There is usually a physical description of the character, but this is often omitted in modern and postmodern novels. These works may focus on the psychological state or motivation of the character. The choice of a characters name may give valuable clues to his role in the work.

Characters are said to be "flat" or "round". Flat characters tend to be minor figures in the story, changing little or not at all. Round characters (those understood from a well rounded view) are more central to the story and tend to change as the plot unfolds. Stock characters are similar to flat characters, filling out the story without influencing it.

Modern literature has been greatly affected by Freudian psychology, giving rise to such devices as the 'interior monologue" and "magic realism" as methods of understanding characters in a work. These give the reader a more complex understanding of the inner lives of the characters, and enrich the understanding of relationships between characters.

Analytical reading

It is important for the reader to look carefully at a work of fiction being studied. The plot or action of a narrative can become so entertaining that the language of the work is ignored. The language of fiction should not simply be a way to relate a plot, but should yield many insights to the judicious reader. Some prose fiction is based on the reader's engagement with the language, rather than the story. A studious reader will analyze the mode of expression as well as the narrative. Part of the rewards of reading in this manner is to discover how the author uses different language to describe familiar objects, events, or emotions. Some works focus the reader on the authors' unorthodox use of language while others may emphasize characters or storylines. What happens in a story is not always the critical element in the work. This type of reading may be difficult at first but yield great rewards.

Reading slowly

Reading novels and novellas offer a different experience than short stories. Our imagination is more active as we review what we have read, imagine ourselves as characters in the novel, and try to guess what will happen next. Suspense, surprise, fantasy, fear, anxiety, compassion, and a host of other emotions and feelings may be stirred by a provocative novel.

Reading longer works of fiction is a cumulative process over a period of time. Some elements of a novel have a great impact, while others may go virtually unnoticed. So as novels are read with a critical eye to language, it is helpful to perceive and identify larger patterns and movements in the work as a whole. This will benefit the reader by placing characters and events in perspective, and will enrich the reading experience greatly. Novels should be savored rather than gulped. Careful reading and thoughtful analysis of the major themes of the novel are essential to a clear understanding of the work.

Narrative technique

Who is the narrator of the novel? What is the narrator's perspective - first person or third person? What is the role of the narrator in the plot? Are there changes in narrators or the perspective of narrators? Does the narrator explain things in the novel, or does meaning emerge from the plot and events? The personality of the narrator is important. He or she may have a vested interest in a character or event described. Some narratives follow the time sequence of the plot while others do not. A narrator may express approval or disapproval about a character or events in the work.

Tone is an important aspect of the narration. Who is actually being addressed by the narrator? Is the tone familiar or formal? Intimate or impersonal? Does the vocabulary suggest clues about the narrator?

All these are important questions to understand if the voice and role of the narrator are to be clearly understood and incorporated into the understanding of the novel.

Drama

Any work where actors or actresses assume roles before an audience, either in a theatre, motion picture, television, or radio. Drama is a major literary genre which may be subdivided into three major groups:

1. Tragedy - a drama in which the leading character has a disastrous end. The character usually represents something significant, good or bad. Tragedy may be seen as an attempt to extract a value from human mortality, giving the sub-genre a positive view of human life, despite its inevitable end.
2. Tragicomedy - a drama that includes both comic and tragic elements. Tragicomedy thus results in a bittersweet mix of literary value. As George Bernard Shaw once commented," tragicomedy is a much deeper and grimmer entertainment than tragedy".
3. Comedy - this type of drama satirizes the misadventures of its characters. Comedy often emphasizes society and its mores, rather than the individual (more common in tragedies). Its origins may be traced to the primitive celebrations of spring.

Dramatic plot
When studying dramatic works, significant events in the story should be recognized. Major shifts or reversals in the plot, and subsequent action should be followed carefully. Aristotle's "Poetics" described a typical progression pattern of a plot as follows:

1. Exposition
2. Complication
3. Reversal
4. Recognition
5. Resolution

This progression is still valid today as we study and analyze plots. The plot may follow the pattern of comedy (ending with a celebration), or tragedy (ending with death). The plot may be explained through dialogue, stage action, and off-stage events or by a chorus. Plots of well known plays are easily understood and analyzed, but more esoteric drama requires careful attention to the complexities of the plot.

Characters
To understand dramatic works detailed knowledge of major characters is essential. Details of their past, motivations for their actions, fatal flaws, romantic relationships, antagonistic characters, and historical context all weave a tapestry of characters that fill out a drama's skeleton. It is vital to distinguish between major and minor characters, which are only functional, and which are central to the drama. The extent to which each character is developed is a good clue in identifying major and minor personae. Details of the relationships between characters often is an excellent guide to plot development and resolution. Who loves whom, who hates whom, who are allied, who are enemies, and the implications of these tangled webs form the structure of plot and drama. Of the many possible relationships in a play, only a few will be crucial. These should be identified and followed closely.

Other important elements

Theme: Ideas or concepts given sustained attention in a drama highlight the major themes of the work. Often the title of the play reflects themes to be presented. Some works are really expositions of argument and points the author wants to make. Arguments and themes are given dramatic force through the form in which they are expressed. This could be action, speech, or narration.

Imagery: Patterns of imagery include the use of symbols and keywords. These are recurring motifs that form themes and plot development together. Some plays focus on a particular image. Symbols are subtle devices used by authors for a variety of reasons, and they are usually a key to the major themes of the drama. Symbols may change as the play progresses, and these changes are important in plotting and action. Some key words are used as symbols, and are repeated and emphasized to enrich the material. These keywords may be tied to one character or shared by many.

Tension: Authors build tension between characters, creating difficult situations that cannot easily be resolved, and highlighting conflict and romance. Often authors choose not to reveal some information that increases tension.

Action: Action is the physical events in a play. Action can be important or have little dramatic impact. Some plays depend on spectacles rather than dialogue to emphasize plot and characters. Staging is an important element in the action of a drama. The play may be written for a particular acting space, necessary for the action employed. The theatre the play was written to be performed in often dictates the scope of action in the work. A work requiring lavish spectacles are usually not written for small theatres. Adaptations may be made in specific productions to allow more or less" action space".

Agony: Agony is the Greek word for struggle or conflict. As used in classical Greek drama, it indicates a portion of the play in which two characters engage in a heated argument or debate. Each of the characters is supported in their arguments by a part of the Greek chorus. The agony was a device used extensively in both comedies and tragedies. It is often the part of Greek drama when climaxes of the plot unfold. The opposing characters usually represent conflicting themes or ideas in the drama. In tragedies the anon is sometimes followed by the death or exile of the protagonist.

In modern literature the term is used in literary criticism to denote a competitive battle. Harold Bloom used the term as an element in literary history in terms of the conflict between a major poet and his or her predecessor whom the poet feels he must displace.

Devices of drama

Apostrophe occurs when a character addresses an abstract idea or a persona not present in the scene. This differs from a soliloquy where a character seems to be speaking to him, or thinking out loud. The soliloquy was used extensively in English Renaissance drama and made popular by Shakespeare in his dramatic works. The soliloquy has evolved into interior monologues in fiction where the musings of a character are used to develop depth and advance plots. Apostrophe and soliloquy are often confused, and it should be remembered that a soliloquy occurs when there is only one character on the stage, while in apostrophe there may be other characters in the scene but not addressed.

Antistrophe is a device in Greek drama where the chorus responds to a previous stanza of verse. Antistrophe is rarely seen today outside of the production of classical Greek drama.

Types of dramas

Chronicle plays are historical dramas based on English history written primarily during the Elizabethan and Jacobean periods. The source of many of these plays was Holinshed's "Chronicles of England, Scotland, and Ireland", thus the title "Chronicle Plays".

Mystery Plays are dramatic works based on the bible. These dramas were usually produced by local trade guilds for the pleasure of their villages. They were presented in cycles that sometimes dramatized the entire New and Old testaments. Mystery plays were performed in England, France, Spain, and Italy among other countries. Passion plays are specialized mystery plays based on the passion of Christ.

Heroic Dramas featured heroes of epic deeds. Usually written in blank verse or heroic couplets, these plays reached the apex of their popularity during the Restoration period.

Interludes refers to a very short form of drama sometimes performed between courses of a banquet but also the term came to refer to any kind of musical or dramatic entertainment. These were usually performed for private parties and fell out of favor with the opening of public venues. Their popularity peaked in 16th century England.

No is a form of traditional Japanese theatre that use music, dance, and poetry. They make no claim to be realistic, rather creating a serene and peaceful mood through spectacle and imagery. No are based on eastern religions, reflecting themes from Hinduism and Buddhism. The plays have a fixed repertory which has been constant since the 1500's. William Butler Yeats adapted No for western audiences in a series of short plays. They remain popular with drama critics and certain classes of Japanese.

Problem plays

Problem plays focus on social problems and movements. Alexander Dumas, son of the great French novelist, wrote a series of short plays attacking the ills of society. The early 19th century was the heyday of problem plays. Henrik Ibsen is perhaps the most celebrated of the problem plays playwright, particularly with his treatment of women's rights in "The Doll House". Lillian Hellman and Arthur Miller have both written popular problem plays in the 20th century.

The term, problem plays, is used in a different context by Shakespearean scholars. These critics use the term for plays that have caused interpretation problems for audiences. Plays such as "All's Well That Ends Well", "Troilus and Cressida", and "Measure for Measure" lend themselves to various interpretations and pose literary problems for students of the bard.

Farce

A dramatic comedy that is full of action, escapades of characters always on the brink of disaster, and full of stereotypical characters filling stock roles. The farce is one of the oldest forms of comedy, found in folk plays, Greek drama, the Renaissance and modern theatre.

The 'Bedroom farce' is a special type of comedy based on the foibles of attempted seductions. It continues to be popular in modern theatre, notably in the work of Alan Ayckbourn.

The theater of the absurd uses farce to represent the essential meaninglessness and chaos of life. Specialized forms of this are tragic force which combines farce with tragedy.
Farce is perhaps best known by the public through silent films, where Charlie Chaplin, the Keystone Cops and many other slapstick comedians made film an excellent example of farce enjoyed by a wide audience.

Poetry

In its most basic sense, any type of literature that uses the principle of meter. Poetry may be divided into three subdivisions:

1. Lyric poetry - a type of poetry where the voice if the poem evokes a particular feeling or attitude. Originally designed for musical accompaniment, it evolved to embrace a wide variety of literary forms.
2. Epic poetry - an extended narrative telling the story of a hero or group of heroes usually taking a journey and experiencing many dramatic adventures. Although usually not directly historical, the stories narrated are often the disguised versions of actual events or processes.
3. Dramatic poetry - poetry in which a single speaker, not the poet, addresses a silent listener. The delivery of the address occurs in a dramatic situation, and reveals something about the character of the speaker and the historical time in which the poem is set.

Poetry relies on sound as well as sense in creating an impact. It makes use of multiple literary devices to convey moods, emotions, narratives, and settings.

Reading poetry

1. Understand the relationship of the title to the work. Does the title suggest anything about the subject?
2. Ascertain who the "speaker" of the poem is. Determine what type of narrative is employed.
3. Know the major theme or argument that dominates the work.
4. Poems deal with private or individual matters or subjects in the public spectrum. Determine which the poem is addressing.
5. What type of meter is used in the poem? Is rhyme employed as a device?
6. Carefully examine the poem for figurative language and note how it is used.
7. Be aware of the poems historical and cultural setting to place the meaning in context.
8. Notice whether the poem fits a formally defined genre within poetry.

Problem

Poetry is usually viewed as the most difficult and unapproachable literary genre. Both the reading and study of poetry present obstacles and barriers for many people.

Poetry has a number of technical, formal, features that differ from prose. These features and formalities are what distinguish poetry from prose, and make it seem esoteric. Some view poetry as an indirect and oblique mode of expression that is available only to those who have the technical ability to decipher it. The language of poetry often seems both obscure and alien. Poetry seems crammed full of symbols, imagery, allusions, and other literary devices some find daunting. Much of this seems true. It clearly takes more preparation and effort to study poetry than prose. The richness of poetic language can be beautiful, but also difficult to understand. A study of the formal analysis of poetry dispels much of the mystery and makes the genre much more accessible.

Analysis

The formal analysis of poetry is essential to its full enjoyment. Understanding poetic form and devices is an important part of interpreting a poems meaning. Some major poetic devices include:

- Meter - is the regular recurrence of a rhythmic sound pattern. It is created by a repetition of a certain number of stressed syllables together with a number of unstressed syllables. The process of determining the meter of a poem is called scansion. This is done by marking accented and unaccented syllables in a poem. Poetry without a meter is called free verse.

- Foot - in English verse lines are divided into units, each called a foot, with a different pattern of accented and unaccented syllables. Common types include iambic, trochaic, dactylic, anapestic, and spondaic. Lines of verse are also classified by the number of feet it contains. A line may be monometer (one foot), diameter (two feet), trimeter (three feet), tetrameter (four feet), pentameter (five feet), hexameter (six feet), or heptameter (seven feet).
- Rhyme - a duplication of sounds usually occurring at the end of a line of verse. Rhyme may include assonance, the rhyming of vowel sounds, or consonance, rhymes where vowels are the same but pronounced differently.
- Accent is a recurring stress in a line of verse. In poetry written in English, the number and order of accented syllables determine the meter of a line or poem.

Understanding the meaning

Poetry creates its meaning from the interactions between the meaning of words and the effects of them being arranged in metrical patterns. To fully derive a poems meaning, the understanding of the formal qualities of poetry is useful. An initial reading of a poem uncovers the main theme of the poem as well as the author's attitude toward the main subject. The narrative situation and the basic features of form usually emerge from a first reading.

Rereading and study of a poem should include the details of form and how these are contributing to understanding. Formal features are most useful when they yield a tangible result. Form and meaning must be considered together for a full understanding of the work. Integrating formal features of a poem does not require great technical skill. It

is really a question of becoming familiar with the language of formal analysis and using this to enhance understanding and enjoyment of the poetry. These skills are easily learned and greatly enrich the reading of a work.

Identifying meter

1. Read the poem and decide where the grammatical and semantic stresses are placed.
2. Mark the pattern of stressed and unstressed syllables.
3. Determine whether the poem follow a regular meter.
4. Count the number of feet in each line.
5. Identify the predominant types of foot and line.
6. Read the poem again, preferably aloud, and listen for rhythm variations in the whole poem.
7. Mark changes of rhythm and the new type of feet.

This process will help understand both the formal structure and meaning of a work.

Poetic oddities

- Aubades are poems in which lovers must part, usually at the breaking of the dawn.
- Cadence is the rhythmic rise and fall of a line of verse, rather than the regularity of meter.
- Cantos are major sections of long poems. Dante's "Divine Comedy" consists of 100 cantos which include the introductory section.
- Couplets are a pair of contiguous lines that rhyme. All of Shakespeare's sonnets end in a couplet.
- Dithyrambs are dramatic and structurally irregular lyric poems. The original form was a hymn sung by the Greek chorus at pagan festivals honoring the god Dionysus.
- Ecologies were originally poems set in pastoral environments, usually featuring Shepard's in dialogue. In modern poetry, it has come to mean a

poem that evokes serious reflection and meditation.

Ryhme

Rhyme is an important device for many poems. There are two main divisions of rhyme:
1. End rhyme - occurs at the close of a rhyme. End rhyme is "perfect", it involves identical sounds.
2. Half rhyme - also called slant rhyme, involves a closeness of sounds but are not identical.

Rhyme may be masculine (rhyming elements comprise single stressed syllables), or feminine (rhyming elements comprise unstressed syllables). Eye rhyme joins similarly spelled words that are pronounced differently. Internal rhyme involves repeated elements in a line rather than at its end. The usual method for describing a rhyming scheme uses letters to signify the sounds of line endings, with the first sound called" A" and the second sound called "B" and so on. For example, rhymes could have AABBCC patterns based on the line endings. As with other formal elements of poetry, rhyming schemes have the most relevance when contributing to the understanding of a work.

Enriching poetry
Rhymes enrich poetry in many ways. Some of the major impacts include:
1. Rhymes add a degree of aural enhancement to poetry. This enhancement fosters the overall meaning of the work. It imposes a pattern on the poem that can be used to emphasize or minimize meaning in lines of poetry.
2. Rhymes tend to strike a chord in memory. Cultures depending on an oral tradition found rhymes an easy way to tell a story that people could remember. Rhymes are used by poets to stress major points in a work, and their use often adds to the popularity and readability of a poem.

3. Rhymes can summarize the major meaning of a poem in an exclamatory manner.
4. Rhyme is used to emphasize words and make connections between them.
5. Rhymes challenges a poet to engage in a literary device as a strategy for understanding, drama, and literary appeal.
6. Reading a poem always begs the question of how rhyming (or lack there of), affects the reading experience.

Figurative language

Poetry is a genre in which language is used in all its variations and embellishments to convey a sense, mood, or feeling the poet feels important. Poetry uses elaborate linguistic constructions to explain the world in creative ways.

Poetry manipulates language itself to convey impressions in new and innovative constructions. It makes extensive use of figurative devices such as conceits, similes, metaphors and many more to express things in fresh ways. These devices will be treated separately later. Together poets use figurative language to suggest rather than give direct meanings. This language provides a creative experience for the reader who is asked to understand meaning in unconventional terms. Poets relish the opportunities to express themselves in creative and unusual words. Figurative language provides both poet and reader an opportunity for unique expression and understanding. Emotions, feelings, and moods are invoked by the skillful use of figurative language.

Movements in poetry

Free Verse
Free verse is generally poetry without a regular meter and usually omits rhyme. The first poet to use free verse as a major mode of

- 34 -

expression was Walt Whitman who's "Leaves of Grass" is written entirely in free verse.

Free verse gives the writer a great deal of latitude in constructing the poetry, by letting her select an individual rhythm for each work. It does however, place unusual demands on the technical skill of the writer, who must develop an original scheme for each poem written in free verse. Some poets have decried free verse, Robert Frost stating that a poet writing free verse is "like playing tennis without a net". Despite these criticisms free verse continues to be a popular mode of poetry, particularly among modern poets who eschew the conventions of formal poetry. The "beat generation" poets like Alan Ginsberg used free verse extensively, perhaps as an expression of their rebellion, in the 1950's and 1960's.

Imagism
In the early years of the 20th century, a new school of poetry called imagism flourished. The imagist ideal posited three poetic goals:
1. To address the subject directly, without symbolism or other obfuscating devices.
2. To use only absolutely essential words necessary for the poetry, without excess ornamentation, or detail.
3. Rhythm was to be guided by musical principles and examples, rather than a sequence of standard meter.

These principles were in part a revolt against romanticism and an argument for the use of free verse. The founders of the imagist school were Ezra Pound, T.E. Hulme, and F.S. Flint, all renowned poets of their day. Amy Lowell helped promote the movement in America and published a set of anthologies of imagist poetry in 1915.

Imagist principles were important in later schools of poetry including Objectivism, and Projectivism. These principles can be seen in much of the modern poetry written in the last 100 years.

Objectivism and Projectivism
Objectivism began in the early 1930's as a further extension of imagism. The phrase was coined by William Carlos Williams, who wrote" the poem is an object that formally presents is case and meaning by the very form it assumes". This movement was another step away from the school of romantic poetry. An excellent example of objectivism is William's poem "The Great Figure", describing a fire truck racing through city streets.

Projectivism originated in the early 1950's with the publication of an essay by Charles Olsen called "Projective Verse". In this essay he endorsed the ideas of both Imagism and Objectivism, calling for poetry more attuned to the ear than critical analysis. This was largely an argument against cerebral poetry and a plea to make poetry reflect the unity of mind and body. Poetry should be more physical, even muscular in language and impact. Influences of both Objectivism and Projectivism can be seen in many examples of modern poetry.

Elegy

An elegy is a mournful or sorrowful poem, usually lamenting the dead. It typically expresses the poet's sorrow for the loss of a friend or lover, or more generally for the sadness of the human condition. Consolation is a recurring theme in an elegy, in some way consoling the audience for the brevity of human existence.

The first elegy was "The Idylls of Theocritus", in early Greek literature. More modern examples include Milton's "Lycidas", Thomas Gray's " Elegy Written in a Country Church Yard", Shelley's "Adonais", and W. H. Auden's "In Memory of W.B. Yeats".

In formal poetic convention, an elegy refers to any poem, regardless of subject, written in elegiac distiches (alternating lines of dactylic hexameter and pentameter).

The usual understanding of the term in poetry is the sorrowful or mournful mood that is the signature of the elegy. This type of work is much less common in modern poetry although it still occurs.

Epic

Originally epics were long narrative poems, focused on a hero's adventures and triumphs. The hero generally undergoes a series of trials that test his courage, character, and intellect. Epic poems have certain conventions such as the use of a muse and exhaustive lists of armies, ships, and catalogues. There were written and oral epics that transmitted folk culture from generation to generation.

The best known of the original epics were written by Homer and Virgil. Milton's "Paradise Lost" is an example of a more recent epic as is Cervantes" Don Quixote".

Epic theatre, pioneered by Bertolt Brecht, is a father refinement of the form.

Epics have come to mean any dramatic work of poetry, prose, drama, film, or music that depends on spectacles and lavish productions sometimes based on historical events.

Essay

Essays are usually defined as a prose composition dealing with one or two topics. The word essay is from the French 'essayer', meaning to try or attempt. The term was coined by Michel de Montaigne (1533-92) who is still regarded as a master of the form. Essays tend to be informal in style, and are usually personal in approach and opinion.

Francis Bacon (1561-1626) pioneered essays that were dogmatic and impersonal, leading to a division of essays called formal and familiar respectively. Some essays have been adapted to verse, while others are a hybrid of essay and fiction.

Essays usually begin with an observation or musing on a subject. Formal essays tend to present an argument while familiar essays are less dogmatic and reflect the personal views of the author. they do not try to convince, but proffer opinions and observations on a subject.

Essays have been written about countless subjects, from public policy to existential anxiety. Literary essays are popular, and some of the best were written by notable authors such as Henry James, Virginia Woolf, and T.S. Eliot.

Literature movements

Aestheticism
Aestheticism, a term originally used in French and English literature, this held that art has no need to serve a moral or ethical purpose. It maintains "Art for art's sake" is its own justification. The French author Theophile Gautier stated the only purpose of art is to be beautiful.

In England, James Swinburne and Walter Pater led the aestheticism movement. Its most famous advocate was Oscar Wilde, who in his last work, "De Profundis", wrote " I treated art as the supreme reality and life as a mode of fiction".

Formalism
Formalism, a modified and less extreme movement, approached literature from its internal features, without regard to historical, social, economic, or political context. Formalism is most closely associated with modern schools of criticism, namely Russian Formalism, and New Criticism.

Literary devices

Literary devices are used to enrich and emphasize observed qualities. They are present in all genres.
- An analogy is a literary device that compares two things. It functions as

an extended metaphor. In a broader sense analogies refer to the process of reasoning from parallel examples.

- Similes are figures of speech that use a grammatical connection such as 'like', 'as if', or 'as' to explain comparisons.
- Metaphors in a narrow sense are figures of speech that highlight the similarities between two elements, conventionally called 'tenor' and 'vehicle'. Metaphors may be direct or indirect. A direct metaphor states the comparison directly, while an indirect metaphor only implies the comparison. Metaphors have always been a major device in poetry, and are now seen in every aspect of language.
- Irony is an expression that conveys something other than its literal meaning. It is also a literary style using this device. Types of irony include:
  1. Verbal irony conveyed by voice inflection as in sarcasm.
  2. Structural irony where an alternative meaning is produced by using a narrative feature.
  3. Dramatic irony used in plays where the audience has important information which is not available to other key characters.

The term irony is derived from the Greek for "dissembling, feigned, ignorance". It was originally used in Greek comedy where the sly Icon usually outwitted his slower rival, Amazon. Irony is used in all forms of literature and is very common in modern works. It is particularly effective in poetry and drama but is also used in fiction and nonfiction.

Characters

A protagonist is the central character in a play or story. The character opposing the protagonist is called the antagonist. Either may be the hero or villain of a drama or work of fiction. In modern literature the protagonist-antagonist struggle is often represented as an internal conflict in one individual. Freudian thought has had a great influence on this inward battle of psychological forces in a person. The hero or heroine is also the major figure in a literary work. The term may be used instead of protagonist. Finally, the villain is the major evil character in a literary work. Usually the villain opposes the protagonist but sometimes is the protagonist of a work. The roles of heroes and villains are exaggerated in melodrama and often seen in early films. The conflict in these cases usually involves a "fair damsel". Modern literature usually reflects a more mixed character, with both qualities present in a character.

Ballads

The original meaning of ballad was song closely associated with dance. Over time, the ballad formed a branch of narrative using verse. Folk ballads, the most common form, typically deal with love affairs, tragic endings, and occasionally historical and military subjects. The narration is often told in dialogue form, arranged in quatrains with the second and fourth line rhyming. Ballads are derived from folk tales and oral traditions, and use direct, descriptive language. Ballads have been popular for centuries, and folk music is an extension of the ballad form. The term ballad is still used extensively to note songs that tell a story, usually with a romantic or tragic theme. Ballads are sometimes derived from historical sources, lending them a sense of stories told in verse. Minstrels were the early performers of ballads, and were important in preserving the cultural and historical records of many peoples. Ballads have also been adopted by poets, as in Wilde's "The Ballad of Reading Goal".

Elizabethan Literature

English literature written during the reign of Elizabeth I. This includes the Early Tudor period and ends with the death of Shakespeare.

Elizabethan literature reflect the national pride felt during the reign of The Virgin Queen. The language of the period is highly colored, rich and ornamented. Elizabethan poetry saw the birth of the sonnet, and the epic poem, the Faerie Queen written by Edmund Spenser.

The crowning achievement of the period was Elizabethan drama, which became hugely popular with the people. Authors such as Thomas Kyd and Christopher Marlowe ushered in this golden age of drama, followed by Thomas Dekker, George Chapman, and Thomas Heywood. William Shakespeare's elegant histories, comedies, and tragedies displayed the genius of this dramatic period. The death of the queen followed closely by Shakespeare's passing brought a close to this golden period of drama.

An early chronicle of world literature

3500 B.C. - The first written language is developed by Sumerians in Mesopotamia.
3000 B.C. - The Egyptians begin using hieroglyphics on papyrus.
2000B.C. - "Gilamesh" an epic poem of Mesopotamia is written.
1500 B.C. - The first alphabet is developed by the Phoenicians.
1200 B.C.- The Old Testament is written.
800 B.C. - Homer writes the epic poems "The Iliad" and "Odyssey" on Greek heroism in the Trojan Wars.
800 B.C. - The Chinese spiritual text," The Way of Power" presents Taoist philosophy of harmonious living.
700 B.C. - Hasid's "Theogony" presents the mythology of greek gods.
610 B.C. - The earliest known record of latin appears in Rome.
610 B.C. - Sappho's poems from the island of Lesbos are written.
450 B.C. - Herodotus's history is the first historical work written.

430 B.C. - Sophocles, Euripides, and Aristophane write Greek drama.
400 B.C. - The Indian epic the "Bhagavadgita" is composed.
380 B.C. - Plato's "Republic" elaborates the teaching of Socrates and lays the foundation for western philosophy.
100 A. D. - Papermaking is invented in China.
100 A.D. - The New Testament is written in Greek
633 A.D. - The Koran is recorded in Arabic.
750 A.D. - The epic poem "Beowulf", the oldest extant work in English is composed orally.
1045 A.D. - Movable type is invented in China.
1100 A.D. - Old English evolves into Middle English.
1200 A.D. - European mystery plays combine biblical themes with social satire.
1297 A.D. - Marco Polo's "Travels" introduces Europeans to Asian culture.
1400 A.D. - Chaucer's "The Canterbury Tales" collects stories of pilgrims in a rich evocation of medieval life.
1450 A.D. - Gutenberg invents movable metal type and the printing press.
1516 A. D. - Martin Luther launches the Protestant Reformation in Wittenberg, Germany.
1558 A.D, - The reign of Elizabeth I begins the golden age of English literature.
1589 A.D. - William Shakespeare's first plays are produced in London.
1611A.D. - The King James Bible is published and will have a lasting impact on English literature.
1660 A.D. - The Restoration Period of English literature begins.
1667 A.D. - Milton's "Paradise Lost" is published in blank verse in England.

Important literary contributors

Homer is regarded as the greatest and earliest of the greek epic poets and a literary giant whose innovations had lasting impact on Western culture. Very little is known of his life, although it is generally agreed he was blind. He lived in the latter part of the 8th century B.C., and his greatest works are "The

Iliad" and "Odyssey". The authorship and means of composition of both epics are a source of academic debate, and few facts can be verified. Both of these epic poems related the events of the Trojan War, and are clearly derived from oral traditions. Some scholars believe they were not written down until long after the death of Homer. Others feel that Homer may have been a baric singer, and the poems were derived from his recitals. These epics were so influential that they were the foundation of education in classical Greece and Rome, and they remain as a core of liberal arts today.

Sappho was one of the earliest and most influential of the Greek poets, she lived on the island of Lesbos, from which the word "lesbian" is derived. On Lesbos she is thought to have led a community of young women who she tutored in music and poetry. Sappho's poetry is usually dedicated to these young women for whom she served as a mentor. Sappho's poetry is intimate in tone and often treats themes of love and friendship. Very little is known of her life, and her poetry survives only in fragments. Some scholars think she was exiled to Sicily by a repressive government on Lesbos. There is an apocryphal story about Sappho being committing suicide by throwing herself off a cliff after a tragic love affair. All such stories must be classed as speculation but what is certain is her poetic skill and dedication to her students with who she lived on Lesbos.

One of the greatest Greek playwrights, **Sophocles** wrote powerful tragedies that were considered the highest form of the art. He lived and wrote in the fourth century B.C., and was considered one of the leading citizens of Athens. His major works include "Oedipus the King", "Antigone", and "Electra". Although Sophocles wrote over 100 plays, only seven complete dramas have survived. His tragic heroes value truth above all, even if it brings destruction and death. Sophocles was the master of writing tightly constructed plays, and was an innovator in Greek drama. He added a third lead actor to the original

two, and produced self-contained plays rather than trilogies. Sophocles lived in Athens and was famous as a writer, musician, statesman, and priest. Aristotle considered Sophocles the greatest of the classical Greek dramatists and his plays have been studied for centuries for their plotting and composition.

Euripides is the author of 92 plays, of which only 19 survive. His greatest works are "Medea", "Electra", and "Hippolytus". Euripides lived in Athens from 484 B.C. until the last two years of his life which he spent at the court of King Archelaus of Macedonia. Little is known of his early life, and he built his reputation as a playwright by competing in the dramatic contests in Athens, which he won 22 times. Euripides was a master at creating complex, characters with rich emotional lives. His characterization of women was particularly artful. In Euripide's dramas the gods are indifferent to earthly problems, and he portrays human weakness as the cause of suffering. Many of his plays are about the foolishness of war, and he championed unpopular social clauses such as the equality of women in society. His personal reputation as a pendant inspired two dramatic parodies of him by his rival Aristophanes. Embittered by these attacks, Euripides left Athens for Macedonia where he died in 406 B.C..

Aristophanes was a Greek playwright who was the greatest comedic writer of his time. His plays were noted for their brilliant dialogue, poetic choral lyrics, sharp parodies, and topical allusions. Eleven of his plays survive, the best known being "The Clouds", "The Wasps", and "The Birds". Others include "Lysistrata" and "The Frogs". He wrote in the style of "Old Comedy", combining mime, fantasy, chorus and bawdy humor which delighted his audiences. He loved to satirize social institutions, public figures, and the gods as well. The details of his life are largely unknown, and most of the information comes from his work. A citizen of Athens all his life, Aristophanes launched his dramatic career in

427 B.C.. He wrote two parodies of Euripides, which so incensed his rival that he left Athens. Aristophanes was a popular figure in Greece and his works are still occasionally staged today.

Virgil was one of the greatest of roman poets. He wrote the inscription for his own tomb, one who " sang of flocks and farms and heroes". Virgil's magnus opus is the epic poem, " The Aeneid", which ranks as one of the most influential works in early classical literature. "The Aeneid" tells the tale of the adventures and triumphs of Homer. Virgil's influence extends to the work of Dante, Spenser, Milton, and Shakespeare. His goal was to create works comparable with the Greek poets, and in this he succeeded. His work was uniquely his own and reflected his Roman culture. Virgil was born in northern Italy, and was well educated for a farmer's son. During the civil war of 41 B.C., his farm was confiscated and he moved to Rome to become one of the Emperor Augustus's circle of artists. His first published work was the "Eclogues", followed by "Georgics", and finally the "Aeneid". Much of his early work was about farm life and the joys of a bucolic existence. He became ill on a trip to Greece, and died upon his return in 19 B.C..

Publius Ovidius Naso, known as Ovid, was a great Roman poet applauded for his passionate, technically skilled, an witty poetry. His influence is seen in the works of Chaucer, Milton, Dryden, and Shakespeare. His masterpiece, "Metamorphoses" is written on the theme of transformation in Greek and Roman myth, is widely respected as a seminal work in Roman literature. His love narratives, 'Amores", were kept alive during the middle ages despite the opposition of the Church. Ovid also wrote an instruction manual on the art of love which established him as a major writer. Born in Sulmo in eastern Italy, Ovid moved to Rome to join the court of Emperor Augustus. He was exiled to the Black Sea for unknown reasons in 8 A.D.. Ovid's pleas for forgiveness were published as his "Sorrows" and "Letters from Pontus",

but he was not pardoned and remained in exile until his death in 17 A.D. . His legacy is one of the most influential in all of classical poetry.

Dante Alighieri, the greatest of the Italian poets, was a major figure in the Renaissance's revolution of arts and letters. His epic masterpiece," The Divine Comedy", ranks as one of the truly great literary works in history. "The Divine Comedy" presents a panoramic view of man and his place in the cosmos, describing a mans journey through the divine realms of Hell, Purgatory, and Paradise. The traveler is helped first by Virgil, then by the woman Beatrice, who was based on Beatrice Portinari, a figure Dante idealized as a figure of Divine love. Combining deeply religious themes with sharp commentaries on social and political institutions, "The Divine Comedy" used Tuscan dialect that had a great influence on the development of modern Italian. Dante was an aristocrat born in Florence in 1265 A.D., and his political activism led to his exile in 1302 A.D..

Thereafter he lived in different Italian cities, finally settling in Ravenna on the Adriatic. He was a prolific writer, treating subjects as varied as uses of the Italian language, and Christian political philosophy. Dante died in Ravenna in 1321.

Geoffery Chaucer is regarded as the greatest of the Middle English authors. Chaucer wrote works of narrative poetry, and his greatest achievement is "The Canterbury Tales". "The Canterbury Tales" presents 24 stories told by a group of pilgrims traveling to Canterbury. The tales range over many subjects, including romances, religious themes, and bawdy verses. The genius of the work is the rich characterization of the pilgrims, done with consummate skill, insight, and humor. Chaucer was influenced by Dante, and Boccacio whom he read on visits to Italy. Chaucer's writing expanded the scope of Middle English writing beyond provincial life and moral ideals, to a more inclusive view of the world. Chaucer was born in England in 1343, and entered royal service in his teens. He held numerous political and diplomatic posts over the years, traveling and serving across Europe. Chaucer was widely read, and incorporated much that he learned in his travels in his writing. Chaucer died in England in 1400.

Sir Thomas Malory is thought to be Sir Thomas Malory of Warwickshire, although this is still the subject of academic debate. his major work, "Le Morte D'Arthur", is a collection of prose stories based on Arthurian legend and oral traditions. These tales were the first collection of works on the legends of King Arthur and the Knights of the Round Table. They tell the stories of the kingdom of Camelot and the epic adventures of its characters. Famous characters such as King Arthur, Sir Lancelot, Sir Gawain, and Queen Guinevere have served as models for countless adaptations and are familiar figures in folk literature. The details of Thomas Malory's life are a mystery, but certain facts are known, chiefly from his works. Born in 1408 in England, Malory completed his literary masterpiece while imprisoned for criminal activity. Malory petitioned for release upon completion of his manuscript, but this was denied and he died in jail in 1471. His great work was published posthumously in 1485.

Francois Rabelais major work was a five volume masterpiece, "Gargantuan and Pantagreul" published in Paris in 1564. This work was a unique combination of social satire, licentious comedy, and humanist philosophy. Shocked by this material, the Church placed the work on Catholic Librium Prohibitorium, and it was banned in France during his lifetime. His literature inspired the word "Rabelaisian" which has come to mean a character with qualities of coarse humor, ribaldry, and boisterousness. His literary influence is seen in the works of Voltaire, Hugo, and Swift. Rabelais was truly a Renaissance man, being a Benedictine monk, physician, teacher, translator, and renowned

for his knowledge in many fields. His role as a monk no doubt was part of the reason his work was seen as controversial by the church and banned. He died in France in 1553.

Michel de Montaigne's great contribution to be the introduction of the essay to Western literature. His seminal work, "Essays" introduced the genre, and the French term "essay", meaning to try was the name given the new form. "Essays" was published in three volumes from 1580-88, and drew heavily from established literary forms such as the treatise and religious confessions. Montaigne commented on social issues, as well as the human condition in a brief, personal voice. His insights into major historical issues such as religious conflict and exploration of the New World were admired throughout Europe. The son of a wealthy landowner in southern France, Montaigne received a classical education and studied law. He counseled Parliament until 1571, when he retired to his family estate for study and writing. During the turbulent periods of civil war in France, he was drawn back to politics as a mediator and eventually Mayor of Bordeaux. He died on his family estate in 1592.

Christopher Marlowe was an English author and playwright who produced a remarkable body of work in his short life. He gained acclaim as the most important Elizabethan dramatist prior to Shakespeare. Among his most successful plays include" Edward II", "Tamburlaine the Great", "Dr. Faustas", and "The Jew of Malta". Marlowe's writing is characterized by developing passionate protagonists, the strength of his verse, and his brilliant plotting. Scholars believe that some works attributed to Shakespeare may have been written in whole or part by Marlowe. Marlowe's poetry is accomplished, the best known being the verse that begins" come live with me and be my love". Marlowe, the son of a cobbler, was born in London in 1564, and educated at Cambridge. He lived a turbulent and sometimes violent life, engaging in criminal activity ranging from forgery to espionage. He was killed in 1593 at age 29 in a brawl over a tavern bill, cutting short a brilliant talent.

William Shakespeare, arguably the greatest playwright ever to live, had influenced world literature for the last 400 years. Shakespeare's genius was the ability to create works that capture the drama of human conflict and weakness, while developing characters that suffer man's deepest existential anxieties. Master of drama and poetry alike, his writing is without peer in literary history. He wrote tragedies, histories, comedies. and sonnets and narrative poems. His works have been translated into scores of languages and adapted for film, opera and ballet. Some of his best known works include "Hamlet", "Henry V", "Romeo and Juliet", and "Macbeth". Shakespeare was born in Stratford-upon-Avon in 1564 and received a classical education. He married Ann Hathaway and spent most of his professional life in London where he used the Globe theatre as his base from 1599. He was well established as an actor and playwright as early as 1592, and wrote a series of brilliant sonnets in 1609. Shakespeare died in England in 1616 and is buried in Stratford.

Edmund Spenser was one of the greatest Elizabethan poets famed for his evocative sonnets and rich epic poetry. His most famous work is "The Faerie Queen", a heroic romance narrating the exploits of 12 knights. Published in 1596, it introduced a new poetic form, the Spenserian stanza based on an Italian poetic scheme. " The Faerie Queen" includes a moral allegory in an epic narrative. Spenser was a prolific author, penning sonnet sequences and notable short verse. Born in London in 1552, Spenser was educated at Cambridge and joined the household of the Earl of Leicester where he wrote his first work," The Shepherdess Calendar", comprised of 12 pastoral poems, in 1579. Spenser moved to Ireland in 1590, where he ran an estate in Cork. Here he wrote an elegy for his friend Sir Philip Sidney called "Astrophel". Spenser returned to London where he died in 1599, his place in literary history assured.

Miguel de Cervantes was an accomplished Spanish novelist, poet, and playwright. A giant in literary history, Cervantes is best known as the author of "Don Quixote", a early masterpiece of prose fiction. Many view him as the originator of the novel, and it is agreed that Cervantes demonstrated the possibilities of satirical narrative and fictional realism. His work has inspired novelists for almost 400 years. Born into a poor family outside Madrid, Cervantes became a soldier and was captured and enslaved by Algerian pirates for five years. Ransomed by Trinitarian friars, he worked as a businessman in Andalusia until the success of "Don Quixote" allowed him the freedom to devote himself to writing. He was productive in later life, writing "Exemplary Stories", a work of 12 diverse narratives. He authored at least 30 plays of which about half survive. Cervantes completed an epic romance," The Trials of Persiles and Sigismunda" only three days before his death in 1616.

Ben Jonson was a commanding figure in English letters. Playwright, poet, and critic, Jonson was famed for his elegant writing and brilliant intelligence. Jonson was the master of satires with his savage portrayals of human follies and corruption. The best known of these are "Valpone", "Epicine", and "The Alchemist". Jonson also wrote epic poetry including the well known "Song to Celia" that was widely influential in the Restoration period. Jonson published his collected works in 1616 and was named Poet Laureate the same year. Born in London in 1572, Jonson had no formal education and went to war as a youth against the Spanish in Flanders. He became a popular writer of masques, a form of court entertainment that featured great spectacle, music, and poetry. Jonson was second only to Shakespeare in reputation among his peers. His followers, whom he served as a mentor, became known as "Sons of Ben".

Francis Bacon, Viscount St. Albans, Baron Verulam, was one of the greatest English essayists and philosopher. Bacon wrote primarily on science and scientific inquiry, championing the method of scientific investigation and empirical observation against the scholastic philosophy favored by the Church His greatest work was "Instaruratio Magna", a sweeping argument against the Renaissance and Scholastic philosophy. Bacon's"Essays,"published in 1612, covered a wide range of subjects including English history, law, and society, and employed a aphoristic style. His vision of utopia was described in "New Atlantis" published in 1627. Bacon was born in London in 1561 and was active in politics, serving in Parliament several times. He served as Solicitor General under James I , but was charged with bribery in 1621 and barred from parliament. He remained an active writer until his death in London in 1626.

John Donne the greatest of the Metaphysical poets, wrote highly original verses on both religious and secular poetry. His love verses were written prior to his secret marriage to 17 year old Ann More. The best known of these are "The Sunne Rising", "The Bait", and "To Catch a Falling Star". His reputation as a religious poet rests on "The Holy Sonnets" written in a period of spiritual search. Donne was born into a Catholic family with strong ties to the Church. He converted to Anglicanism in 1614 after suffering a crisis of faith. Donne's marriage to Ann More without her fathers consent caused a scandal for which he served a short prison sentence. His ambitions for a government career were dashed by this incident, and he turned to a career as an Anglican priest and dean of London's St. Paul's Cathedral. His reputation as a passionate preacher grew, but his poetry was not published until two years after his death. Donne wrote his own funeral sermon that was delivered in 1631.

John Milton, the great English poet, wrote one of the great masterpieces of English literature in "Paradise Lost". This great Christian epic poem describing "mans first disobedience" was published in 1667. Milton followed this with the more severe "Paradise Regained", and his final work, the verse drama "Samson Agonistes" both published in 1671. Milton was born into a wealthy family and attended St. Paul's school and Cambridge before undertaking seven years of independent study. Several of his best known works, "L'Allegro" and "Il Penseroso" emerged from this period. Milton was a strong supporter of the Puritan and Commonwealth cause, and wrote extensively defending civil freedom. He served as s secretary in the Cromwell government, and was severely disillusioned by the Restoration in 1660. Blind since 1652, he turned his power to the writing of his majestic work for which he is best remembered. Byron called him "the prince of poets", a well deserved sobriquet.

Jeb-Baptiste Poquelin, known as **Moliere**, was the greatest playwright of his time. Combining an acute ear for language, sharp character portraits, and the ability to evoke both profound and absurd moods, Moliere delighted his sophisticated Parisian audiences. His most popular plays include "La Tartuffe", banned by the Church, "The Misanthrope", and "The School for Wives". Moliere's unique combinations of talents produced a new type of comedy of manners, which brought him both fame and wealth. Moliere was born into a well-to-do Paris family in 1622. He eschewed a promising business career to devote himself to the theatre. He was active as an actor, writer, producer, and director, and toured France for ten years. Moliere became a favorite of King Louis XIV who offered him a theatre in the Louvre. Here he flourished becoming a favorite of French society. Moliere continued his dramatic work in Paris when during a performance of his last play, "The Imaginary Invalid", he collapsed and died in 1673.

Samuel Pepys fame rests on his "Diary", published in full in 1828. This work provides an insightful and unusually candid view of

17th century court life. Pepys chronicles events in his own life as well as important historical occasions such as the coronation of Charles II. Pepys leaves us the most dramatic account of the great fire in London, and the black plague. His legacy is to provide a window into the history of his time through his "Diary". Pepys was born in London in 1633, the son of a tailor. Educated at Cambridge, he served as a naval officer, member of Parliament, and President of The Royal Society. These positions gave him an entree into the high society of London, where he was feted and honored over the years. His personal life was marred by tragedy with the death of a beloved young wife. Pepys's "Diary" went undiscovered for over 100 years until it was found in Cambridge in 1825. Pepys died in London at age 70 in 1703 at the height of his fame.

John Dryden was a man for all seasons, a poet, playwright, and literary critic. He wrote a number of popular plays, the most important being "The Wild Gallent", "All For Love", "The Maiden Queen", and "The Indian Queen". Equally adept as a poet, Dryden won royal favor with his poem," To His Sacred Majesty", written for Charles II restoration to the throne. His verse satires were considered masterpieces. He served as Poet Laureate of England from 1668-88 and was revered in English society. Born in rural England in 1631, Dryden moved to London in 1655 where he remained for the rest of his life. He was appointed the royal historiographer in 1670. When James II was crowned, Dryden converted to Catholicism in the 1680's. His last years were spent translating several of the ancient classics, and he died in London in 1700. His career was illustrious and he became one of the most honored men in England.

John Bunyons literary reputation rests on his masterpiece," The Pilgrims Progress", written in 1684. This work was a religious allegory that became the best seller of its day. Read by both Catholics and Protestants, it recounts the spiritual journey of mankind. Bunyan was

born in Bedford in 1628, in the English countryside, and served in Cromwell's army during the English civil war. A spiritual maverick, he joined a nonconformist church in 1653 and became a popular preacher. In 1660 Bunyan was arrested for preaching without a permit, and spent 12 years in prison. This was a time of productive writing for Bunyan, who penned "Grace Abounding to the Chief of Sinners", "The Holy War", and other spiritual tracts. Bunyan also began work on his magna opus, "The Pilgrims Progress" while in prison. He was a vocal opponent of Quakerism, which he denounced in "A Vindication" in 1657. Bunyan was an active writer and preacher until his death in 1688.

Alexander Pope, the great English poet and satirist, was born in London in 1688. Pope's style featured biting wit, excellent command of formal poetry, and a particular kind of verse that was both insightful and dramatic. Among his numerous works is his great satire, "The Rape of the Lock", narrating a feud started over a lock of hair. "An Essay on Criticism", Pope's poem about writing, launched his career in 1711. He was to produce a body of work noted chiefly for satire and brilliant essays, including translations of Homer's "Iliad" and "Odyssey". Pope also edited a controversial edition of Shakespeare which won him notoriety. Pope had little formal education, and was raised a Catholic at a time that anti-Catholic feeling ran high in England. He contracted an unknown illness when he was a child, leaving him a semi-invalid, and stunting his growth. Despite these handicaps, Pope became one of the giants of English literature until his death in London in 1744.

Daniel Defoe born in London in 1700, had a varied and prolific literary career. He produced over 500 books, the most important being "Robinson Crusoe", and "Moll Flanders". Generally considered to be England's first novelist, Defoe was a keen observer of life, and was able to translate this into riveting characters in his novels. Defoe was an eclectic author, writing essays, non-fiction, and working as a journalist during his productive years. His editorship of the "Review" from 1704-13 made him the finest journalist of his day. Defoe was successful in both business and politics, becoming a strong supporter of William of Orange. His political pamphlets earned him a short term in prison. rescued by a Tory politician, Defoe became a well known political pamphleteer writing arguments for the Tory party. Defoe died in London in 1731 at the apex of his journalistic career.

Jonathan Swift, Irish satirist, wrote on a wide variety of subjects including economics, politics, society, and manners. His legacy was established by "Gulliver's Travels", his blistering satire on the human condition published in 1726. Other well known works include " Tale of a Tub", a satire on the church, "Drapier's Letters", an inluential tract on Irish politics, and "A Modest Proposal", suggesting Irish children be fattened and used as food for the rich. Born in Dublin in 1667, Swift received an excellent education at Trinity College and Oxford. Ordained a priest in the Church of Ireland in 1694, Swift served for ten years before becoming secretary to a prominent diplomat. Swift lived for years in both London and Dublin, where his reputation as a satirist grew. His began to decline in the 1730's, and he was declared incompetent and assigned a guardian. Upon his death in 1745, his estate granted a large sum to found a hospital for the mentally ill.

Henry Fielding , English novelist and playwright, is considered to be a pioneer in novel writing. Fielding wrote over 25 plays before turning his talent to novels. His best known work is "Tom Jones", and other notable works include" Joseph Andrews", "Amelia", "Shamela", and "The Life of Mr. Jonathan Wild the Great". He also published a newspaper, "The Champion", which was highly successful. He was adept in social satire and comedy which are best exemplified by "Tom Jones". Born in London in 1707, Fielding became active in politics in his late

20's. His strong anti-Jacobite essays gained Fielding political favor, and he served for many years as a judge in London. When political favor turned against him, Fielding concentrated on his writing, producing several late novels of note. Fielding died in London in 1754.

Samuel Johnson, the English poet, essayist, biographer and lexicographer, dominated the literary period of mid 18th century England. in 1746, he began to organize the first dictionary of the English language. He completed the task in 1755 and it was hailed as a major literary accomplishment and made Johnson's reputation. A prolific essayist and journalist, his prose was celebrated for its keen observation of human folly and frailty. Johnson's other major works include" Lives of the Poets", "Rasselas",and "The Vanity of human Wishes", considered his greatest poem. "Irene", a verse tragedy, was produced for the stage in 1746. Johnson was born in Litchfield in1709, and worked as a schoolmaster there for many years. He moved to London to become a writer, and succeeded beyond his dreams. Johnson was immortalized by James Boswell, his friend and confidant, in the" Life of Samuel Johnson". Johnson was such a giant literary figure, that upon his death in 1784, his era became known as "the age of Johnson".

Jean-Jacques Rousseau was a Swiss born novelist, essayist, philosopher, and intellect, who was very influential in the affairs of nations. Writing in French, Rousseau most important work was "The Social Contract" which was his polemic for changing society. The ideas expressed in this work helped ignite the French and American revolutions. He wrote two hugely successful novels," Julie", and "Emile", and numerous essays on a wide variety of topics. His autobiography, " Confessions", were a candid self-examination and self criticism. Born in Geneva in 1712, Rousseau moved to Paris and established his reputation as a writer with his essay, "Discourse on the Science and Arts" which argued science and art degraded the natural man. Rousseau's works became increasingly controversial and he was derided and exiled from several countries. Finally, he found refuge in England, but his last years were marked by paranoia and mental illness. He died in Paris in 1778, a largely broken man.

Robert Burns, the famed Scottish poet, became the most well known literary figure in Scotland. Burn's work includes some other best known poetry in the English language, including "Auld Lang Syne", "A Red, Red, Rose", and the long narrative poem "Tam o Shanter". His first anthology of poetry was "Poems, Chiefly in the Scottish Dialect", which became an instant success and led to his long and distinguished career. Burns spent much of his life collecting and editing traditional Scottish airs. Born to a poor family in 1759, Burns spent much of his life working the land on the family farm. He was a rebel by nature, and supported the French Revolution openly. Burns was to die in 1796, having lived only 37 years but enshrining his poetry in the hearts of all Scots. His reputation has grown over the generations and Burns is recognized as a major poet who transcended his nationalistic feelings.

James Boswell, was a Scottish biographer, and essayist. His most important work was "The Life of Samuel Johnson", still regarded as one of the finest biographies in the English language. He also wrote a political history, "An Account of Corsica" which narrated that island's movement for independence. Boswell's diaries, which included astute observations on society and manners of his day, were published after his death. Born in Edinburgh in 1740, Boswell immigrated to England where he met Samuel Johnson in 1763. Boswell neglected his own law practice to devote his life to Johnson and his biography. He spent much of the next 25 years traveling and living with Johnson. This was a unique friendship of two notable literary figures that resulted in a biography of great power and feeling. Boswell died at age 55 in his native Scotland but left a legacy for all future biographers.

William Blake, poet and artist, launched his career in 1789 with the publication of "Songs of innocence". His most important prose work, "The Marriage of Heaven and Hell", rejects rationalism in favor of mystical faith. His masterpiece, "Songs of Innocence and Experience", was written in 1794. Blake pioneered what he termed "prophetic books", which purported to predict the futures of America and Europe. His epic poem "Jerusalem", sought to imagine the existence of spirit after death. Blake was a master illustrator and true mystic. Born in 1757, he had visions of angels, devils, and poets as a young child. His illustrations were extraordinary, and he worked on Dante's "Divine Comedy" and other major works. Blake's art and poetry are a heady mix of symbolism, mystic vision, and powerful emotion. Thought by many to be mad, Blake remained true to his vision and died in England in 1827 at the age of 70. Few men or women equaled Blake's extravagant perceptions and his ability to put them into words and art.

Johann Wolfgang von Goethe was a German poet, novelist, and playwright. He was an initiator of the "Storm and Stress "movement which preceded German Romanticism. Goethe's best work included the lyric poem "Hermann and Dorothea", and his drama "Faust", which narrates the tale of the scholar who trades his soul for knowledge and pleasure. Goethe also wrote scientific essays and an autobiography, "Poetry and Truth". One of his most popular works was the novel "The Sorrows of Young Werther", which narrated the emotional pain of the protagonist/author. Goethe was born in Frankfurt in 1749, and served as a public official in Weimer for ten years. A long sojurn in Italy influenced his writing style and cultural outlook. Goethe developed a close friendship with the writer Frederich von Schiller and they remained confidants for many years. Goethe and Schiller shared many literary interests and their relationship enriched both authors work. Goethe remained active into old age and died in Weimar in 1832.

William Wordsworth was a catalyst for the romantic movement in English literature. A close friendship with Samuel Taylor Coldridge resulted in the publication of a joint venture, "Lyrical Ballads" which sounded a new voice in poetry. The neoclassical model then in vogue was renounced for poetry written in the manner in which people actually spoke. Wordsworth's best known volumes include "Poems: in Two Volumes", and Wordsworth's greatest work," The Prelude", an epic based on the author's own life. Wordsworth was born in the Lake District of England in 1770. Educated at Cambridge, he traveled extensively in Europe and became fired with the spirit of the French Revolution. In his early 30's, Wordsworth married and retired to his home in Grasmere where he lived the remainder of his life. He held the position of Poet Laureate of England from 1843 until his death in 1850. One of the most loved poems in the English language is "Tintern Abbey" published in his first slender volume of poems in 1798.

Samuel Taylor Coldridge was a leading figure in English Romanticism. His partnership with the young William Wordsworth blossomed with the publication of "Lyrical Ballads" in 1798. The first poem in this book was Coldridge's " The Rime of the Ancient Mariner", a spectacular start to a most successful career. Coldridge's creative ideas on poetic form and his original and striking use of language are his contributions to English literature. Other poems of this period include "Christobel" and "Kubla Kahn". Coldridge was a tragic figure in English literature. Born in the West Country in 1772,, and educated at Cambridge, he married hastily and unhappily. In later life he moved to the Lake District to be close to William Wordsworth, his lifetime friend. Coldridge became an opium addict and his marriage failed during this time. He had an unrequited love affair with Sara Hutchinson, the sister of Wordsworth's fiancé. These travails

prevented Coldridge from creative work for many years and his body of poetry is small. This unhappy, but brilliant figure died in 1834.

Jane Austen was an English novelist of enduring popularity. Considered by some to a founder of the modern novel, Austen narrated the everyday life of country gentry in the latter part of the 28th century. She combined keen observation, sharp wit, and memorable characters to create a much loved body of work. "Northanger Abbey"," Sense and Sensibility", and "Pride and Prejudice" were written in the 1790's but not published until ten years later. "Emma, "Mansfield Park", and "Persuasion" were the fruits of her later work. Her parodies of Gothic romances and novels of courtship are unequaled in English literature. A brilliant plotter, her view of character relationships against the complex web of social manners and mores of the day is unequaled. Austen was born in 1775, she was educated at home in the Bath area, where she lived her entire life. All of her novels were published anonymously and she wrote productively until her death in 1817. Austen's work was a critical success as well as being loved by the public. They have been adapted to plays, television, and cinema.

George Gordon Byron was an English poet who captured the imagination of the literary world. His most famous work is "Childe Harold's Pilgrimage", a work of fiction set as a travelogue. Perhaps his masterpiece is the epic satire "Don Juan", a lengthily poem largely autobiographical. Later works of note include "The Prisoner of Chillon and other Poems", "Manfred", and the satirical poem "Beppo". Byron was born in 1788 in London, and reared in Scotland. Byron was educated at Cambridg, He was unusually handsome, but suffered from a club foot. Byron took his seat in the House of Lords briefly, before setting out on travels in Europe. He left England for good in 1816, traveling widely in Switzerland, Italy, and Greece. Byron engaged in passionate love affairs, became a revolutionary, and generally captured the

- 47 -

imagination of the literary world. He died of a fever in Greece in 1824 and was sent back to England for burial.

William Cullen Bryant was an American poet, critic, and prose writer. His most famous work is "Thanatopsis", a revelry on death, published in 1817. He enjoyed nature and much of his work touches on natural beauty. "To a Waterfowl" (1821), is an example of this affection for the natural world. This poem became a milestone in American poetry, viewing nature as the guiding principle of life. Bryant was also a critic, and his volume "Early American Verse", was instrumental in building the foundation for the American literary tradition. Bryant was born in Massachusetts in 1794. He began a career as a lawyer but soon realized his interests were in writing. He moved to New York in 1825, where he served as editor of the "New York Evening Post", a liberal newspaper dedicated to abolition of slavery and workers rights. Bryant became a champion of these causes, and much of his energy was used to advocate for them. He became the dean of American journalism, and was active until his death in New York in 1878.

Sir Walter Scott was a Scottish poet and novelist. He began his literary career by collecting traditional ballads of Scotland and publishing them in an anthology. He specialized in narrative poetry with a romantic theme, usually set in medieval times. His breakthrough poems include" The Lady of the Lake" and "The Lay of the last Minstral". Scott is best known for his historical novels published as the "Waverley Novels". Included in this group are "Rob Roy", "Ivanhoe", "Kenilworth", and "The Bride of Lammermoor". Scott was born in 1771 on the English-Scottish border and spent his early life there. His formal training was as a barrister, but he did not practice law for a living. He relied on his popular fiction for his income and was most successful at first. A publishing partnership failed, and Scott was burdened with large debts he spent most of

his life repaying. He eventually became financially stable through his popular fiction and works of literary criticism. He died in Scotland in 1832.

Washington Irving was an American novelist, essayist, and short-story writer. Some of his best work was the now familiar stories, "Rip Van Winkle", and "The Legend of Sleepy Hollow" now immortalized as children's fiction. Irving was an astute critic, essayist, and folklore expert. Irving's later works include "Legends of the Alhambra", "Christopher Columbus", and his impressions of the American west, " A Tour of the Prairies". a well known biographer he wrote volumes about George Washington and Mohammed. Irving was born in 1783 and grew up in New York. Irving lived abroad for many years, serving as a diplomat in Spain for two separate periods of his life. He was a founder and co-publisher of a literary journal,"Salamagundi" which was popular with American literary figures. He toured the American west several times and was an accurate observer of pioneer America. Upon his death in 1859 he was called the "first American Man of Letters".

Percy Bysshe Shelley was a renowned English poet who used the themes of love, romance, and imagination as his topics. Shelley had a powerful lyrical voice, and his best known poems "To a Skylark", "Prometheus Ubound", "Ode to the West Wind", and "Adonais" exhibit this narrative power. He has remained an inspiration to romantic poets for centuries. Born in England in 1792, Shelley attended Eton and Oxford before being expelled for publishing a tract on atheism. He traveled widely in Europe, sometimes in the company of Lord Byron. He had a passionate relationship with Mary Shelley, whom he would marry after the death of his first wife. Tragedy stalked Shelley, with the loss of two children and his wife's subsequent breakdown. Besieged by creditors, and in failing health, he continued to write productively until his death by drowning in Italy in 1822. His 29 years were filled with literary accomplishment and personal sorrow.

Mary Wollstonecraft Godwin (later Shelley) was an English novelist who won lasting fame with her Gothic horror story, "Frankenstein", published in 1818. This classic narrates the creation of a monster from human body parts. This work has been adapted countless times in many ways, always retaining the flavor of horror and responsibility. Shelley's later works include "Valperga", "The Last Man", and "Lodore". She also edited numerous editions of Percy Shelley's prose and poetry. Shelley was born in England in 1797, the only child of radical reformer William Godwin, and feminist pioneer Mary Wollstonecraft. She eloped to Europe with Percy Shelley who she married in 1813. Mary Shelley suffered greatly from several miscarriages, the death of two children, and ultimately her husband's drowning. She continued to write effectively through these travails, but never again equaled the success of "Frankenstein". She died in 1851.

John Keats was an English poet of great imagination and a romantic nature. His work is best known for six odes written in 1819, "Ode to a Grecian Urn"," Ode to a Nightengale","Ode to Psyche","Ode on Melancholy", "Ode on Indolence", and "To Autumn". This poetry abounds in symbolism exploring the frailty of life and the power of creative art. They are felt to be some of the best English poetry extant. Keats's other notable works include" Lamia", "The Eve of St. Agnes", and "Hyperion". Keats was born in London in 1795 and studied medicine for a time. He soon turned to poetry, mentored by the political radical and writer Leigh Hunt. In 1818 he published his first poetry, "Endymion", an epic based on Greek mythology. Keats contracted tuberculosis, and fell upon hard times. His engagement to Fanny Brawne would end as his health failed. As his disease advanced, Keats moved to Rome hoping the change would help heal him. He died there in 1821 at the tender age of 25.

James Fenimore Cooper has a legitimate claim to being the first American novelist. Cooper was a prolific writer and his best known novels are "The Leatherstocking Tales" which include "The Pioneers","The Last of the Mohicans", "The Pathfinder" and "The Deerslayer". Cooper wrote a series of adventure novels in nautical settings, the most important being "The Pilot". The three novels of the "Littlepage"' manuscripts address American social issues. His later work includes "The Sea Lions" and "Red Rover" which enjoyed popular success. Cooper was born in upper New York state in 1789. Expelled from Yale University for unknown reasons, he spent eight years in the Navy, mustering out in 1809. Enriched by an inheritance from his father, Cooper devoted himself to politics and writing. Cooper's political writing embroiled him in many lawsuits which he often won. He began a period of writing social criticism including "The American Democrat", and "A Letter to his Countrymen"attacking American democracy. Cooper was active until the end of his life in 1851.

Victor Hugo, French playwright, novelist and poet, was a giant figure in the Romantic revolution in the French arts. Best known for his great historical novels,"Les Miserables", and "The Hunchback of Notre-Dame", Hugo wrote drama, verse plays, and poetry. Important later works include "The Punishments", and an elegy for his drowned daughter, "Les Contemplations". Hugo was the most popular author in France for three decades. Born in Besancon, France in 1802, Hugo began his literary career by founding "Conservauteur Litteraire", a literary journal in 1819. Hugo was a giant figure in French letters and politics, becoming vocal advocate of the Republican cause. Hugo left France for 19 years after Napoleon III came to power. The creation of the Third French Republic in 1870, led to Hugo's triumphant return to Paris among adoring throngs. Hugo' revolutionary spirit can be seen in many of his works, particularly "Les Miserables" with its vivid depiction of the Revolution. Hugo died in his beloved Paris in 1885.

Heinrich Heine was perhaps the greatest poet of the German post-Romantic period. his first collection of poetry was published as "The Book of Songs" in 1827. His most controversial work was "Germany, a Winters Tale", an epic satire on German politics. Heine wrote scores of impressive poems, and his works have been translated into most of the world's major languages. Heine's poetry has been set to music by both Schubert and Schumann. Born in Dusseldorf, Germany in 1797, Heine studied law in order to enter government service. He moved to Paris in 1831 and wrote articles on political, social, and economic issues of the day. Heine's works were banned in Germany in 1935, and he was forbidden to return to his homeland. His political views were considered radical for the time, and he was discriminated against for his Jewish heritage. Heine fell victim to a chronic illness that confined him to bed for the last years of his life. Despite this, he transcended his suffering in his last volume, "Romanzero". Heine died in Paris in 1856.

Honore' de Balzcac was a writer of prodigious output. He named his body of literature "The Human Comedy". This French novelist wrote almost 100 works of fiction in his 51 years. His realistic description of 19th-century French society and manners provide a window in history. His first major success was "The Physiology of Marriage" in 1830. He followed this with "Lost Illusions" an autobiographical novel of the corruption of a young poet in Paris which is considered to be his greatest work. Later works included "The Black Sheep", and Cousin Bette" which were both successful. Balzac wrote in great detail and was an excellent plotter. His works were influential in the development of the novel. Balzac was born in Tours in 1799, and educated in Paris. He tried business and failed; then gave his full attention to writing. Balzac was an obsessive worker, sometimes writing for days without rest. His tales could be melodramatic, but readers loved them and

his reputation soared. Balzac died in Paris in1850 at age 51. His productivity in writing novels is unmatched.

Stendal was the pen name of Marie Henri Beyel, a French novelist of great technical skill. His novels reflected deep and subtle psychological themes, irony, cool, detached prose, and great realism. His greatest works include "The Red and the Black"(1830), and "The Charterhouse of Parma" (1839). Both books narrate the adventures of young men and their rise and fall. Later important novels include" The Life of Henry Brulard", an autobiographical novel, and "Memoirs of an Egotist". Stendahl also wrote several excellent biographies including one on Rossini. Born in Grenoble, Stendhal joined the Ministry of War and later fought with Napoleon in his European and Russian campaigns. After the fall of Napoleon, he worked as a minor diplomat in Italy from 1831 until his death in 1842. Unappreciated in his own time, Stendhal's reputation has grown with the years. Modern novelists feel he is a major figure in the development of the genre.

Allen Ginsberg, American poet, was a major figure in the "Beat Generation". He, Jack Kerouac, and William S. Burroughs led a group of artists in opposing the conformist society of America in the 1950's. Ginsberg's epic poem "Howl"(1956), became a rallying cry for the counterculture revolution. Ginsberg's poetry draws from traditions of free verse and symbolism, in a probing voice demanding to be heard. Always socially and politically engaged, Ginsberg's later works include"Kaddish"(1961), "The Fall Of America"(1973), and "Reality Sandwiches"(1966). Born in New Jersey in 1926 to a working class family, Ginsberg was educated at Columbia University. He moved to San Francisco in the 1950's, where he found a flourishing counterculture of rebellion. Ginsberg and his friends lived a bohemian life, and challenged all the accepted mores of society. Ginsberg died in 1997.

Eugene O'Neill, American playwright, was a pioneer in American drama. O'Neill was an innovator and experimented with aspects of realism and naturalism to his work. O'Neill was one of the most critically honored dramatist of his time, winning four Pulitzer Prizes and the Nobel Prize for Literature in 1936. Financial success did not come with his critical acclaim, and O'Neill struggled for a long time. His most outstanding play was "Long Day's Journey Into Night" was written in 1941 but not produced until after his death. O'Neill was born in New York to a show business family in 1888, and attended Princeton University. Suffering from tuberculosis, O'Neill turned his attention to drama and by 1920 had a play in production in New York. His later success was highlighted by "The Iceman Cometh"(1946), and "Strange Interlude"(1928) for which he would win a Pulitzer Prize. O'Neill remained an active writer until his death in 1953.

Voltaire, the pen name of Francois - Marie Arouet, French novelist , poet, playwright, and philosopher. Voltaire was a vocal and literate advocate for freedom of thought, political justice, and humanism in 18th-century France. Voltaire's fame is for his essays and letters defending human rights and arguing for reason and tolerance. Best known of his literary works are "Candide", and "Zadig", fiction that blends philosophy and humanism. Nonfiction works include "Essays on the Manner and Spirit of Nations", a seven volume history, and a dictionary of philosophy. Voltaire was born in Paris in 1694 and educated by the Church. He soon abandoned the study of law for writing, philosophy, and advocating human rights. His sharp tongue and pen found ready targets in this Church, nobility, and government. A short stay in England exposed him to the ideas of John Locke and other liberal minds of the times. Many of his works were banned during his lifetime which ended in Paris in 1778.

Aleksandra Pushkin was an immensely talented poet, playwright, and short story writer. Possibly the most revered Russian writer, Pushkin began his literary career with narrative poetry including "The Prisoner of Caucasus", and" The Gypsies". In 1831 he wrote his famous verse-tragedy, "Boris Goduvov". His verse novel " Eugene Onegin" (1833), became his most important work. Master of the short story, Pushkin produced many great ones including "The Queen of Spades"(1834). Puskin's later work is innovative and experiments with language, form, and characterization. Born in Moscow in 1799, he was educated at the Imperial Lyceum, and served in the Russian government until his exile for writing poetry critical of the Tsar. Allowed to return to Moscow by the new Tsar in 1826, Pushkin married and continued his literary career. Puskin was killed in a duel with his wife's lover in 1837, only 38 years old. His impact on Russian literature is immeasurable.

George Sand, the pen name of Amadine-Auroe-Lucile Dupin was a French woman of letters who was an accomplished essayist, novelist, and playwright. Her novels often touched on themes of love, romance, and early feminist philosophy. Best known were " She and He "(1859), "Little Fadette" (1849), and "The Country Waif"(1850). Her four volume autobiography " Story of my Life," chronicled her exciting life in detail. Sand's novels mixed socialist and feminist ideas, with erotic language and criticisms of society. Sand was born in Paris in 1804, and received a Catholic education. She married at 18, but began a series of love affairs that ended in her divorce. She was a striking figure, wearing men's clothes and having open affairs with Musset, Chopin, and others. She fascinated the public with her personal escapades, and was an extremely popular writer in her day. Sand died in Paris in 1876.

Ralph Waldo Emerson was an American essayist, poet, and Transcendentalist philosopher. His first major work "Nature" was published in 1836 and proclaimed the unity of nature and the universe, and his belief that each man finds his way to the

Divine through individual apprehension. His two volume "Essays" (1841-44) include his most famous essays including "Love", "Friendship", and "The Oversoul". "Poems" (1847), and "May Day" (1687), contain his best poetry. Emerson founded "The Dial", a journal for Transcendentalist writers in 1840. Emerson was born in New England in 1803, and educated at Harvard University. Ordained as a Unitarian minister, he left the church after being disillusioned with orthodox Christianity. Returning to America he became a leading figure in the Transcendentalist movement, joining such notables as Margaret Fuller, David Thoreau, and Louisa May Alcott.

Henry Thoreau was an American essayist and naturalist who published only two books in his life. His first book, "A Week on the Concord and Merrimac", was a failure and his prospects seemed dim. Then came "Walden"(1854) his masterpiece, which narrated Thoreau's experiment in simple living in a cabin on Walden pond for two years. Initially unsuccessful, "Walden" became a classic and guide to a simpler, more natural life. Thoreau's "Journals" appeared in 1906. Thoreau was born in Concord, Massachusetts in 1817 and graduated from Harvard in 1837. He was a teacher and major figure in the Transcendentalist movement in New England. He wrote extensively on nature, society, and the spirit of individualism for many years. Often at odds with authorities, Thoreau spent a night in jail and defended his actions in a famous essay, "Civil Disobedience" (1849). He died in 1862 in his beloved Concord.

Nathaniel Hawthorne was an American fiction writer. Hawthorne had a tragic vision of life, believing man is imperfect, and a mixture of good and evil. His work reflected this view, starting with the publication of "Twice Told Tales " in 1837. Hawthorne gained public fame with "The Scarlet Letter"(1850), a novel of adultery in puritan New England. He followed this with the successful "House of the Seven Gables", a novel tracing the history of a family hiding a dark secret. Hawthorne was born in Salem Massachusetts in 1804 to a prosperous family. he graduated from Bowdoin College in 1825, and vowed to devote his life to literature. Living in semi-seclusion in Salem for 12 years< Hawthorne produced his first stories. After briefly working in government, he joined a utopian community at Brook Farm, later satirized in his novel "The Blithedale Romance (1852). Appointed American counsel in Liverpool, he lived in Europe for many years.

Charles Dickens is thought by some to be England's greatest novelist. In 1837, "The Pickwick Papers", a comic novel, launched his career. This was followed quickly by " Oliver Twist" (1838) "Nicholas Nickelby"(1839), and "A Christmas Carol" (1843). Dickens had a genius for creating memorable characters, and his ability to evoke a sense of 19th-century England is unmatched. His later works include " David Copperfield"(1850), "Great Expectations" (1861), and " A Tale of Two Cities" (1859). Charles Dickens was born in London in 1812. He worked as a journalist until the success of his novels. Dickens founded and edited several literary magazines, including "Household Words", and "All the Year Round". Dickens gave reading tours in Europe and the United States that were very popular and drew large crowds. Dickens died in London in 1870 and is buried in Westminster Abbey.

Henry Wadsworth Longfellow was one of the most popular American poets of his day. Longfellow gained lasting fame with his long narrative poems, "Hiawatha" (1855), and " Evangeline" (1847). His "Tales of the Wayside Inn" (1863) contain "Paul Reverie's Ride", a poem known and beloved by American schoolchildren. Among the best known of his shorter poems are "The Arsenal at Springfield", "The Wreck of the Hesperus", " A Psalm of Life", and "The Village Blacksmith". He also wrote essays and translated Dante's "Divine Comedy." Longfellow was born in Maine in 1807 to a wealthy family. He was educated at Bowdoin College and studied in Europe for several years before returning to Bowdoin to teach languages. He later became a faculty member at Harvard and was a well respected professor. He died in New England in 1882.

Edgar Allen Poe was an American poet, novelist, and short-story writer of particular talent. His tales of terror and arresting poems have gained him lasting fame in American literature. Poe published a great anthology of short stories with "Tales of the Grotesque and Arabesque" in 1840. He cemented his fame with "The Raven and other Poems" in 1845. Some of his greatest poems include "The Bells" (1849), "Annabel Lee" (1849), and "Ulaume" (1847). His best known short stories include "The Pit and the Pendulum" (1843), "The Tell-Tale Heart" (1843), and "The Gold Bug" (1843). Poe was born in Boston but was orphaned at an early age. Raised by a wealthy Virginia businessman, he attended the University of Virginia and West Point. Poe's marriage to a young cousin would end with her early death. Poe would never recover from this loss and sank into a morass of drug addiction and alcohol abuse. He would die in Baltimore 1849.

Alfred, Lord Tennyson was an important English poet of his day, publishing his first work, "Poems, Chiefly Lyrical" in 1830. His subsequent volumes of poetry include "Maud, and other Poems" (1855), "Idylls of the King" (1885), an epic poem based on the legend of King Arthur. Later works of note are "Enoch Arden" (1864) and "Demeter and other Poems" (1889). His best loved individual poems are "The Charge of the Light Brigade", "Crossing the Bar", and "Mariana". Tennyson wrote of history, honor, and faith, championing Victorian values and mastering the technical elements of poetry. Born in a small village in the North of England in 1809, he was educated at Cambridge and published his first book of verse there. Tennyson was named Poet Laureate of England by Queen Victoria in 1850 succeeding William

Wordsworth. He died in England in 1892, his place in history secure.

Nikolai Gogol was a Russian playwright, novelist, and short-story author who wrote sharp satirical prose in an innovative style. Two collections of his short stories " Mirgorod" and "Arabesques" were published in 1835. His best known work, the novel "Dead Souls", a biting satire on feudal Russia, appeared in 1842. The sequel to "Dead Souls" was to have been Gogol's crowning work, but he burned the manuscript in 1852, shortly before his death. Only fragments of the manuscript remain. Gogol was born in 1809 in the Ukraine. Moving to St. Petersburg, he worked in civil service and teaching as he began to write. Gogol began displaying symptoms of mental illness in the 1840's. He became obsessed with religion, and fell under the influence of a fanatical priest who urged him to destroy the manuscript of the second part of "Dead Souls" to atone for the original book. Increasingly, Gogol became delusional and destroyed the manuscript, then starving himself to death in 1852.

Known as **Alexander Dumas** pere (father), this great French novelist and playwright was the most popular literary figure in France in his time. Best remembered for his exciting historical novels "The Three Musketeers "(1844), and "The Count of Monte Cristo" (1845), Dumas published many other popular novels including "The Man in the Iron Mask" (1850), as well as many dramas based on his stories. His forte' was the historical novel, usually with heroic figures and imaginative plots that captured the fancy of the public. Dumas was born in Paris in 1802, the son of one of Napoleon's great generals. Dumas led a life worthy of his novels, having many mistresses and winning and losing fortunes regularly. He was a flamboyant character in the cafe society of Paris, living with the joy that seemed to permeate his fiction. Dumas left several volumes of his memoirs documenting his exciting adventures. He died in Paris in 1870.

Charlotte Bronte, beloved English novelist, wrote stories of independent women in a very personal voice. Her characters were enmeshed in romance and love affairs, even as they lived lives of creativity unusual for the period. Her first novel, "The Professor" was not published until after her death. Her most powerful work is "Jane Eyre"(1847), a narrative of a young woman and her travails in love and society. Other works include "Shirley" (1849), and "Villete"(1853) based on her sister Emily's experiences living in Europe. Bronte was born in 1816, the daughter of a Yorkshire clergyman. She was sent to a boarding school with harsh living conditions and strict rules of behavior. She would later use the school as a model in "Jane Eyre". The death of her three siblings in quick succession clouded her life with sadness. She died in England in 1855 at the tender age of 38.

Emily Bronte, sister of Charlotte Bronte, and English novelist and poet, produced only one novel in her lifetime. However her novel "Wuthering Heights (1847)" stands as a testament to her literary talent. A harsh tale, it is the story of the passionate bond between Catherine and Heathcliffe, in which jealously destroys two families. It is a signature novel of English Romanticism. Emily Bronte was a poet of some skill, her works appearing jointly with her sister's in "Poems by Currier, Ellis, and Acton Bell" (1846). Emily Bronte was born in 1818 in Yorkshire. A unique and mysterious personality, she had few friends except her sister Anne, with whom she maintained a strong bond. Together they created the world of Gondal, an imaginary society that she used extensively in her poetry. In Charlotte's words, Emily was "stronger than a man, simpler than a child. Emily contracted tuberculosis and died at age 29 in 1848.

William Makepeace Thackeray was a gifted Victorian English novelist and satirist. He started his writing career doing satirical pieces for magazines and weekly's. "The Book of Snobs"(1848), and his masterwork,

"Vanity Fair"(1849) both appeared first as serials in periodicals. "Vanity Fair" follows Becky Sharp as she attempt to climb the social ladder of English society. Thackeray's later work includes "Barry Lyndon"(1852), "The Virginians"(1859), and the fictional autobiography," Pendennis"(1850). Thackeray was born in India, but returned to England for his education at Cambridge. Thackeray was a popular lecturer, and he toured England and America giving talks. His strength as a writer was his ability to describe the moralistic hypocrisy of British society. "Vanity Fair" is his lasting legacy and remains a popular vehicle for adaptations today. Thackeray died in London in 1863.

Fydor Dostoyevsky, Russian novelist, journalist, and short-story writer who was the master of the psychological character. He also had unusual skill as a prose writer and ranks as the greatest of Russian writers. His first major work was "Crime and Punishment"(1867), narrating a murder and its aftermath. This was followed quickly by a series of important works including "The Idiot"(1874), "The Possessed"(1872), and " The Brothers Karamazov"(1880). All these works deal with the criminal mind and the struggles within the human psyche. Dostoyvesky was born in Moscow in 1821, the son of a physician who was murdered by serfs when Dostoyevsky was in his late teens. He suffered from epilepsy and was a chronic gambler that left him in constant debt. Arrested for subversion, he spent eight years in Siberia before his release. With Tolstoy he is considered the greatest Russian writer. He died in Moscow in 1881.

Herman Melville was one of America's rare talents, excelling in short-stories, poetry, and above all, the novel. Melville wrote adventure stories, "Typee"(1846), and "Omoo"(1847), before writing his master novel," Moby Dick"(1851). This novel was an allegory about men, life, and obsession. It is usually considered to be one of the greatest American novels. Unpopular at first, it was rediscovered in the 1920's and given the accolades it so richly deserved. Mellville's later work included "The Piazza Tales", a collection of short-stories, and novels "The Confidence Man"(1857), and "Billy Budd"(1888). Mellvile was born in new York in 1819 and went to sea as a teenager. In 1866, Melville became a customs inspector in New York. Stalked by tragedy with the death of two sons and his financial reverses, Melville persisted with his writing. He is now considered one of literature's finest novelists. Melville died in New York in 1891.

Harriet Beecher Stowe, American novelist, rests her reputation on "Uncle Tom's Cabin" (1852), a polemic that brought the horrors of slavery to the world. The book became a bible for the Abolitionist cause, and some credit it as a catalyst for the American Civil War. Three million copies were sold in the decade after it was published, and it was translated into more than 25 languages. Stowe's later works include"Oldtown Folks"(1869), and "The Minister's Wooing"(1859). Stowe was born in Litchfield Connecticut in 1811. In her late teens she moved to Cincinnati and married a clergyman. She became heavily involved in the Abolitionist movement, which led her to write "Uncle Tom's Cabin". Enriched and honored by her book, Stow continued to campaign for social justice until her death in 1896.

Walt Whitman, the American poet and journalist, sought to develop an American voice for poetry. His style mirrored the American ideal: democratic, idealistic free flowing, and panoramic in perspective. His life's work," Leaves of Grass"(1855), embodied what Whitman conceived as the American spirit. Using free verse Whitman produced an American original. Whitman was born on Long Island, in New York state, and reared in nearby Brooklyn. He worked as a teacher, typesetter, and journalist, becoming editor of the "Brooklyn Eagle" in 1846. He lived most of his life in Brooklyn, until the publication of "Leaves of Grass". During the Civil War, he traveled to Virginia to nurse his wounded brother. He stayed on as a hospital volunteer until the end of the war. Crippled by a stroke in 1873, he retired to New Jersey where he died in 1892.

Anthony Trollope was an English novelist of great dexterity. Famed for his evocation of Victorian life, and his vivid characters, Trollope was one of the most popular writers of his day. His finest works were two novel sequences, " The Barsetshire Novels" consisting of four volumes, and the politically themed "Palliser Novels". His fiction created characters that have stood the test of time and remain fresh today. Trollope's stories have been adapted many times for film, television, and the stage. Trollope was born in rural England in 1815 and reared there in modest circumstances. He became a civil servant, working for the Royal Mail for many years. He wrote with great energy during his life, producing prose collections, travel books, biographies, and 47 novels. His two volume "Autobiography" appeared posthumously in 1883. Anthony Trollope died in 1882 at the age of 67.

Elizabeth Barrett Browning, the well known poet of Victorian England, is best remembered for her lyrics of love in her "Sonnets from the Portuguese" published in 1850. Her verse " How do I love thee? Let me count the ways" have inspired lovers for over 150 years. Her other major works include" Aurora Leigh" (1857), a verse novel clearly autobiographical, and "Last Poems"(1852). Browning's poetry evokes England and Italy, where she also lived, and has themes of social justice throughout. Browning was born in Hertfordshire in 1806, and reared on the family farm. Smothered by an overly protective father, the poet suffered poor health and was a semi-recluse. She met Robert browning and in 1845 and they wed the next year. The couple moved to Italy where Browning improved both her health and disposition. She spent the next 16 years with Browning in a devoted and tender marriage. Elizabeth died in 1861 at age 55.

Robert Browning was a major Victorian poet known for his skill in characterization, psychological nuances, and his colorful and dramatic dialogue. His early work was not well received but Browning persisted, publishing the successful "Dramatic Lyrics" in 1842. His next collection, "Dramatis Personae" (1864), was his most popular. His technical skill as a poet remains his greatest legacy. Browning was born in London in 1812 and was largely self educated. He did not achieve public acclaim until later in life. In 1845, Browning began a correspondence with the reclusive Elizabeth Barret. Against all odds, the couple married in 1846 and created one of the great literary romances. The pair lived a full and devoted life together until Elizabeth's death in 1861. Robert Browning survived and enjoyed his greatest success until his passing in 1889, 28 years after Elizabeth died.

Charles Baudelaire was a French essayist, poet, and critic. His reputation as one of the great French poets of his time was based on his seminal work, "The Flowers of Evil"(1857). "The Flowers of Evil" combine macabre imagery and a profane, cynical tone, to produce a book of much power. Baudelaire was prosecuted and fined for obscenity following its publication, and a few of the poems were banned from future edition. Baudelaire was born in Paris in 1821 to a wealthy family. He turned to writing almost immediately, and began friendships with Courbet, Delacroix, and Manet. After squandering a large inheritance, Baudelaire became addicted to opium and alcohol, and began to deteriorate. His later years were poverty stricken, and he was heavily in debt. The publication of "The Flowers of Evil" made further alienated the public. His writing career was essentially over, and he died of syphilis in 1867 at the age of 46.

Gustave Flaubert was a French author of fiction, a master of the novel and adept at short-stories. After an unsuccessful first manuscript, Flaubert spent five years writing his best known work "Madame Bovary",

published in 1857. This narrative of the adulterous affairs of a middle class French woman shocked much of France, and Flaubert was prosecuted for the book's "immorality". His other novels include " Salaambo" (1862), and "A Sentimental Education"(1869). Flaubert is recognized as a pioneer in modern fiction writing. Flaubert was born in Rouen, France, in 1821 and began writing fiction as a child. He enrolled in law school but soon suffered a breakdown and abandoned his education. He committed himself to writing with great energy and gave up many of the distractions of Paris life to concentrate on his craft. Flaubert died suddenly and somewhat mysteriously at his home in Croisset, France, in 1880. He was 59 years old.

Emily Dickenson is ranked as one of America's greatest poets. Dickenson's poetry is highly formal, her language both subtle and creative, and reflect the quiet life she led. Dickenson's topics include death, art, love, pain and betrayal, all couched in her wonderful poetic language. She wrote over 1800 poems, yet only 10 are known to be published in her lifetime. Her fame has grown through the generations and she is at last recognized as a poetic genius. Born in Amherst, Massachusetts in 1830, she was educated at Mt. Holyoke seminary. She returned to Amherst, and went into virtual seclusion in her parent's home. She saw very few people socially, and rarely left the house. Despite this isolation, Dickenson's work is vibrant and alive, reflecting her keen observation of the world. Dickenson is a true American literary voice, rivaling Walt Whitman. She died in Amherst in 1886.

Willkie Collins, English novelist, is considered to be the pioneer of the mystery story and novel. His first novels were "Antonia, or The Fall of Rome" (1850), and "Basil" (1852), his first novel of suspense. Collins reputation was made with the publication of "The Woman in White in 1860. He followed this success with the hugely popular " The Moonstone" in 1868. His later works include " Armadale"(1866), "The New

Magdalen"(1873), "The Haunted Hotel"(1879), and "Heart and Science" (1883). Collins was born in London in 1824, and studied law in college. Although admitted to the bar, he never practiced and soon turned his energies to writing. Befriended by Charles Dickens, who published much of his early work serially in his literary magazines, Collins soon became popular and the demand for mystery and suspense fiction has never waned. He died in London in 1889.

Christina Rosseti was an accomplished English Victorian poet. Her best known poetry is contained in "Goblin Market and other Poems"(1862), and " The Prince's Progress and other Poems"(1862). Rosseti published a successful book of children's poetry, "Sing-Song" in 1872. Her later work is highlighted by "Time Flies" published in 1885. In 1904, William Rosseti compiled his sister's "Poetical Works followed by a collection of her letters. A devout high Anglican, her work often reflects her piety. Rosseti was born England in 1830, into a cultured and well-to-do family. After her initial successes, Rosseti was afflicted with Grave's disease, and never really recovered her health. Increasingly reclusive, she devoted herself to melancholy religious prose. Rosseti never married, spurning several Catholic suitors, and died at her family home in 1894. She was 64 years old.

Ivan Turgenev, Russian novelist, playwright and short-story writer, wrote politically inflammatory stories criticizing Russian serfdom and government. His work managed to inflame both the tsarist generation and the young radicals of his time. Best known for his "Fathers and Sons" published in 1862, he continued fiction writing for over 30 years. some of his more successful novels include" On The Eve"(1860), "Smoke"(1867), and "The virgin Soil"(1877), a controversial novel about Russia. His best known play is "A Month in the Country" first produced in 1855. Turgenev was born in Moscow in 1818, and educated in universities in Moscow and St.

Petersburg before moving to Berlin. Here he became " a Westerner for life". This was reflected in his work that became increasingly critical of Russian society and economics. He left Russia in 1863, and lived in France and Germany for most of the rest of his life. Turgenev died in France in 1883.

Lewis Carroll is the pen name of Charles Lutwidge Dodgson, author of "Alice's Adventures in Wonderland" (1865), and its sequel " Through The Looking Glass" (1871). His literary reputation rests on these two children's books, although he wrote several other novels including " The Hunting of the Shark"(1876), "A Tangled Tale"(1885), and "Sylvie and Bruno"(1889). Carroll also wrote several significant works on logic and mathematics. "Alice" was inspired by his favorite child-friend, Alice Liddell, and her two sisters to who he related the story. Carroll was born in England in 1832 and became a mathematics teacher and resident Scholar of Christ Church college, Oxford. He assumed his pen name to protect his academic reputation that might be affected by authoring children's books. "Alice" brought him instant celebrity, and served as an entree' to Victorian society. Carroll remained at Oxford until his death in 1898.

Matthew Arnold, English poet and critic, published six volumes of collected verse in his life, covering a wide range of subjects and moods. Much of his poetry evokes sadness and despair. Best remembered for "Dover Beach"(1867), a poem concerning the loss of faith in the modern age, Arnold was a critic of great importance. Arnold believed that literature and culture should be inculcated into society for moral and spiritual reasons. He was a prolific essayist, writing on religion, social issues, literature, and economics. His literary criticism was influential throughout the world. Arnold was born in Middlesex and educated at Rugby School and Oxford University. He worked for many years as an inspector of schools, a position he valued highly. In 1857 he became professor of poetry at Oxford, where he taught for ten years. His lectures at Oxford became the basis for many of his influential essays over the years. Arnold died in 1888.

Count Leo Tolstoy was Russia's leading novelist and moral philosopher. Tolstoy's two great masterpieces of fiction are " War and Peace" (1869), and "Anna Karenina" (1878). "War and Peace" is s love story set in the Napoleonic wars and provides a panoramic view of Russian life. "Anna Karenina" is the story of a woman who gives up everything for her love. Both are novels of great philosophical and psychological depth. Tolstoy described his spiritual crisis and its resolution in" Confessions"(1882). Tolstoy had a productive writing period in his later life, publishing novellas and a final novel "The Resurrection"(1899). Tolstoy was born in Moscow in 1828, and was educated at home by tutors. He served in the Russian army and fought in the Crimea and Caucasus campaigns. He returned to his estate in 1859, married and taught the children of surfs while he wrote his great novels.   Tolstoy retired to his estate and died there in 1910.

Louisa May Alcott is one of America's beloved children's writer, novelist, and short-story writer. Alcott began her publishing career writing popular "dime novels" under pseudonyms to make a living. The publication of "Little Women" in 1868, and its huge popularity allowed her to pursue serious fiction thereafter. "Little Women" is a fond narrative of family life based partially on her own family. It is a romantic, yet realistic novel with strong and memorable characters. Alcott's later novels include "Little Men"(1871) and "Rose in Bloom"(1876), both written for young readers. Her best adult fiction includes" Moods"(1864), a novel of married life, and "Work"(1874), a story based on her financial problems. Alcott was born in Boston in 1832 and reared in nearby Concord. Her father was the famous Transcendentalist   thinker, Bronson Alcott. She died in 1888.

Emile Zola, French novelist, wrote finely detailed narratives with a realistic eye. Zola believed objective observation was necessary to maintain the integrity of his work. His first novel, "Therese Raquin"(1867) was written in this dispassionate style. His reputation rests on a mammoth 20 volume novel cycle, called "Les Rougon-Macquart", narrating the fortunes of a 19th-century family over several generations. Topics in this series were often on the seamy side of life, including prostitution, labor unrest, and alcoholism. Zola was born in Paris in 1840, and raised in Provence. His education was mediocre, and he worked in a publishing house before becoming a journalist. He wrote for several French periodicals on a variety of topics as he honed his new style of writing. His mature novels were very successful and provided Zola with a comfortable life. He died in France in 1902.

W. S. Gilbert was an English playwright and humorist who teamed with Arthur Sullivan to produce the most popular light verse and comic opera in the English language. The partnership was formed in 1870, and they produced 17 operettas together. The most popular include "The Pirates of Penzance"(1879), "The Mikado"(1884), "H.M.S. Pinafore"(1878), and "The Yeoman of the Guard"(1888). Gilbert and Sullivan became the most successful writers of light opera ever. Gilbert was born in London in 1836 and educated at King's College. He began his writing career as a journalist, creating humorous pieces for magazines and weeklies. In 1866 he wrote his first play, "Dulcamara" for a Christmas presentation. His partnership with Sullivan lasted 20 years and proved to be one of the most successful in music history. Gilbert died in London in 1911.

George Eliot, the pen name of Mary Ann Evans, English novelist and essayist, started her literary career with the publication of "Scenes of a Clerical Life" in 1858. Her most beloved novel is "Middlemarch" (1872), a richly evocative narration of life in an English country town. Her characters are vivid and memorable, particularly her protagonist Dorothea Brooke. Eliot went on to publish a number of fine novels, including "Silas Marner"(1861), "Daniel Deronda" (1876), and "The Mill on the Floss" (1860), thought to be largely autobiographical. Her writing was bold and powerful, and brought new prestige to the 19th-century English novel. Eliot was born in the English countryside in 1819. After her father's death, she served as an editor of "The Westminster Review", a leading literary journal. Eliot was a free thinker who had a long relationship with a married man causing a scandal in English society. She died in London in 1880.

Arthur Rimbaud, French poet was a literary figure unlike any other. A revolutionary in every sense, he pioneered the use of free verse in his poetry, and lived a life of adventure and daring. At the age of 17 he wrote " The Drunken Boat" (1871), a surreal poem which would remain his greatest work. Rimbaud's " A Season in Hell" (1873) plumbed the depth of his despair, a cry of spiritual longing and the inability to love. His literary career was over at the age of 19, and he experimented with alcohol, drugs, and sensory deprivation. Rimbaud was born in Northeastern France in 1854. His family was impoverished, and he left home as at age 15 to live on his own. Rimbaud met and fell in love with Paul Verlaine, who served both as a mentor and lover. The relationship was a violent one, and Rimbaud left Paris to wander the world as a merchant, arms dealer, and vagabond. He returned to France and died in Marseille in 1891 at the age of 37.

Paul Verlaine, French poet, was the leading light of the Symbolist movement, which stressed the importance of suggestion and shading, rather than direct description. Symbolism intuited subtle connections between the spiritual and physical worlds. Verlaine's best work was reflected in his "Song Without Words" (1874) and "Fetes Galantes"(1869). His poetry in later life was influenced by his conversion to Catholicism

when he embraced positive values and wrote" Wisdom"(1880), " Love" (1888), and "Happiness" (1891). Paul Verlaine was born in Metz in 1844. Educated in Paris, he joined the radical poets in the salons and cafes of literary Paris. He shocked society when he left his family for 17 year old Arthur Rimbeau, with whom he carried on a tempestuous and violent affair. Verlaine embraced the Church in his 40's, and achieved a peace that had eluded him. He died in Paris in 1896.

Henrik Ibsen, Norwegian poet and playwright, is known for his realistic descriptions of modern social problems and psychological dilemmas that haunted his characters. Perhaps his most popular work is "Peer Gynt" published in 1876. His more mature work is composed of a number of plays written with marked realism. Those include "A Doll's House"(1879), "Hedda Gabler"(1891), "The Wild Duck" (1885), and his final play, "The Master Builder" (1893), perhaps his most autobiographical drama. Henrik Ibsen was born in near Oslo in 1828, to a wealthy family. When he was a child, his father's business failed and he was apprenticed to a pharmacist. Ibsen abandoned this and moved to Oslo to work in the theatre. He became a jack -of-all-trades, managing and directing groups of players. Ibsen died in Oslo in 1906 at the age of 72.

Mark Twain, the pen name of Samuel Langhorne Clemens was a true American voice in literature. Humorist, novelist, and travel writer, he is best known for "Tom Sawyer"(1876), and "The Adventures of Huckleberry Finn" (1884), beloved novels with memorable characters and undertones of social concern. "Life on the Mississippi " (1883) was an autobiographical account of his days on a riverboat. Twain's acid humor, stories of a fading rural America, made him one of the most popular figures of his day. Born in 1835 in Hannibal, Missouri, Twain who was self-educated, became a journalist and sometimes printer. His literary success made him a popular lecturer in America and Europe. His travels abroad provided Twain with the material for the satirical " A Connecticut Yankee in King Arthur's Court " (1889), and " The Innocents Abroad" (1869). His later life was marred by tragedy including the death of his wife and two daughters, as well as financial difficulty. He died in America in 1910.

Robert Louis Stevenson was a Scottish essayist, novelist, poet, and short-story writer. After writing for weeklies for a few years, his "Treasure Island"(1883) brought him acclaim and wealth. Stevenson followed this success with "Kidnapped" (1886), "The Strange Case of Dr. Jekyll and Mr. Hyde"(1886), and "The Master of Ballantrae"(1889), all critical and financial successes. Stevenson also wrote a book of verse for children, "A Child's Garden of Verses"(1885). His swashbuckling tales and colorful language engaged the fancy of the public, and he retired a wealthy man. Stevenson was born in Edinburgh in 1850 and was educated in law. His life was tainted by chronic tuberculosis, and he sought cures and more healthy climates all over the world. Stevenson finally found the relief he sought in Samoa, where he settled and lived the last years of his life. He died there in 1894, at the young age of 44.

Sir Arthur Conan Doyle contribution to literature was the enigmatic detective, Sherlock Holmes. Conan Doyle based his character on a former professor at the University of Edinburgh. Holmes first appeared in 1887 in " A Study in Scarlet", and more stories of the master of deductive reasoning appeared in magazines of the day. These stories were collected and published as "The Adventures of Sherlock Holmes" in 1892. Most memorable among the Holmes novels include "The Hound of the Baskervilles" (1902), " The Valley of Fear" (1915), and "The Sign of Four" (1890). Holmes also wrote a number of popular historical romances. Conan Doyle was born in London in 1859, and educated at Edinburgh. He trained as a physician practiced medicine in South sea from 1882-

90. The success of his writing allowed him to largely retire from medicine.

Thomas Hardy was an English novelist, playwright, and short-story writer. His dark works, often drawn from his own experience, include his first novel "Far from the Maddening Crowd" (1874), a tale of a strong woman and her three lovers. Hardy followed this modest success with four powerful novels," Jude the Obscure"(1895), " The Return of the Native"(1878), " Tess of the D'Urbervilles" (1891), and "The Mayor of Casterbridge"(1896). All these volumes showcased Hardy's skills as storyteller and creator of strong characters. Hardy's poetry is also considered to be some of the best of his time. Hardy was born in Dorchester in Southwest England in 1840. Hardy was trained as an architect, which he gave up for writing when he achieved success. With death of his wife, Hardy was guilt ridden and his grief fueled the writing of his greatest poetry, "Poems of 1912-13". Hardy married again and lived until 1928.

Oscar Wilde, (originally named Fingal O'Flahertie Wills Wilde), was an Irish writer, poet, critic and, playwright. Famed for his wit, repartee, and flamboyant life-style, Wilde's first success was "The Importance of Being Ernest" produced in 1895. Some of Wilde's most famous works include "The Picture of Dorian Gray" (1891), a moral allegory, "An Ideal Husband"(1895), "The Happy Price"(1888), and a French drama "Salome"(1896). "De Profundis"(1905) was taken from a letter written in prison. His final work," The Ballad of Reading Gaol" (1897), is his most famous poem. Wilde was born in Dublin in 1854 and had a classical education. He moved to London becoming a leader in the Aesthetic movement. Wilde was imprisoned for his homosexual activity, after losing a libel suit against the father of his lover, and spent two years at hard labor. On his release from prison he moved to France where he resided until his death in 1900 at the age of 45.

Charlotte Perkins Gilman was an American writer of short-stories, essays, and poetry. She was an early feminist and leader in the women's movement in the early part of the 20th-century. She challenged gender stereotypes in her writing. Her most influential work was "The Yellow Wallpaper" (1892), a tale of the abuse of women, medical science, and madness. Other important works include "Women and Economics" (1898), and her utopian novel, "Herland", published in 1915. Gilman was born in Hartford, Connecticut in 1860, to a family that included Lyman Beecher, and Harriet Beecher Stowe. An unhappy childhood and difficult first marriage contributed to her clinical depression. She divorced her husband and moved to California where she did her best work. Gilman committed suicide in 1935 after a period of failing health. Her autobiography was published soon after her death.

H.G. Wells was an English journalist and novelist. Known as a founding father of science fiction, he is now best known for "The Time Machine"(1895), "The Island of Dr. Moreau"(1886), and "The War of the Worlds'(1898) futuristic novels that captured the fancy of the public. He was also admired in his day for his traditional novels, chief of which is "Tono-Bungay"(1909). Wells wrote a respected "The Outline of History" (1920), which was a warning to society to recognize and remedy its problems. Wells was born in London in 1866 and attended the Normal School of Science. He incorporated his scientific knowledge in his work, which gave it a ring of truth. Wells was a socialist who believed the salvation of society would be its technology. He was active politically his entire life, and became an influential advocate of socialism. Wells died in London in 1946, having witnessed the birth of the atomic age.

Stephen Crane was an American journalist, short-fiction writer, and novelist who produced a number of memorable works in his 29 years. Best known for his unflinching evocation of a soldier in battle, "The Red Badge of Courage" (1895), Crane ironically never fought in a war. He published a collection of poetry, "The Black Rider and other Lines"(1895) that was a critical success. Crane traveled the world as a journalist, and his experiences provided him with ample material for his fiction. Crane was born New Jersey in 1871 and became a journalist in New York City. He was what we now term an investigative reporter, writing grim and harshly realistic articles about the poor. Crane eventually settled in Sussex, England, and became an associate of the important literary figures of the day. His short stories are included in many anthologies, and are the strength of his writing. He died in England in 1900.

Bram Stoker, born Abraham Stoker, was an Irish novelist. His reputation is based the creation of one of the most feared and imitated characters in literature, Count Dracula of Transylvania. Count Dracula was a polished and urbane aristocrat, and a supernatural creature who feasts on human blood to transform his victims into monsters. This Gothic novel, published in 1897, is based on folklore and the historical figure, Vlad, the Impaler. Born in Dublin in 1847, Stoker received a classical education at Trinity College, Dublin. He worked in local government for a short time, and then became secretary and manager of Sir Henry Irving, a prominent actor in London. Their association would last 27 years before Stoker retired to concentrate on his writing. Bram Stoker died in 1912, his legacy assured in the ever popular figure of Dracula.

Kate Chopin, American novelist and short-fiction writer whose breakthrough work was the novel, "The Awakening" (1899). The story of a woman's struggle to attain independence has become a landmark in feminist literature. The book was roundly condemned for its bold use of sexuality, particularly the heroine's illicit affairs. The criticism was so overwhelming it almost ended Chopin's writing career. Her later works are collections of stories of Creole and

Cajun life. Kate Chopin was born in St. Louis in 1851. She married and moved to New Orleans in 1870. Chopin continued to live and write in Louisiana until her death in 1904. She is now regarded as an early victim of anti-feminist opinion in literary circles. Her inquiries into the nature of female identity are remarkable for her period, and prepared the ground for future feminist literature.

Theodore Dreiser was an American novelist who was a leader in the literary movement known as "naturalism". Naturalism sought a literary ideal base on an objective, dispassionate, description of the world. Dreiser's first novel, "Sister Carrie" (1900), was so controversial the publisher refused to promote it. His magna opus, "An American Tragedy (1925)" was based on a true story of the day. Dreiser later published three successful novels, "The Financier"(1912), "The Titan"(1914), and a late book," The Stoic"(1947). Dreiser was born to a poor family in Indiana in 1871. He worked as a journalist for many years as he polished his writing skills. Besides his novels, Dreiser wrote short-fiction, plays, and an autobiography. His work is understood to have had a major impact on novel writing in America, by its rough portrayal of urban life. Dreiser died in 1945.

Anton Chekov, Russian playwright and short-story writer, is regarded as one of the greats in Russian literature. Known for his skillful blend of symbolism and naturalism, Chekov combines comedy, tragedy, and pathos, into a heady brew. His greatest short stories include" The Black Monk"(1894), " A Dreary Story"(1889), and "Ward Number Six"(1892). His fame as a dramatist rests on his four later plays, "The Cherry Orchard"(1904), " Uncle Vanya"(1897), "The Three Sisters"(1901), and " The Seagull"(1897). Chekov was born in southern Russia, and studied medicine at Moscow University. As a student, he wrote for periodicals to supplement his income. After his early successes, he concentrated on

his writing, and only occasionally practiced medicine. He suffered from tuberculosis, and moved to the Crimea in hopes of a more healthy environment. In this he was unsuccessful, and he died in 1904.

Rudyard Kipling, the favorite writer of the British Empire, was a novelist, poet, and short-fiction writer of great skill. His novels of British imperialism, such as "Kim"(1901), carved a unique literary niche for Kipling. His poetry was much beloved, outstanding examples are "Gunga Din", "Mandalay", and "Danny Deever". Kipling's story collections for children include "The Jungle Book (1894), and "Just So Stories"(1902). Kipling's descriptions of British Colonial life became a window for the world to understand the glory and excesses of the Empire. Kipling was born in Bombay in 1865, and educated in England. He returned to India for several years, working as a journalist and fledgling poet. Returning to England, his prose collection captured the fancy of the nation. Kipling lived for four productive years in Vermont, then came home for good. The first English writer to win a Nobel Prize in literature, he died in England in 1936.

Joseph Conrad , born Josef Teodor Konrad Korziniowski, was a Polish-born English novelist who found success with his early adventure novels of the sea such as "Almayer's Folly"(1895), "Lord Jim"(1900), and "Typhoon"(1903). He is perhaps best known for his adventure and psychological thrillers such as "Heart of darkness"(1902), and "The Secret Agent"(1907). Conrad was noted for his treatment of moral questions and his adroit use of language in his work. Born in Poland in 1857, Conrad moved with his exiled family to Russia. Conrad went to sea with both the French Merchant Marine, and the British Merchant navy eventually commanding a ship. His travels provided the raw material for his fiction, which is now highly regarded by critics. Conrad became a British citizen and lived in London until his death in 1924.

American novelist, short-story writer, playwright, and essayist, **Henry James** is a founder of the modern American novel. His mature fiction includes" The American"(1877), "The Europeans"(1789), "Daisy Miller"(1879), and "Washington Square"(1880). James's middle period features novels of social concern and artists, "The Bostonians"(1886). James's mature works use the technique of presenting events through each character's limited perspective, as in "Turn of the Screw"(1898), and "Wings of the Dove"(1902). James was an excellent literary and art critic, writing for a number of newspapers and periodicals. James was born in New York City in 1843 but spent much of his time in Europe. From 1876 until his death he lived in London, eventually becoming a British citizen. Many of his works involve Americans living abroad, particularly in England. James died in London in 1916.

Samuel Butler, English essayist, critic, and novelist, is best known for his biting satire and savage wit. His first major work "Erewhon", published in 1872, was a satire on the public's belief in universal progress. He wrote two additional novels," The Fair Haven"(1873), an attack on the Resurrection, and "Erewhon Revisited"(1901), before the publication of his best known work, "The Way of All Flesh", published posthumously in 1903. "The Way of All Flesh" is a largely autobiographical work describing Victorian middle-class life. Samuel Butler was born in Nottinghamshire in 1835, and educated at Cambridge. He emigrated to New Zealand and became a sheep farmer and occasional writer on scientific theory. Returning to England in 1864, he turned to writing full time, and produced most of his major work. Butler died in England in 1902.

Jack London was an American novelist, short-fiction writer, and essayist. London's first collection of short-stories, "The Son of the Wolf" was published in 1900. "The Call of the Wild"(1903) is the story of a sled-dog that becomes the leader of a wolf pack, was hugely successful, bringing the author both stature and riches. London's best known other novels include "The Sea Wolf"(1904), and "White Fang"(1906), another tale of survival in the wild. His later works are more ideological, and the best known is "The People of the Abyss"(1903). London was born in Oakland California in 1896 into a poverty stricken home. A vagabond who worked as a gold miner, cannery worker, and seaman, London went to the Klondike on a failed expedition to find gold. London was a passionate socialist, and he spoke and wrote often as an advocate. London, destitute and an alcoholic, committed suicide in 1916.

Edith Wharton was born Edith Newbold Jones and was a prolific American novelist, poet, short-fiction writer, and essayist. She was expert at narrating the foibles of Old New York society of which she was a member. Wharton' first success was "The House of Mirth"(1905), a novel depicting an individual's struggles against society's mores. Writing from France , she published "Ethan Frome"(1911), and her most popular work, "The Age of Innocence"1920", which won a Pulitzer prize for literature. "The Age of Innocence" chronicles a long and stormy love affair. Wharton was born in New York in 1862, and raised in elite society. Her marriage to Edward Norton after he suffered a number of nervous breakdowns, and was caught embezzling her accounts. She divorced Wharton which presaged her most productive writing period. She moved to France in 1907, and her writing career became the focus of her life. Wharton, much honored and loved, died in 1937.

Upton Sinclair was an American novelist, journalist , and essayist. He was the best known of the "muckrakers, a socially minded band of writers who decried and attacked perceived immoral conduct in business and government. His most popular novel, "The Jungle"(1906) attacked and exposed abuses in the Chicago meat packing industry. "The Jungle" was instrumental in forcing the passage of the Pure Food and Drug Act. Sinclair's later works include "King

Coal"(1917), and a novel based on the Sacco-Vanzetti trial, "Boston" (1928). Born in California in 1878, Sinclair was an ardent socialist who ran (and lost) for the governorship of California in 1934. He remained a muckraker to the end, advocating socialism, and attacking social ills, Upton Sinclair died in California in 1968.

Henry Adams was an American editor, biographer, and historian famed for his autobiography, " The Education of Henry Adams" published in 1907. Adams produced two novels, "Democracy, an American Novel" (1880), and "Esther" (1884), both published anonymously. His life's work was a nine volume "History of the United States of America During the Administrations of Thomas Jefferson and James Madison", published in 1889-91. Adams was born in 1838, in Boston, grandson of John Quincy Adams. Educated at Harvard, he chose a profession of scholarship, rather than government service. Editor of the "North American Review", for six years, he then accepted an appointment as medieval history Professor at Harvard. He remained there until he retired to write full time. Adams died in Boston in 1918.

Johan Strindberg was a Swedish novelist, playwright, essayist, and short-fiction writer. His initial success was a novel of bohemian life in Sweden, "The Red Room" published in 1879. His writing was noted for blending realism and naturalism together in a unique manner. His best novels include "The Father"(1887), "Miss Julie"(1889). Strindberg later turned to Symbolism mixed with Expressionism for his "Ghost Sonata" (1908), and "The Great Highway"(1910), both autobiographical plays. Strindberg was born in Sweden in 1849. An unhappy childhood followed by three failed marriages influenced his work greatly. His public life was full of controversy, and he flirted with debilitating mental illness all his life. A near breakdown is described in "Inferno"(1897), Strindberg turned to Symbolism and Expressionism. He died in 1912.

Ford Madox Ford, born Ford Hermann Hueffer, was an English novelist and critic. His most honored work is "The Good Soldier" published in 1915. "The Good Soldier" narrates an unhappy marriage in the English upper class. Ford collaborated on two novels with Joseph Conrad, "The Inheritors"(1901), and "Romance"(1903). His other major works include, "Parade's End", a trilogy of novels set in America and Europe. Editor and founder of the "Transatlantic review", a literary journal of excellent reputation, Ford spent his later productive years writing a general survey of world literature for lay readers. Ford was born in England in 1873, and fought in France in World war I. He returned and settled in Paris after the war, where he was active in literary society. He lived for a time in America, before returning to Europe to die in 1939.

Gertrude Stein was an American poet, essayist, novelist, and short-story writer. Her major work is "Three Lives"(1909), a novel of working class women. Her poetry collection, "Tender Objects, Food, and Rooms" published in 1914 was well received. Her autobiography, "The Autobiography of Alice B. Toklas"published in 1937, has become an icon to millions of individuals. Born in America in 1874, spent most of her childhood in Europe. She studied psychology with William James in Baltimore before moving to Paris for good. With her secretary and partner, Alice B. Toklas, Stein became the center of the modernist literary scene in Paris and was a close friend of Picasso, Hemingway, and Ford Madox Ford. Stein was a flamboyant figure in Paris famous for her acid tongue and repartee. Stein died in Paris in 1946.

Rabindranath Tagore was an Indian poet, playwright, novelist, short-fiction writer, and songwriter. Best known for his spiritual poetry written in Bengali, his first collection was "The ideal One"(1890). Noted for his lyrical, spiritual poetry, also written in Bengali, Tagore dominated the Indian literary scene for decades. His most popular work,

"Song Offerings"(1912), won him a Nobel prize in literature in 1911. Tagore published a number of poetry anthologies, and his stories of village Bengal life were published as "The Hungry Stones"(1916), and "Broken Ties"(1925). His best novel, "The Home and the World"(1916), was adapted for film by Satyagit Ray. Tagore was born in Calcutta in 1861, to a wealthy Hindu family. He studied law in London, and traveled widely in the West before returning to India to live. He died in India in 1941.

D. H. Lawrence, English novelist, poet, essayist, and short-fiction writer brought an intensity to his work and life that sometimes scandalized his peers. His autobiographical novel, "Sons and Lovers", was published in 1913. His greatest works, "The Rainbow"(1915),"Women in Love"(1921), and "Lady Chatterly's Lover"(1928), (banned in England and America for 30 years), focus on love, class, social standing, and sexuality. "The Complete Poems of D.H. Lawrence"(1964) is the best anthology of his verse. Lawrence was born in industrial England in 1888, his childhood was marred by an unhappy home. In 1915, Lawrence and his wife left England for good and traveled extensively. Suffering from tuberculosis, Lawrence sought a climate that would benefit his health. He died of the disease in 1930.

George Bernard Shaw was an British playwright and critic. Shaw published his collections of drama in "Plays Pleasant and Unpleasant"(1898), which included some of his best work including his critical prefaces. Shaw's plays also include "Caesar and Cleopatra"(1901), "Major Barbara"(1907), "Pygmalion"(1913), and "St. joan"1924). He was awarded the Nobel prize in literature in 1925. Shaw chose controversial topics for his dramas, stressing realistic social problems. He satirized social class and gender discrimination, but with a light touch that made its points without anger. Shaw was born in Dublin in 1856 and soon moved to London. An ardent progressive, he spoke and wrote passionately on the social issues of the day. He was renowned for his literary criticism, and was a major contributor to literary digests of his day. A leading figure in world literature, Shaw died in London in 1950.

Marcel Proust, French novelist, owes his reputation to his epic seven-part masterpiece, "Remembrance of Things Past", published between 1913-27. This monumental work, examines the existential problem of finding meaning and value in the maelstrom of life. Using the device of interior monologue, Proust views the transient nature of life and the flux of consciousness using observation of minute detail in a manner rarely done with such skill. Proust was forced to publish the first volume himself, but subsequent books were well received. The final three volumes were published after Proust's death. Proust was born in Paris in 1871 in Paris and educated at the Lycee Condorcet. As a young man, he was a favorite in the literary salons of Paris, a setting he used repeatedly in his novels. Suffering from chronic asthma and the early death of his mother, Proust withdrew into semi-seclusion where he devoted himself to his life's work. Proust died in Paris in 1921.

Thomas Sterns Eliot, American poet, playwright and ,and critic, was a major poet of the modernist school of poetry. Eliot first success was in 1915 with the publication of "The Love Song of J. Alfred Prufrock" originally appearing in "Poetry", a small literary magazine. Eliot struggled with his own despair at the futility of life, and the spiritual barrenness of modern life. He addressed these themes in "The Waste Land", a powerful and influential work in the history of modern poetry. Eliot wrote several dramas in verse including "Murder in the Cathedral"(1953), and "The Cocktail Party"(1950). Eliot was born in St. Louis in 1888 and educated at Harvard and Oxford University. He moved to London and worked as a banker before becoming an editor at Faber and Faber in 1925. In 1927 he became a British citizen and converted to

Anglicanism. He was a distinguished figure in literature until his death in 1965.

Robert Frost, American poet, who is remembered as a master the technical aspects of poetry while remaining true to his New England heritage. Frost will always be remembered for his masterful simplicity in such poems as "Stopping By the Woods on a Snowy Evening"(1923), and "The Road Not Taken"(1916). While living in England before World War I, Frost published two collections of poetry. Returning to New England, he published a number of anthologies including "Complete Poems"(1945), "West Running Brook"(1928), "A Witness Tree"(1942), and "In the Clearing"(1962). Frost was born in California in 1874 and was educated at Dartmouth College and Harvard. He received the Pulitzer Prize four times and capped his career by reading "The Gift Outright" at the inaugural of John Kennedy in 1961. Frost died in 1963.

Frantz Kafka was a Prague born and German writing novelist and short story writer. Using powerful symbolism ,and addressing the anxieties and chaos of modern society, Kafka wrote penetrating stories and novels. during his lifetime, the novella," The Metamorphosis"(1915), "In the Penal Colony"(1919), and the collection, "The Hunger Artist (1924). Kafka instructed his executor and literary agent, Max Brod, to destroy his unpublished manuscripts after his death. Recognizing Kafka's genius, Brod published the works including the great novels "The Trial" (1925), "The Castle"(1926), and "Amerika" (1927). Kafka was born in Prague to a middle class Jewish family with whom he lived most of his life. He attended law school, but worked in an insurance firm for many years. His fiction was dark, wounding, and sometimes painful, but always arresting. Kafka died in 1924.

James Joyce, Irish novelist and short-story writer, developed a style rich in innovative literary technique and creative language. His first major work was a collection of short stories, "The Dubliners"(1914), followed by an autobiographical novel, " A Portrait of the Artist as a Young Man"(1916), and a drama, "Exiles" (1918). Joyce published "Ulysses" in 1922 to critical acclaim. Joyce spent many years on his next novel, finally publishing "Finnegans Wake" in 1939. James Joyce was born in Dublin in 1882 and most of his fiction was set in that city. Rebelling against the constraints of Catholic society, Joyce left Ireland and lived in Europe most of his life. He lived in a number of European cities with his wife Nora Barnacle, often in poor circumstances and plagued by an eye disorder that caused near blindness. Joyce died in 1914.

Edna St. Vinceny Millay was one of the best known American poets of the 1920's. Millay won a poetry contest in 1902 with "Renascence" which became her best known poem. Millay won the Pulitzer Prize for her poetry, "The Ballad of the Harp-weaver" in 1923. She published a number of successful collections of poems, including " A Few Twigs from Thistles"(1920), "Fatal Interview"(1931), "Wine From These Grapes"(1934), "Conversation at Midnight"(1937), and "Make the Bright Arrows"(1940), and the posthumously published "Collected Poems"(1956). Millay infused traditional sonnets with the voice of an independent, modern woman. Millay was born in Rockland, Maine in 1892. Educated in liberal arts at Vassar College, she worked as a reporter for "Vanity Fair" magazine New York. Millay died in 1950 at the apex of her career.

Virginia Woolf, born Adele Virginia Stephen, English novelist, short-fiction writer, essayist and critic, was one of the most creative and influential writers of the 20th century. After publishing two traditional novels, Woolf wrote "Jacobs Room"(1922), using her "steam of consciousness" method of interior monologues to develop an absent character. She continued her experimentation in "Mrs. Dalloway"(1925), "To The

Lighthouse"(1927), and "The Waves"(1931). Woolf was born in England in 1882, and educated by her father, a distinguished literary figure of his own. After her father's death, she and her family moved to the Bloomsbury section of London, where their home became the center of the group of authors, artists, and thinkers known as the Bloomsbury Group. She married Leonard Woolf, with whom she would found the Hogarth Press, a publisher of many important modernist writers. Woolf committed suicide in 1941by drowning.

Gerald Manley Hopkins, English poet, published his first successful poem, "The Wreck of the Deutschland", in 1875. He followed this with a series of sonnets, including "The Windhover", "Pied Beauty", "God's Grandeur", and "Carrion Comfort". His later poems were written in a period of personal, depression, and religious doubt. He developed a style called "sprung rhythm", which attempts to duplicate human speech. The first collection of his work, "Poems", was published 30 years after his death. his reputation has grown over the decades, and he is now seen as a major influence on modern poetry. Hopkins was born in Startford, Essex, in 1844. He attended Oxford, where he received a classical education. Following his decision to convert to Catholicism and study for the priesthood, Hopkins abandoned poetry for seven years. Poverty and spiritual doubt haunted the rest of his life. He died in England in 1889.

Willa Cather, American novelist, short-story writer and, essayist. Her breakthrough came with the publication of her second novel, "Oh Pioneers" which narrated the story of an immigrant family's struggle in the new world. "My Antonia", a story of a woman's struggle and eventual triumph on the prairie met critical acclaim in 1918. Cather won the Pulitzer Prize in 1922 for "One of Ours". Cather's later work bemoaned the loss of pioneering spirit in America which were the theme for "Death Comes for the Archbishop" (1917). She published a successful essay

collection , "Not under Forty" in 1936. Other writing examines the topics of art, loss, and disillusionment, including a novel on the American Civil War, "Sapphira and the Slave Girl"(1940). Cather was born in Virginia in 1873, and moved to the Nebraska frontier as a child. Her experiences on the in Nebraska furnished much of the material on which she based her work. She died in 1947.

Wilfed Owen is regarded as the greatest English poet of World War I. Owen's work is best known as a scathing indictment against war based on his experiences in France in 1917-18. Stylistally innovative, his language is starkly realistic in depicting the horrors of war. Most of Owen's work was published after his death, with the collected "Poems" introduced by Sassoon, which include "Strange Meeting", and " Anthem for Doomed Youth". Owen's verse was used in Benjamin Britten's "War Requiem", a powerful choral piece that became an instant classic. Wilfred Owen was born in Shropshire, and had a mundane education at Shrewsbury Technical College. He taught until 1915 when he enlisted in the army. Wounded in 1917, he was recovering in Scotland where he met Siegfried Sasson who encouraged his poetry. Returning to the front in 1918, he was killed only a week before the war ended.

Born **Katherine Mansfield Beauchamp**, Mansfield was a New Zealand short story writer. Her first collection of short-fiction, "In a German Pension" (1911), was well received. She was to publish a number of anthologies of her work, including "Bliss" (1920), "The Garden party and Other Stories(1922), and "Prelude"(1918). Her style and strength was the complex and subtle development of her characters, probing their psychological depths. She was a prolific contributor to magazines, working with her editor-husband, John Middelton Murry. He was to collect all of her letters and journals and publish them after her death. Mansefield was born in New Zealand in 1888. She emigrated to England in 1907, where she would spend the rest of her life. Mansfield died in London in 1923.

Dame Agatha Christie, English novelist and playwright, is one of the most successful writers of all time. The author of over 80 detective novels, her work has been translated into over 100 languages. She created two memorable characters , the eccentric Hercules Poirot, and the elderly spinster, Miss Jane Marple, who are the protagonists of most of her books. Christie wrote and adapted many works for the stage, including her famous " The Mousetrap", which is the longest running play in the history of drama. The play is still running in London, where it opened in 1952. Many of her works have been adapted for television and film. Born and raised in the West Country in 1890, she worked as nurse and chemist in World War I, where she gained a working knowledge of poisons, which she utilized in her fiction. Christie died in London in 1976.

Edward Estlin Cummings, E. E. Cummings, American poet and novelist was noted for his unique writing style, using unconventional punctuation and typography, innovative language and imagery, made him a leading modernist voice in poetry. His first book and only novel," The Enormous Room"(1922). His verse is often light and joyful, but contains a great depth of irony and complex feeling. His major works include" Tulips and Chimney's"(1923), "50 poems"(1940), "Ninety-five Poems"(1958),and "73 Poems" published after his death. Cummings also published works of non-fiction and prose. Cummings was born in 1894, educated at Harvard, and served in France in World War I. He became a popular and important lecturer on the literary scene before his death in 1962.

Rene' Maria Rilke was a German poet and a much beloved figure throughout the world, where his work is universally admired. Struggling with themes of life, and death, Rilke explored man's relationship to the Divine, and particularly humanity's perception of the universal. His major works include" The Book of Images"(1906),"Duino Elegies"(1923), "Sonnets to Orpheus"(1923),

and "New Plans", his first volume published in 1908. Rilke is one of the most widely translated poets in the world, some done by well known poets such as Robert Bly and Randall Jarrell. Rilke was born in Prague in 1875, he lived across Europe, with sojourns in Germany, France, and Switzerland. Rilke visited Russia twice, which inspired his first book of poetry. Rilke died in Paris in 1926 a giant man of letters.

Edward Morgan Forster, English novelist, essayist, and critic, is a major figure in modern literature, published his first four novels between 1905-10. The best known of these are "A Room With A View"(1908), "Howard's End"(1910), "The Longest Journey"(1907), and "Where Angels fear To Tread"(1905). Forster addressed subjects such as social justice, materialism and spirituality, and the dissolution of the English upper classes.

His masterpiece, "A Passage To India"(1924) was inspired by several visits to India and Forsters service in Egypt in World War I. Forster also published volumes of literary criticism and essays. Forster was born in 1879 in London into a upper-middle-class household. He was educated at King's College, Cambridge, and became a contributor to a number of literary journals. His eclectic and prolific work made him a major figure in world literature. Forster died in England in 1970, at age 81.

Thomas Mann, German novelist and essayist, was a writer of great importance in the early 20ty-century. His work usually focused on art and the struggle of the artist to flourish in European society. This conflict is the theme of the novels "Buddenbrooks"(1903), and "Death in Venice"(1912). Ultimately Mann turned to Spirituality in his long allegorical novel, "The Magic Mountain" published in 1924. Later works include "Dr Faustus"(1947), "Joseph and His Brothers"(1933-43), a tetra logy of novels about the biblical character. Mann won the Nobel Prize for literature in 1929. Thomas

Mann was born in Germany in 1875, and fled Nazi Germany in the early 1930's after clashing with Hitler's policies. He became a United States citizen in 1944 but remained active in world affairs and visited Europe frequently after the war. He died in Switzerland in 1955.

F. Scott Fitzgerald was an American novelist and short-story writer. Fitzgerald has transcended his early reputation as a period novelist, now being viewed as a great modern novelist. He launched his writing career with "This Side of Paradise"(1920), a novel of the jazz age. His masterpiece, "The Great Gatsby"(1925), chronicles the life of a bootlegger who reforms. "Tender is the Night"(1933), a largely autobiographical novel about a psychiatrist's failing fight to save his wife from mental illness. Fitzgerald was born in St. Paul, Minnesota, in 1896. Educated at Princeton University, became a productive short-story writer after the success of his first novel. His marriage to the flamboyant Zelda Fitzgerald, spiraled downward with alcoholism and her increasing mental illness. He worked in Hollywood as a screenwriter, before his death in 1940.

Ezra Pound American poet, critic, and editor was a most controversial in world literature. He published his most important work of poetry," The Cantos", late in his career. His influence as a critic was formidable, and he fostered the work of Robert Frost, Ernest Hemingway, James Joyce, and T.S. Eliot. Pound was an important Imagist, advocating the use of free meter and the extravagant use of image. His first book of verse, "A Lume Spento", was self published inn Europe. Pound was born in Idaho in1885, reared in Pennsylvania, and educated at Hamilton College, and the University of Pennsylvania. He moved to Europe after college, where he became an influential critic and editor. Associated with Mussolini and his fascist regime, Pound was arrested for treasonable propaganda. Committed to an asylum in

America for mental illness for 12 years, he returned to Italy until his death in 1972.

Ernest Hemingway, American novelist and short-story writer, was a modernist master who became a legendary figure in his own lifetime. He achieved fame with his novel "The Sun Also Rises"(1926) and " A Farewell to Arms"(1929), based on his World War I experiences. Other important works include "For Whom the Bell Tolls"(1940) based on the Spanish Civil war, and "The Old Man and the Sea"(1952), a novel about a Cuban fisherman. Hemingway was awarded the Nobel Prize in Literature in 1954. Hemingway was born in the American Midwest in 1899, and worked as a ambulance driver in World War I. He joined a group of expatriate writers in Paris in the 1920's, a rich literary experience for a young man. Hemingway moved to Cuba in the 1940's, and lived there for many years where he became a local hero. Returning to America, he fell into a period of declining mental health, committing suicide in Idaho in 1961.

William Butler Yeats, Irish poet and playwright, originally made his name as a dramatist, with such plays as "The Countess Cathleen"(1892), " The Land of Heart's Desire"(1894), and "Cathleen in Houlihan"(1902). The poetry of Yeat's later years show a spare, realistic style, with much symbolism. Examples of this are "Easter 1916"(1916), celebrating the Easter rising in Dublin, and "The Second Coming"(1921). Yeats was awarded the Nobel Prize in literature in 1923. Yeats was born in Dublin in 1865, and raised in London. He maintained a strong interest in Irish nationalism, folklore, mysticism, and painting his entire life. In love with the political activist Maud Gonne, he suffered when his love was not returned. Yeats was a founder of what became the Abbey theatre in Dublin, a center of Irish literary life. Yeats died in Dublin 1939.

William Faulkner, American novelist and short-story writer, wrote almost solely about southern history in his fiction. After the publication of his first successful novel,"Sartoris"(1929), Faulkner reeled off a series of impressive novels including "The Sound And The fury"*(1929), "As I Lay Dying"(1930), "Absalom, Absolom"(1936), "Sanctuary"(1931), and "Go Down, Moses" in 1942. Winner of the Nobel Prize in literature in 1949, Faulkner also won two Pulitzer Prizes. He is remembered as a giant in American literature. Faulkner was born in Mississippi in 1897 and spent most of his life there. His recurring themes include Southern aristocracy's attempt to survive in the modern world, racial inequality in the South, and the burdens of slavery carried by his characters. Much of his work is based on his own family history, both colorful and tragic.

Erich Maria Remarque is the pen name of Erich Paul Remark, German novelist and literary figure. His experiences as a soldier in World War I formed the subject of his first and greatest novel, "All Quiet On The Western Front" published in 1929. Detailing the experiences of ordinary German soldiers, the book became one of the more important literary works to emerge from the World War. Remarque was born in a small town in Northern Germany in 1898. Drafted into the German army, he was gravely wounded and abandoned behind the French lines. He survived to write his fictional history of the conflagration that impacted millions of lives. Remarque never again achieved the fame following his first novel, but he remained active and lived in Europe until his death in 1970 at the age of 71.

Hart Crane, American poet, left behind one work on which his reputation rests. "The Bridge", Hart's 18 part epic poem based on the Brooklyn Bridge, celebrates America's muscular industrial strength in a manner that precedes Carl Sandburg. The poem, published in 1930, was a popular and critical success. Combining bold imagery with technical dexterity, the sweeping American themes captured the fancy of the public and critics alike. His complete works, including a manuscript found after his death was

published in 1966. Crane was born in Ohio in 1899, and was an industrial worker during World War I. Hart suffered from depression his entire life, and on a trip returning from Mexico he committed suicide by jumping off of the ship into the ocean. This bizarre death ended a promising talent in 1932 when Hart was only 32 years old.

John Dos Passos, American novelist, wrote sobering fiction and prose about the decline of the United States both spiritually and socially. His literary reputation rests on a trilogy of novels published as "U.S.A." in 1937. His jaundiced view of America is based on his observations of a country deeply divided by class and coarsened by commercialism. Early novels polished his stream-of-consciousness style he would employ so effectively in "U.S.A.". Dos Passos was born to a wealthy Chicago family in 1896. Educated at Harvard, he worked with Hemingway as a ambulance driver in France in World War I. Dos Passos's essentially negative view of American society is a recurring theme in his literary work. He worked as a journalist most of his life and published several works of biography and history before his death in 1970 at age 74.

Aldous Huxley, English novelist and social critic, created a hellish vision of the future in his "Brave New World" published in 1932. Describing a society based on technology and social control, "Brave New World" was the summation of a generation's fears about the future. Huxley's early novels are full of biting satire and criticism of society. His later works include" Island"(1962), reflecting his interest in eastern spirituality and metaphysics. "After Many A Summer Dies The Swan" (1939) indicate Huxley's growing distrust of politics and social trends. Two later works discuss his experiments with hallucinogenic drugs. Huxley was born in Surrey, England in 1894 and educated at Eton and Oxford. He emigrated to America in 1937, where he lived for the rest of his life. Huxley remained active as a teacher, writer, and social critic until his death in 1963.

Henry Miller, American novelist, short-fiction writer, and essayist, is best known for two books that were banned initially in the United States, "Tropic of Cancer"(1961), and "Tropic of Capricorn" (1962) both of which were published in France first. These two autobiographical novels caused an uproar because of their controversial treatment of sex . The Supreme Court ruled in Miller's favor in 1964, and the books were then legal in America. Miller's later works include "The Rosy Crucifixion", a trilogy based on Miller's life., along with anthologies of essays and stories. Henry Miller was born in Brooklyn, New York in 1891. He moved to Paris as a young man and celebrated his bohemian lifestyle. His works were a great influence on the "Beat " generation of the 1950's. Miller returned to the United States and lived in the Big Sur in California until his death in 1980.

Lillian Hellman was an American playwright and diarists who burst on the literary scene in 1934 with "The Children's Hour", a play about two schoolteachers who are accused of Lesbianism. She followed this with 'The Little Foxes", a portrait of a ruthless southern family. Other notable plays by Hellman include "Nazi Watch On The Rhine'(1941), and "Toys In The Attic"(1960). She published several volumes of her autobiography which were lauded for their eloquence. Lillian Hellman was born in New Orleans in 1905 to a middle class Jewish family. She grew up in New York and moved to Hollywood to work as a script reader. Blacklisted in the 1950's for her political activism, she fought a long battle to clear her name. Lillian Hellman grew to be a much loved liberal icon until her death in 1984.

Clifford Odets, American playwright, was an important figure in the theatre of the 1930's. His forte was social protest theatre, in which he became a leader. Odet's found his first success in "Waiting For Lefty "(1935) and "Awake And Sing"(1935), both powerful depictions of class struggle. Odets other notable plays include "Golden Boy" (1937), "The Big Knife"(1949), and "The Country Girl" (1950). The "Country Girl", a story of an alcoholic actor's attempt at a comeback was later adapted to an award winning film starring Grace Kelly. Clifford Odets was born in Philadelphia in 1906 and raised in New York. He began his career as an actor with the Theatre Guild and later became a founding member of the famous Group Theatre. Odets remained active on Broadway as well, working in legitimate theatre. Clifford Odets died in Hollywood in 1963.

Anna Akmatova, pen name of Andreyevna Gorenko, Russian poet whose work is set against repression in the Soviet Union. She was a leading light of the Acemist school of poetry, which valued accuracy, precision, and realistic clarity as a reaction to Symbolism. A collection of lyrical love poems, "Vecher"(1912), was her first book. Her epic poem "Requiem"(1940), was a response to her husband's execution by the Soviets. Regarded as her masterpiece, "Poem Without A Hero" (1965) narrated the difficulties of an artist working in a repressive regime. Akmatova was born near Odessa in 1889. Stalinist officials banned her work for almost 20 years, judging it to be too concerned with love and God. Expelled from the Writer's Union in 1946, she was not published again until the late 1950's. She is now ranked as one of the great poets of the 20th century. She died in the Soviet union in 1966.

Margaret Mitchell rests her reputation on one book, "Gone With The Wind" published in 1936. The novel won Mitchell a Pulitzer Prize, and was made into one of the most popular films of all time, starring Clark Gable and Vivian Leigh. The book narrates a Southern Belle's rise and fall set against the panorama of the planter South and the American Civil War, The protagonist, Scarlett O'Hara, suffers the end of her Southern society and her values, before becoming a resilient and successful survivor. Margaret Mitchell was born in 1900 in Atlanta and lived all of her life there. She attended Smith College in Northampton Massachusetts and worked as a journalist in Atlanta. She wrote

"Gone With The Wind" over a ten year period completing it in 1934. The unprecedented success of the book and film changed her life forever. She spoke, taught, and lectured over the next ten years until her death in Atlanta in 1949.

John Steinbeck, American novelist and short-story writer, wrote with a realistic style about the lives of common people. Steinbeck's most important work describes the plight of itinerant workers set in rural and industrial California. His best known works include "Of Mice And Men"(1937), and his Pulitzer Prize winning novel. "The Grapes of Wrath"(1939). The latter evokes the depression stricken "dust bowl" and a refugee family's travails. Other important books include "Cannery Row"(1945), "East Of Eden"(1952), and his whimsical "Travels with Charley (1962). Steinbeck won the Nobel Prize in literature in 1962. John Steinbeck was born in California in 1902. He was educated at Stanford University where he studied Marine Biology. Most of his fiction is set in California and the themes of the sea are evident in his early work. His writing exhibits a lyrical quality combined with a stark realism that was his trademark. John Steinbeck died in California in 1962.

Robert Penn Warren was an influential American novelist, poet, and critic. His most famous work is the Pulitzer Prize winning novel "All The King's Men" published in 1946. Based loosely on the life of Huey P. Long, it was adapted into an Oscar winning motion picture in 1949. Other important fiction includes the novel "World Enough And Time"(1950), and the short-story collection, "The Circus In The Attic"(1947). Warren published 14 collections of poetry, and won the Pulitzer Prize for "Now And Then"(1978). He was an influential literary critic, promoting the New Criticism in important textbooks. Robert Penn Warren was born in Kentucky and attended Vanderbilt University. He taught for many years at Louisiana State University where he founded the "Southern Review". He was named Poet Laureate of the United States in 1985. Penn Warren died in 1989.

Richard Wright, American novelist, and short-fiction writer, was one of the most influential black voices in American literature. His first book, "Uncle Tom's Children"(1938), included four novellas and won critical acclaim. Wright's publication of the best-selling "Native Son" in 1940, insured his place in literary history. In addition to "Native Son", Wright's other important work includes "The Outsider"(1953), and his autobiography, "Black Boy" published in 1945. Richard Wright was born in rural Mississippi in 1908, the grandson of slaves. Reared in Memphis, largely self-educated, he moved to Chicago at age 19 and entered the Federal Writer's Project. During the Depression, Wright joined the Communist party, and lived in Mexico before settling in Paris. Richard Wright died in Paris in 1960 at the age of 51.

Carson McCullers, born Lula Carson Smith, American novelist, set her fiction in the small Southern towns she grew up in as a child. Her themes were alienation, loneliness, and spiritual longing. Her best known novel, "The Member Of The Wedding" narrates the story of a lonely adolecesent girl in a Southern town, who lives vicariously through her brother. Her literary reputation was established with the appearance of "The Heart Is A Lonely Hunter" in 1940. Other well known works include "Reflections In A Golden Eye"(1941), "Clock Without Hands"(1961), and a posthumously published story collection, "The Mortgaged Heart"(1971). Carson McCullars was born in Georgia in 1917, and studied music at Julliard before attending Columbia to study writing. She was ill most of her life and a series of crippling strokes began in her 20's. She died in 1967 at age 50.

Wystan Hugh Auden was an English born man of letters, an accomplished poet, playwright, critic, editor, and translator. Perhaps best known for his verse, which was witty, musical, and innovative in the use of rhythms, Auden published a number of collections. "The Age Of Anxiety"(1947), won him a Pulitzer Prize for poetry. Other important works include "Another Time"(1940), "The Double Man"(1941), "Nuns"(1951), and the National Book Award winner "The Shield Of Achilles"(1955). An opera librettist of great skill, he worked with such luminaries as Brittan and Stravinsky. Born in England in 1907, Auden was educated at Oxford, where he became a political activist for leftist movements. Auden moved to the United States, becoming a popular teacher and lecturer while producing work of the first order. Auden died in his adopted country in 1973 at the age of 65.

Eudora Welty , American novelist, short-fiction writer, critic, and essayist, was one of the great writers of the South. She mastered the Southern vernacular, the culture and customs of the South, and produced an impressive body of work. Her first collection, "A Curtain Of Green"(1941), contained many of her most popular stories. Her novel "The Ponder Heart"(1954), is a classic of absurdist humor. "The Optimist's Daughter"(1972) won her a Pulitzer Prize in 1972. She holds many honors, including the French Legion of Merit, and the American Medal of Freedom. Welty was born in Jackson, Mississippi in 1909, and attended Mississippi State University and the University of Wisconsin. She lived in New York until her father's early death caused her to return to Jackson where she would live the rest of her life. She was a literary figure of great importance in the South until her death in 2001.

Bertolt Brecht, born Eugene Berthold Freidrich Brecht, was a German playwright and poet whose major contribution to drama was to utilize the stage as a platform for political and social commentary. Brecht believed that the stage was a forum for presenting patterns of human behavior, outlined in his theory of "Epic Theatre". His success dated from the writing of the "Three Penney Opera" in 1928, a work of biting

satire coauthored with composer Kurt Weill. Two other plays of interest are "Mother Courage And Her Children"(1941), and "The Life of Galileo"(1943). An anthology of English translations appeared in 1979. Brecht was born in Augsburg, Germany, in 1898. Brecht embraced Marxism, and was forced to flee Germany in 1933 by the Nazis. He lived in Europe and the United States for many years until returning to East Germany in 1949. He died there in 1956.

Albert Camus, French philosopher, poet, novelist, and playwright, who explored the philosophy of the absurd through his work. He examined man's existence in an indifferent universe, and stressed the need for humanistic and moral values in this situation. Success came with his novel "The Stranger" in 1942, and his essay, "The Myth Of Sisyphus"(1942), both arresting explorations of the absurd. Other significant works include the novel, "The Plague"(1947), and "The Fall"(1956), and his influential essay, 'The Rebel" (1951). Camus was born in Algiers in 1913 to a middle class family. He studied philosophy at the University of Algiers and later worked as a journalist. He was an intellectual leader of the French Resistance under Nazi occupation, and served as the editor of the underground paper "Combat". Camus was awarded the Nobel Prize in literature in 1957. He died in an automobile accident in 1960.

Jorge Luis Borges, Argentinean poet, novelist essayist, and short story writer, combines fantasy, myth, and philosophy in the fabric of daily life. His work is highly original, and his collection of essays," Other Inquisitions"(1952), explain the writer's philosophy of life and art. Other important works are a book blending poetry and prose, "The Book Of Imaginary Beings"(1967), a collection of stories," The Book of Sand", and a collection of his poetry in English translation. Born in Argentina in 1899, Borges studied abroad and received his degree from College de Geneva in Switzerland before returning home. During the dictatorship of Juan Peron, Borges was a vocal critic of the government. After the fall of Peron, Borges was appointed Director of the National Library of Argentina in Buenos Aires. Borges died in Argentina in 1986.

Jean Genet, French novelist and playwright, is the master of drama and fiction depicting criminal life and anti-social behavior. His absurdist dramas are existentialist nightmares, and mix violence and erotic content in a powerful blend. Genet breakthrough novel was "Our Lady Of The Flowers"(1983), written in prison while serving a life sentence. Sartre and Cocteau successfully argued for Genet's release, and he published his shocking autobiography " The Thief's Journal" in 1949. Genet then turned his attention to drama, writing several successful pays including "The Maids"(1947), "The Balcony"(1956), and " The Blacks"(1948), all of which were influential in the development of avant-garde theatre. Genet was born in France in 1910,, an illegitimate child abandoned by his mother. After spending his youth in unhappy foster homes and orphanages, he joined the Foreign Legion and promptly deserted. Genet died in France in 1986.

Tennessee Williams, born Thomas Lanier Williams II, American playwright, is regarded as one of the greatest American playwrights of the 20th century. His subject matter was drawn from the earthiest topics and treated with a lyrical touch in a romantic, yet realistic view of America's South. His rise to fame was meteoric with "The Glass Menagerie" in 1945, followed by his Pulitzer Prize winning "A Streetcar Named Desire" in 1947. Other important plays followed, including "Cat On A Hot Tin Roof"(1955) which earned Williams another Pulitzer, "Suddenly Last Summer"(1958), "Sweet Bird Of Youth"(1959), and his last hit, "The Night Of The Iguana" in 1961. Williams was born in Mississippi in 1911, and educated at the Universities of Washington and Iowa. After his dramatic success had slowed, he published a collection of poetry and his

memoirs. Williams is generally regarded, along with Eugene O'Neill and Arthur Miller as the greatest American dramatists. He died in 1983 at the age of 72.

William Carlos Williams, American poet, novelist and short-story author, found inspiration for his work in the experiences of everyday life. He wrote 45 volumes of prose and poetry, typically American, using his realistic or objectivist style. His best poetry was his five volume" Paterson"(1946-58), based on the city near his home. His "Pictures From Brueghel"(1962), a three volume work, won Williams a Pulitzer Prize in 1962. He also published numerous short fiction, and the Steche trio logy of novels. His prose included a book of essays and an autobiography. William Carlos Williams was born in Rutherford, New Jersey, in 1883 and studied medicine in college. He returned to his birthplace and practiced as a pediatrician for over 50 years, while turning out a huge body of innovative and very American work. Williams was unusual in literally having two full time careers his whole adult life. Williams is now regarded as a leading modernist writer. Williams died in New Jersey in 1963.

Norman Mailer, American novelist, short story writer, essayist, and journalist, Mailer won his initial success with "The Naked And The Dead", his autobiographical novel of World War II published in 1948. Blending gritty realism with a unique and arresting writing style, Mailer was granted instant celebrity. His future novels never approached the success of "The Naked And The Dead" and his reputation today rests largely on his journalism. Mailer won the Pulitzer Prize for "Armies Of The Night", and "The Executioner's Song", both non-fiction books. Norman Mailer was born in New York in 1923 and educated at Harvard University. After his initial success in fiction, he developed his own blend of journalism, political commentary, fictional allusions, and autobiography into a rich style with colorful language. Significant later works include "Ancient Evenings", and "Harlot's Ghost".

Arthur Miller, American playwright, described the pain of the common man in his stirring dramas. Perhaps his best known play, "Death Of A Salesman"(1949) earned him a Pulitzer Prize. "The Crucible"(1953), a drama about the Salem witch trials is regarded as an American classic. Miller was an extremely productive author, penning dramas over six decades. Some of his better early works include" A View From The Bridge"(1955), "The Price",(1968) and "The American Clock"(1980). Notable later works include "The Misfits And Other Stories"(1987), and a novella, "Homely Girl"(1995). Arthur Miller was born in Harlem in 1915. Educated at the University of Michigan, he began writing plays in the 1940's. Haunted by his father's failure during the depression, Miller returned to the subject of failure in many of his plays. Arthur Miller had an extremely productive career, ending with his death in 2004.

George Orwell, the pen name of Eric Arthur Blair, English novelist, critic, and playwright, is best known for his novels damning totalitarian regimes, and doing so with crushing satire. His two major works are "Animal Farm" (1945), and Nineteen-Eighty Four"(1949), which established him as a leading satirist and novelist. His writing was fueled by his passionate economic and political views, and they are the keystones of his work. Aside from his two successful novels, he wrote several lesser ones, a collection of essays, and his four-volume "Collected Essays, Journalism, and Letters of George Orwell" (1968). Orwell was born Bengal, India in 1903, and educated at Eton. He then joined the Indian Imperial police in Burma, but became disillusioned by imperialism and returned to Europe to live. Orwell fought for the Republicans in the Spanish Civil War and wrote of his experiences. After his success in the 1940's, he enjoyed an all too brief period of fame until his death in 1950.

Simone de Beauvior , French novelist, philosopher, and memoirist was a powerful intellectual figure in post World War II Europe. Perhaps her most important work is "The Second Sex'(1949), a ground-breaking feminist polemic about the secondary status of women in the world. Her best known novel is " the Mandarins"(1954) which relates her struggles with the repressive regimes of Vichy, follower by Stalinist excesses. de Beauvior wrote extensively about her life and published five volumes of memoirs that offered a window of history into her time. Born in Montparnasse in Paris in 1908, she met and formed the defining relationship of her life with Jean-Paul Sarte. This was a friendship, a love relationship, and a partnership of philosophy and art. She focused on the themes of individual freedom, particularly between the sexes. She died in Paris in 1986.

Nelson Algren, born Nelson Ahlgren Abraham, was an American novelist and short-story writer. His work in noted by the stark reality with which he depicts the lives of the poor. Algren's is best remembered for his novel, "The Man With The Golden Arm"(1949), which brings the reality of drug addiction to the literary world. The book earned him a National Book Award and gave him a national reputation. The book was later adapted into an award winning film. Later works include a story collection, "The Neon Wilderness"(1947, and a novel about Bohemian life in New Orleans, "A Walk On The Wild Side". Algren was born in 1809 in Detroit and raised in Chicago. Educated at the University of Illinois, he set much of his fiction in the Midwest, where he explored the seamy side of urban life. Always viewed as a radical personality, his work nevertheless reflects a slice of American urban life largely unnoticed. He died in 1981.

Jerome David Salinger, American novelist and short-fiction writer, is one of the most enigmatic figures in 20th century literary history. Salinger wrote one novel, "The Catcher In The Rye", published in 1951 that has been a bible to coming -of-age youth for over 50 years. His hero, Holden Caulfield, seeks meaning in a world he finds contrived and artificial. The book has been required reading in countless college courses over the years. Salinger also wrote several collections of short stories including "Nine Stories"(1953), and 'Franny And Zooey"(1961) which again narrates young people's alienation from society. Salinger was born in New York in 1919 and little is known about his early life. After the success in the early 1950's, Salinger became a recluse in New England and withstood all attempts to interview or even meet him. He has written almost nothing since the early 1960's.

Anthony Powell, English novelist, produced on the staggering achievements of 20th century fiction with his writing of the 12 volume opus, "A Dance To The Music Of Time" published between 1951 and 1975. grouped in three series of four novels each, is the story of a man's life over 50 years, from public school through adulthood. His narration is sometimes humorous, often melodramatic, and it has been consistently overlooked by critics. His earlier works focus on satirizing the British upper class. After completing his masterwork, Powell remained productive, including a four volume memoir. Anthony Powell was born in London in 1905, and educated at Eton and Oxford. He worked for many years in journalism and publishing, until his success allowed him to concentrate on his novels. Anthony Powell had a long and active career which ended with his death in 2000.

Ralph Ellison, American novelist and essayist, published only one novel in his lifetime. His hugely successful "The Invisible Man", published in 1952, was a candid and realistic examination of race relations in the United States. The unnamed protagonist, a black man, realizes his color makes him essentially invisible in American Society. Winner of The National Book Award in 1952, "The Invisible Man" has become a classic in the study of race relations in modern

America. Ellison remained a productive writer, publishing books of essays and short stories. Ralph Ellison was born in Oklahoma, and originally trained as a musician. He joined the Federal Writers Project in 1936 and met and befriended Richard Wright. He lived most of his adult life in New York City where he was held an endowed chair at New York University. Ellison died in New York in 1994.

Frank O'Hara, American poet playwright and art critic, was a leader of a group of poets known as "The New York School", which captured the spirit of New York in conventional and conversational verse. Drawing from expressionism and the sounds of jazz and cadences of New York, this school produced poetry that was truly American. O'Hara was known for his improvisational writing such as "Lunch Poems"(1964), "Meditations in A Emergency"(1956). and his tribute to Billie Holiday, "The Day Lady Died" (1955). Frank O'Hara was born in Baltimore in 1926 and raised in Massachusetts. Educated at Harvard, and the University of Michigan, he migrated to New York and became editor of "Art News", where much of his art criticism first appeared. Intimates such as William de Kooning, and Jackson Pollock provided much of the inspiration for his improvisational work. O'Hara was killed in an accident at Fire Island in 1966, cutting short his career at age 40.

Samuel Beckett was an Irish-French novelist, playwright, short-story writer, and poet . His work explores the degradation of modern man, with a focus on the essential meaninglessness and absurdity of life. Beckett's work contains little action, meaning coming from dialogue and silences. His best known work, the play, "Waiting For Godot" (1953), is an allegory of life waiting only on death. Beckett was a prolific author, writing short fiction. drama, and prose for almost 50 years. he leaves a huge body of work behind that attests to his technical skills as a writer. He was awarded the Nobel Prize in Literature in 1969 for his contributions. Born in Ireland in 1906, Beckett was educated at Trinity College, Dublin. He moved to Paris where he befriended James Joyce, who had an important influence on his work. He fought in the French Resistance during the war, and was forced to flee Paris where he returned in 1945. He died in France1889.

Dylan Thomas, Welsh poet and prose writer, was a figure bigger than life. Thomas produced his first volume of poetry in his 20's, and won a reputation as a fresh voice in modern poetry. Later volumes include "Death And Embraces"(1946), "In Country Sleep"(1952), which included his best known verse "Do Not Go Gentle Into That Good Night". Thomas was an eclectic writer, developing stories and radio scripts that were very successful. His short-story volumes include" Under Milk Wood"(1954), and "A Child's Christmas in Wales"(1955). Thomas was born in Swansea, Wales, in 1914, the son of a teacher. Perhaps best known by the public for his bouts of drinking, strife-ridden relationships, and flamboyant personality, his work is sometimes overshadowed by his personality. Thomas died of alcoholism on a poetry-reading tour in New York City in 1953 at the age of 39.

James Baldwin, American novelist, playwright, and essayist, Baldwin became the leading black author of his time. His autobiographical novel, "Go Tell It On The Mountain"(1953), is the story of a teenage boy growing up in Harlem. His work almost exclusively deals with intolerance and the struggle for free expression. His own experience of racism in America resulted in his collection of essays, "Notes Of A Native Son", published to critical success in 1955. Several anthologies of his works have been published. James Baldwin was born in Harlem in 1924, the son of a popular clergyman. Depressed by race relations in the United States, Baldwin emigrated to Paris after World War II, and remained in France the rest of his life. Baldwin was heavily involved in the Civil Rights movement in America, and won praise for his activism. Baldwin died in Paris in 1987.

Saul Bellow, Canadian-born American novelist, was noted for the ethical intensity of his work. He depicted the experiences of urban Jews in America in a new voice. Critical and popular success came to Bellow with the publication of "The Adventures Of Augie March"(1953), and "Henderson, The Rain King"(1959). A trio of his best work followed, "Herzog"(1954), winner of the national Book Award, "Mr. Sammler's Planet"(1970), and his Pulitzer Prize winning novel "Humboldt's Gift"(1975). Bellow continued his productivity in the 21st century, and received a Pulitzer Prize in literature in 1976. Bellow was born in Montreal, Canada, in 1915. He grew up in Chicago, and like many young writers of this period, got his start with the WPA Writers Project. He has grown to be a grand figure in American fiction, and is regarded as one of the great modern novelists.

Ray Bradbury, American novelist, short-fiction writer, playwright , and poet, is known primarily as a writer of fantasy and science fiction. He is known for weaving social criticism into his work, and shows a constant wariness of the dangers of technology. Bradbury's best works include "Fahrenheit 451" (1953), " The Martian Chronicles"(1950) , and "The Illustrated Man"(1951), all best sellers in the then exploding field of science fiction. Bradbury, a prolific writer, has also published volumes of poetry, children's books, plays, and television and film screenplays. Bradbury was born in 1920 in the Midwest. He was an early contributor to pulp fiction and fantasy magazines His early success gave Bradbury the freedom to experiment with different styles and genres. Bradbury has been a productive author for over 50 years and continues to develop fresh ideas and creative approaches to his craft.

Wallace Stevens, American poet, is one of the great modernist poets. His verse covers a wide scope of themes, but returns continually to the role of poetry in filling the emptiness created by the lack of God. Stevens did not publish his first book until he was 44. Through the 30's, 40's, and 50,s he produced a body of work that includes" The Man With The Blue Guitar"(1937), "Transport To Summer"(1947), and "Parts Of A World"(1942), to name only a few. Stevens was ignored during his lifetime for the most part, and only in the last year of his life did he win a Pulitzer Prize and National Book Award. Born in Reading, Pennsylvania in 1879, he was educated at Harvard, and studied law in New York City. He became an insurance attorney and worked for almost 40 years with The Hartford Accident And Indemnity Company. During this period he turned out a body of work rarely excelled in modern poetry. Stevens died in 1955.

John Ronald Reuel Tolkien, English novelist, became famous for his mythological fantasies, "The Hobbit" (1937), and the "Lord Of The Rings" trilogy (1954-55). His fantasies were based on bedtime stories he told his children. At the urging of his friend and colleague C. S. Lewis, Tolkien wrote the "Hobbit", and spent the next 12 years writing the sequels, " The Lord Of The Rings". His own favorite among his novels was the Middle earth romance, "The Silmarillion" published by his son after Tolkien's death. Tolkien was an academic, an Oxford professor of Anglo-Saxon and English language and literature. Born in South Africa in 1892, he attended Oxford on a scholarship, and fought in World War I. His fantasies changed his life, but he continued his interest in medieval literature. Tolkien died in 1973 at age 81.

Vladimer Nabokov, Russian-born American novelist, critic, and translator, was a skillful, imaginative, and creative writer who has earned a place in literary history. He published his first few novels under a pseudonym in Berlin. He will always be best known for "Lolita", his landmark novel published in 1955. This highly controversial novel was about the affair of a middle-aged

man and his young step-daughter. Nabokov wrote other excellent novels, including "Pale Fire"(1962), "Pinin"(1957), and "Ada Or Ardor"(1969). He was a translator of talent, his work with Puskin's "Eugene Onegin" winning him plaudits. Nabokov was born in Russia in 1899. He studied literature at Cambridge, then lived in Paris before emigrating to The United states in 1940. He taught at several excellent universities, completing "Lolita" when he was on the faculty at Cornell. He then devoted full time to writing, and died in 1977 at the age of 78.

Importance of deciding to listen

Although it may sound strange, it is actually a good idea to consciously decide to listen when involved in interpersonal communication. Most people fail to listen properly because, not being intentional listeners, they allow themselves to become distracted by secondary stimuli. When a person makes a conscious decision to listen, he or she naturally ignores all the other kinds of activity going on in the background. Also, once a person gets into the habit of consciously listening to others, he or she will find that his or her listening skills improve exponentially. Many people do not realize just how satisfying interpersonal communication can be until they make a conscious decision to listen.

Intercultural contact as a characteristic of speechmaking

An effective speaker always keeps in mind the cultural characteristics of his or her audience. When a speaker is delivering a message to an audience whose culture is different from his or her own, he or she needs to be especially sensitive to the cultural mores observed by the group. For instance, excessive familiarity may be a sign of friendliness to the speaker, but it may demonstrate disrespect in the eyes of some audiences. It is a good idea to familiarize oneself with the basic manners appropriate to the intended audience. A failure to observe the customs of the group may prevent a message from being heard.

Differences between listening and hearing

For most people, listening and hearing are synonyms. In the world of speech communication, however, a subtle distinction exists between the two. Hearing is simply receiving a sound in the ear. In other words, hearing is the physiological and neurological act of converting heard sounds into meaning. Listening, on the other hand, is the more active process of taking in what is heard and interpreting it. People are constantly listening to the words of those around them and using their knowledge of language and cultural values to determine the meaning of what is being said. Listening, then, is a more subjective act than hearing.

Three listening styles

Experts in speech communication distinguish among three listening styles: RRP, VAT, and SUR.

RRP includes reasons-oriented listeners, results-oriented listeners, and process-oriented listeners. Reason-oriented listeners are interested in hearing the logical support for a given argument. Results-oriented listeners, on the other hand, are interested in the overall intention of the idea or argument. Finally, process-oriented listeners are interested in the way a particular idea or argument was conceived. All of these types of listeners will be very interested in the specific details of a speech. To impress an RRP listener, a speaker must have his or her details in order and possess an extensive knowledge of the subject.

VAT listeners are so-called because their listening style emphasizes the visual, auditory, or tactile elements of a speech. A visual listener will focus on the aspects of the presentation that can be seen, whether it is the speaker's body language and physical presentation or any visual aids accompanying the speech. To engage an audience of visual listeners, the speaker should be sure to have sufficient visual aids on hand. On the other hand, an auditory listener will be most interested in the spoken words delivered by the speaker. Auditory listeners will not need the presence of visual aids to hold their attention during a speech. Finally, tactile listeners need some physical contact to truly appreciate what is being described. Physical demonstrations, handouts, and sample materials are all good ways to engage the attention of a tactile listener.

SUR listening style describes those who are self-absorbed, unfocused, and rules-driven. Self-absorbed listeners are preoccupied with their own concerns and have a hard time paying attention to the ideas or interests of others. Unfocused listeners are not skilled or knowledgeable enough to listen well and thus have a hard time understanding an argument or complicated idea. Rules-driven listeners tend to obsess about minor points of reason and logic instead of paying attention to the most important aspects of a speech's message. In other words, rules-driven listeners "cannot see the forest for the trees."

Maintaining proper attention during a speech

It is essential to maintain attention throughout the delivery of a speech. To get the full value of a speech, a member of the audience must understand the entire structure of the speech, and this can only be done by maintaining attention throughout. If a person misses the beginning of the speech, for example, he or she will not understand what all of the speaker's subsequent arguments and evidence are supporting. On the other hand, if an audience member listens to the beginning of the speech but allows his or her attention to trail off, he or she will come away from the speech not knowing the precise reasons why the speaker's thesis statement should be believed.

Concentrating on message structure during a speech

An effective listener will be able to mentally outline the structure of a speech. The basic outline of a speech will include the main argument, supporting arguments, and supporting evidence and reasoning. Only by making sense of structure can an audience member truly assess the strengths and weaknesses of the speech. For instance, an audience member should be able to tell whether the speaker has done a good job of ordering his or her points. If the speaker makes the mistake of initiating the speech with minor points and only later working in more essential arguments, the audience members should be able to identify this error and determine whether it reflects poorly on the speaker or on the argument as a whole.

Relationship between good listening and the emotions

To be a good listener, an audience member needs to keep his or her emotions in check. Of course, this is not always easy. Sometimes a speaker's fiery rhetoric or sentimentality is designed to sweep the audience into a heightened emotional state. Audience members should try as much as possible to maintain control of their critical faculties, however, in order to accurately and objectively appraise the merits of the speech. Indeed, an objective and comprehensive speech analysis includes assessing the methods by which the speaker attempts to engage the emotions of the audience. If the audience member's emotions are roused by the speaker, he or she can say that the speaker's emotional appeal has been successful. This does not necessarily assume the merit of the speaker's argument, however.

Critical listening as it applies to public speeches

Critical listening is perhaps most important in the context of public speeches, since there will be less opportunity for each audience member to clarify the speaker's remarks through questions after the conclusion of the speech. In other words, each audience member will be on his or her own in the task of deciphering and evaluating the speaker's message. For this reason, many audience members try to take brief notes and chart out the structure of a speaker's argument. Speeches delivered to large crowds often involve appeals to the emotions. A speaker can get away with histrionic gestures and exaggerated vocal mannerisms when speaking to a large crowd, whereas these same techniques might seem ridiculous to a small group.

Four basic channels of public communication

Normally, speech delivery is considered a simple transmission of words by one person to a group. However, this is only one of the channels through which information is delivered during a speech. In the technical language of speech communication, the speaker's words are said to pass through the verbal channel. At the same time, the speaker's tone of voice indicates his or her attitude through the aural channel. Some speakers use visual aids, which transmit information through the pictorial channel. Finally, a speaker transmits information about his or her attitude and self-image through gestures and facial expressions. This transmission is said to pass through the visual channel.

Importance of physical setting in the delivery of a speech

The physical setting in which a speech is delivered exerts significant influence over the expectations of the audience and should therefore be taken into account by the speaker beforehand. For instance, an audience that is required to stand during a speech will have less patience for a long-winded and complex oration. On the other hand, if the audience is seated in soft, plush chairs, they may be too relaxed to pay attention to a serious lecture. When the subject of a speech requires a fair amount of technical detail, it is a good idea for the audience to be seated in upright chairs and for the room to have sufficient light. In any case, the speaker should consider how physical setting will influence the mood of the audience and should adjust his or her speech accordingly.

Fundamentals of preparing a speech

To successfully prepare a speech it is best to follow a basic set of established steps. By following these steps, the speaker (or speechwriter) can more efficiently develop an organized and effective presentation. The first step in preparing a speech is to select a subject, if the topic has not been predetermined. Next, the speaker should articulate to himself or herself the key ideas and arguments to be included in the speech. As he or she begin to formulate these ideas and arguments, it is important to take into account the characteristics of the intended audience. At this point, the speaker should begin gathering materials for the speech, whether through research or brainstorming. The next step is to outline the speech, and finally, write a draft of the speech. It is always a good idea to practice delivering the speech and to make revisions or adjustments where necessary.

Select a subject for a speech
Perhaps the most important component of an effective speech is an appropriate and interesting subject. When selecting a subject for a speech, one should look for a topic that is engaging to a general audience. While it is important for the speaker to have some familiarity with the subject, it is not necessarily a good idea to speak about a subject on which he or she is an expert. Too often, an expert delivering a speech to a general audience dwells too much in details and specificities, which has a tendency to bore the audience. It is a good idea for the speaker to have a passing familiarity with the subject, so that he or she will be able to find good research materials and judge what will be interesting to a general audience. However, the speaker should also make sure to emphasize the aspects of the subject that are relevant to the lives of the audience members.

Creativity

Sometimes it can be difficult to come up with a topic for a speech. All the "good topics" may seem to have already been covered, or there may be no one single subject on which a potential speaker has enough information to be effective. Effective speakers develop creative ways to come up with new speech topics. Being creative, however, does not mean sitting back and waiting for the muse of speech topics to visit. Creative speakers work proactively to develop new topics. They list their areas of interest and are constantly considering everything they see and read in terms of how it could be developed into a speech. Most creative speakers discard more ideas for speeches than they ever use.

Creative analysis of a speech topic
After a speaker has decided upon a topic for a speech, the next move is to conduct a creative analysis of that topic—simply a detailed exploration of the topic. To begin with, the speaker assembles as much information as he or she can within the amount of time available. This may include interviews, books, and old periodicals. Experienced speakers will have a good working knowledge of the public or school library and will be able to acquire diverse basic materials in a short period of time. After all this information has been assembled, the speaker will sort through it, looking perhaps for an entry point for his exploration. An interesting narrative, a point of local interest, or a previously overlooked angle on the subject may all be ways for the speaker to engage the interest of the audience on a given subject.

Preparation phase of a speech

During the preparation phase of speech composition, a speaker will begin to organize his or her research material. Once the speaker has decided upon the basic angle and structure of the speech, he or she may need to acquire more research materials for elaboration and support. Of course, it may take the speaker a while to find the appropriate thrust of the speech. Speakers should not be discouraged by numerous blind alleys or false starts during the preparation phase. Even when it seems that progress is not being made, the speaker should remember that each false start eliminates a possible point of entry bringing the ultimate goal closer.

Incubation phase of creative speech analysis

During the incubation phase of creative speech analysis, the speaker actually does not engage in any direct work on the speech. Instead, the speaker allows his or her subconscious to mull over the content of the speech. Even though it seems like no work is being done during this period, the incubation phase is actually very important, as it is during this period that the most creative thinking on the subject occurs. Also, the incubation phase gives the speaker a chance to freely imagine the speech, associate various ideas, and try unique combinations. Many speakers say their most unique and powerful ideas often occur to them when they are doing something totally different than speech preparation.

Illumination phase of creative speech analysis

After the incubation phase, the speaker should have a solid structure as well as a number of creative ideas for the speech. In the succeeding illumination phase, he or she will apply the ideas gained during the incubation phase to the basic outline constructed during the preparation phase. It is very common for a speaker to feel a burst of enthusiasm during the illumination phase, as he or she discovers the unique ways in which his or her original ideas will elaborate and improve upon the original structure. The illumination phase is still basically a brainstorming phase. Speakers are still experimenting with new ideas and combinations of materials.

Verification phase of creative speech analysis

The fourth and final part of the creative analysis of a speech topic is the verification phase. During this phase, the speaker looks over his or her notes carefully. Occasionally, some of the ideas that seemed so brilliant during the incubation and illumination phases turn out to be inappropriate or implausible. Other times, a careful examination of the speech will uncover holes in the reasoning of the argument or reveal the necessity of adding or removing a particular part of the speech. The verification phase of creative speech analysis can be seen as a final polishing of the materials gathered and organized during the first three phases

Necessity of managing creativity during the development of a speech

For the process of creative speech analysis to be effective, a certain amount of discipline needs to be brought to bear on the creative instinct. This is one reason why the process of creative speech analysis includes four distinct phases. By adhering to a set procedural pattern, the speaker will limit the amount of time spent in any one area and will move along toward completion at a predictable pace. Also, by following an organized analysis process, it is easier to avoid the procrastination that commonly occurs during the creative process. As much as possible, a speaker should try to work at specific times without interruption to allow the creative subconscious to do its work.

Basic message units in a speech

In every speech, the content is divided into what are called basic message units. A basic message unit has two parts: the point the speaker is trying to make and the evidence or supporting material he or she has assembled. In order to be complete, a message unit needs to have both components. Otherwise, the speaker will be making points without offering any reasoning or evidence, or he will be giving factual information and argumentation without connecting the dots to make a larger point. The point stated by the speaker needs to be a complete and discrete thought. The supporting material must be pertinent to the point and sufficient to convince a reasonable person.

Value of making a logical analysis of a speech topic

A speaker should always perform what is known as a logical analysis before presenting his or her speech. This is simply an analysis of the message units that make up the speech, as well as the connections between these message units. To be effective, the logic of any speech must progress in a systematic and discernible manner and should include ample evidence and supporting materials. Speakers often create a brief outline for their speech, in which they sketch the basic structure of the speech's logic, leaving out the supplementary material. In any case, it is essential to make sure the logical skeleton of a speech is sturdy before focusing on other aspects.

Assess the logic of a speech topic
As the speaker reviews his prepared speech and performs a logical analysis, he needs to be constantly asking himself whether each point and piece of supporting material is essential. Everything included in the speech should be there for a clear and explicit reason or else it must be considered superfluous. The speaker must also determine whether all of the evidence clearly and directly supports the points it is intended to support. Finally, the speaker must make sure every point in the speech follows a proper order, progressing logically to the speech's climax and ultimate conclusion.

Error of reasoning: faulty attribution of causation
One of the most common errors of logic one can make in a speech is the faulty attribution of causation. This occurs when the speaker erroneously assumes that just because one thing followed another, the second thing was caused by the first. For instance, I may grab my umbrella on the way out the door before it starts raining, but if I later use my umbrella I cannot claim that bringing my umbrella caused the rain. When a speaker describes a major historical or social event and suggests such an event had only one cause, this is almost always a case of faulty attribution of causation. Major social and historical movements are simply too complex to be attributed to a single cause. At the very least, a speaker must provide detailed substantiation for any assertions of causation.

Error of reasoning: circular reasoning
A common logical error in speeches is circular reasoning. A chain of logic is described as circular when the assumptions made at the beginning of the argument depend on the conclusion of the argument being true. For instance, imagine a speaker declaring that the Tigers baseball team will certainly lose their playoff series. As evidence for this claim, the speaker declares that the Tigers always lose their playoff series. This reasoning clearly does not hold up: In order to believe the Tigers will lose their playoff series, we have to assume they always lose their playoff series, which we do not really know yet, and which depends on their performance in the upcoming playoffs series. In other words, the claims made by the speaker depend for their support on the speaker's assumptions.

Error of reasoning: contradictory argument
Occasionally, a speaker will fall victim to the logical error known as the contradictory argument. A contradictory argument is one in which the speaker introduces information that directly contradicts his main argument. For the most part, this error should be easy to avoid. After all, a speaker will be careful not to include information that undermines his main point. Speakers do, however, sometimes include inconsistent arguments in a speech and this can be highly detrimental to their purpose. Contradictory argument is

especially problematic in a persuasive speech, in which the speaker is attempting to persuade the audience from their pre-existing opinions and hoping to sell them on the merits of an alternative view.

Use of expository supporting material
Most speeches include expository supporting material. The word "expository" comes from the same root as "expose" and refers to information that sheds light on areas about which the audience may know little. Some of the common forms of expository information are examples, analogies, and narratives. Expository supporting material is distinguished from argumentative supporting material in that it strives to remain as objective as possible When a speaker claims to be providing objective and impartial information, he or she will be held to that standard by the audience. For this reason, it is especially important for speakers who use expository supporting material to verify their sources.

Use of examples, both real and hypothetical
Successful speakers are likely to use both real and hypothetical examples in the course of a speech. Real examples are appropriate in speeches describing a particular historical or social topic that is grounded in reality. For instance, it would not be appropriate to use a hypothetical example in an argument about the Revolutionary War since there are plenty of real examples to illustrate points regarding that conflict. In more general speeches, however, it may be necessary to use a hypothetical situation as an example. When describing the possible results of some decision, for instance, a speaker might invoke the case of some hypothetical person as a means of dramatizing his or her argument. In general, real examples are treated with more respect by an audience and should be used whenever possible.

How a good speaker uses examples
A good speaker knows that examples can be effective because they provide concrete case studies through which the audience can assess the arguments of the speech. Examples are also good for humanizing an abstract speech. For instance, an audience may have a hard time listening to a speech about water conservation, but if the speaker introduces examples of how drought can affect individual people, they will be more likely to stay engaged. A good speaker includes examples that are appropriate and interesting, but which do not distract from his or her main points. Also, examples should not dominate a speech; they should simply add interest to the body of the speaker's message.

Analogies in a speech
An effective speaker will often elaborate and clarify his or her ideas with analogies. An analogy is simply an extended comparison between two things. For instance, a speech on economics might describe a current downturn in the economy as it relates to the Great Depression. In other words, the speaker is drawing an analogy between a current problem and a known historical event. The important thing to remember about an analogy is that the two things being compared will probably not be identical in all respects. The speaker should take care to indicate this and should not make claims that suggest the analogy is perfect. On the other hand, an effective analogy can be a useful predictive tool and can give the audience a way of engaging with the subject.

Narratives in a speech
Speakers often incorporate narratives into their speeches as a way of engaging interest and indirectly making a point. A narrative is simply a story. Narratives can be either fiction or nonfiction. As with examples, narratives tend to have more impact on an audience when they are true. However, an artfully told fictitious narrative can also captivate an audience. Recent scientific research suggests that audience members are mentally programmed to pay attention to information when it is presented as a story. That is, the human mind is naturally receptive to a narrative. Good speakers take advantage

of this tendency by delivering information in the context of a narrative.

Statistics in a speech

Speakers often use statistics to provide numerical evidence for their assertions. Basically, a loose definition of statistics is any information that contains numbers. To be effective, statistics must be clear and accurate. Statistics can have a great deal of sway over an audience, since they carry with them the impression of objectivity and mathematical truth. That being said, audience members should keep in mind that statistics are often highly subjective. For instance, by manipulating sample size, information taken into consideration, and scope of a statistical survey, a speaker can present information to support his point no matter how incorrect it is. Audience members should always be wary of statistics and should press the speaker to provide more information on the origin and methodology behind any statistics he or she uses.

Numbers in a speech

There are a few different ways to use numbers in a speech. One way is to use numbers as markers of evaluation. When we say a person weighs 120 pounds, for instance, we are using numbers to evaluate their weight. In a similar way, numbers can be used as a basis for comparison. By comparing the prices of two dishwashers, for instance, we obtain an important piece of information we can use in making a consumer decision. Numbers can also be used to make illustrative points. For instance, speakers often cite various statistics in support of an argument. It is important to emphasize that, although numbers suggest impartiality, they are calculated by human beings, who are highly subjective and whose intentions should be rigorously questioned.

Eyewitness testimony in a speech

Many speakers incorporate eyewitness testimony into their speeches to great effect. Of course, this kind of supporting material is only appropriate for certain kinds of speeches. For instance, when delivering a speech about the Battle of the Bulge, it might be very useful to quote some soldiers who fought in the battle. On the other hand, eyewitness testimony seems less appropriate to a speech about climate change , which is so widespread that no one person could view its entire effect globally. When using eyewitness testimony, it is important to establish the credentials of the person being quoted. Also, a speaker should take care to indicate the particular vantage point of the eyewitness, so the audience can consider his or her testimony in light of that point of view.

Expert testimony in a speech

Whenever possible, speakers attempt to incorporate expert testimony into their speeches. Any time a speaker can quote a well-known authority who agrees with his or her point of view, he or she will be eager to do so. Most members of an audience will probably feel relatively uninformed compared to the speaker and will be ready to listen to anyone who may be considered an expert. Of course, testimony is only expert and appropriate when it comes from an expert in that particular field. For example, most people would be less inclined to take seriously the political views of an expert in basketball than they would if those views came from a respected public servant. Nevertheless, an audience should remain skeptical about persuasive arguments, even when they are made by experts. The standards of logic required of experts apply to everyone else as well.

Title of the speech

It is very important to settle on a clear and appropriate title for a speech early on in the preparation process. The title should make explicit the central idea or concept to be discussed in the speech. The title should also indicate the intention of the speech. For instance, if the intent of the speech is to inform the audience about a particular subject, the title should clearly state the name of the subject. If the intention of the speech is to persuade the audience, the title should indicate the main arguments to be made by the speech. To be effective, a title should be succinct, clear, and, if possible, engaging.

Difference between immediate aim and ultimate aim when making a speech

On occasion, a speaker will have a slightly different intention in making a speech than is apparent from the speech itself. In the field of speech communication, this is known as the distinction between immediate aim and ultimate aim. An example would be a particular speech intended to be a small part of achieving a long-term goal. A prominent businessman, for example, might make a speech about ethics in public policy. Whereas on its face the speech might seem to be a simple address about local community issues, it might be also be part of the businessman's plan to develop his reputation in advance of a political campaign. The immediate aim of the speech, then, is to inform, while the ultimate aim is to advance the political ambitions of the speaker.

Location should dictate the characteristics of the speech

When preparing a speech, one should always keep in mind the occasion for which the speech is intended as this will help determine what kind of speech is appropriate. Individuals who have gathered together for a summer picnic, for instance, will not be interested in hearing a long and complicated speech. A short, humorous address would be more appropriate for this setting. A convention of professors, on the other hand, will be receptive to a more substantive speech that might also include relevant technical information. On rare occasions, a speaker may decide it is necessary to deliver a speech not entirely appropriate for the setting; this should only be done, however, when it is absolutely necessary.

Time limits influence the preparation of the speech

When preparing a speech, one must be aware of exactly how much time is available for presenting the material. The time limit will greatly influence the content of the speech. It is rarely possible, for instance, to effectively discuss a complicated subject in a short period of time. Nor will it be possible to hold an audience's interest over a long period of time without having a wealth of information and ideas. Giving an effective persuasive speech in particular requires sufficient time. This is especially true when one is trying to convert an audience's opinion on a subject with which they are unfamiliar or on which they already have firm opinions. Generally, it takes a strong argument, elaborated through a number of points, to alter an opinion already agreed upon by most members of the audience.

Elements of setting a speaker should consider when preparing a speech

When preparing a speech, a speaker should take into account any idiosyncrasies of the speech format or setting. For instance, in some situations a speaker will have specific guidelines and rules for his or her speech. When giving an address to the members of a particular religious or cultural group, for instance, one might need to abide by specific rules. Another thing to consider is the placement of the speech in the overall event. For instance, if other speeches are to follow, one might want to make sure there will be no overlap in speech content. Also, if the speech is to be given directly after a dinner, one should be aware that audience members will be less likely to pay close attention to the details of the speech. Finally, a good speaker will be aware in advance what the physical setting for the speech will be. That is, he or she will know beforehand such details as whether or not the speech is to be given standing or sitting and whether a podium will be available.

Research required preparing for a speech

To adequately prepare for delivering a speech, one needs to assemble all pertinent information and create a complete outline. One of the reasons why it is a good idea to select a familiar topic for one's speech is that less research will be required. At the very least, one should know where to look to find the information necessary to deliver an informative and comprehensive speech. Speakers may need to consult with experts in the given subject or peruse newspapers, magazines, and books for extra information. Many local and school libraries have extensive databases for performing research, and a thorough Internet search can often provide vast amounts of helpful material.

Composing a speech outline

Creating a detailed, comprehensive outline is the first step before actually writing the first draft of a speech. After assembling all the necessary material and information for the speech, the speaker can then begin organizing the main points of the speech and the arguments and evidence supporting his or her ideas and claims. It is important that all secondary ideas and claims also support the speech's main idea or claim. One should always introduce the most important claim, or thesis, at the beginning of the speech. The speaker can then spend the rest of the speech building a case for this thesis and elaborating other related points. When composing an outline, remember that the finished speech should ideally be much more colorful and engaging. An outline is not meant to entertain, but rather to clearly and succinctly indicate the organization of the speech.

Other problems of listening besides the SUR listening style

SUR is an acronym for a listening style in which the audience is self-absorbed, unfocused, and rules-driven. Unfortunately, there are some other common obstacles to listening besides being self-absorbed, unfocused, or rules-driven. Many people simply do not pay attention or they allow their minds to wander off during a digression from the major ideas of the message. In scientific studies of listening behavior, researchers have observed that the human mind can process information much more quickly than information can be delivered in a speech. Thus, while a person is listening, his or her brain is often performing other tasks simultaneously. Obviously, these other tasks run the risk of hindering effective listening and concentration. Some research has suggested, however, that many individuals require a small amount of distraction in order to concentrate effectively. For instance, many people are able to study more intently when listening to music at the same time.

Intentional listening

Ideally, when listening to a speech one will not simply sit back and allow the words being spoken to wash over him or her. Rather, an effective listener will engage in what is known as "intentional listening," an active state of processing, interpreting, and thinking critically about a speech. It is always good for the audience members to ask themselves what they hope to gain from a speech before it begins, as this will focus their attention and give purpose to their listening. While the speaker is addressing them, audience members should be attempting to place each successive idea into an overall framework.

Appreciative and therapeutic listening

Speech communication researchers have identified five basic kinds of intentional listening: appreciative, therapeutic, discriminative, comprehensive, and critical. Appreciative listening is perhaps the most passive form of listening. An appreciative listener is simply seeking to obtain as much pleasure as possible from the words being spoken. Although the intention of many speeches is to entertain the audience, an appreciative listener may not pay enough attention to the actual message being delivered by the speaker. Therapeutic listening, on the other hand, is listening with the intention of obtaining as much emotional support as possible. Many times, those listening to sermons and motivational speeches are engaged in therapeutic listening. The message of the speech empowers them and makes them feel better.

Critical listening

Speech communication researchers have identified five basic kinds of intentional listening: appreciative, therapeutic, discriminative, comprehensive, and critical. Critical listening is the most active form of audience behavior. It entails organizing and interpreting the information contained in a speech. While a speaker is giving his or her speech, the critical listener will be evaluating the arguments or ideas the speaker is presenting, weighing the evidence provided, and thinking of possible problems with the speech. As consumers, people engage in a form of critical listening every time they hear an advertisement. During a speech, however, many people sympathize with the speaker rather than critically evaluating the speaker's message.

Discriminative listening

Speech communication researchers have identified five basic kinds of intentional listening: appreciative, therapeutic, discriminative, comprehensive, and critical. Discriminative listening focuses on the aspects of a speaker's message that are implied rather than spoken directly. A discriminative listener is paying attention to the sound of voice, body language, and the speaker's implicit argument. To a certain extent, everyone is always practicing discriminative listening, although some people engage in this style of listening more than others do. A sophisticated listener obtains information not only from the message but from the medium in which it is delivered.

Listening for comprehension

Speech communication researchers have identified five basic kinds of intentional listening: appreciative, therapeutic, discriminative, comprehensive, and critical. Comprehensive, or listening for comprehension, is probably the most familiar form of listening. Students in a classroom are engaged in listening for comprehension when they take notes during a lecture. Whenever people listen to an informative or persuasive speech in order to gain information about a subject, they are engaged in listening for comprehension. The validity and accuracy of other forms of listening, such as critical listening and discriminative listening, depend on listening effectively for comprehension. If an individual is unable to understand the message being presented, he or she will not be able to critique it insightfully.

Importance of detached, intentional listening

When speech communication instructors describe the ideal listener, they often refer to "detaching" or "decentering." These terms refer to the process of considering the speaker's message on its own terms rather than in the context of the listener's experience and emotions. In essence, this simply means giving a speaker a fair hearing before applying critical thinking to his or her message. Too often, audience members pre-judge a message based on their past experience or existing opinions. This not only prevents such listeners from acquiring a better understanding, but it significantly handicaps their ability to listen for comprehension. Even when a speech is being delivered on a subject with which a member of the audience is quite familiar, he or she should try to keep an open mind in order to gain as much as possible from the speech.

Purposes of an audience member may change during a speech

When speech communication instructors refer to the five kinds of listening (appreciative, therapeutic, discriminative, comprehensive, and critical), they do not mean to suggest that these forms of listening exist independent of one another at all times. On the contrary, the members of an audience may be engaged in several different kinds of listening at the same time. Furthermore, it is quite common for members of an audience to adjust their listening style during the course of a speech. For instance, whereas at the beginning of a speech an audience member may be strictly listening for comprehension, as the speech goes on he or she may begin to listen more critically. Similarly, an audience member may at first pay attention strictly to the speaker's explicit message, but later may become more interested in the implications of the speech and may therefore engage more in discriminative listening.

RRA technique for active listening

When speech communication instructors describe active listening, they sometimes refer to the RRA (review, relate, anticipate) technique. This technique breaks the process of active listening down into three easy steps. To begin with, an active listener is constantly reviewing what has been said and placing new information into the evolving model of the message. As the listener considers the speaker's argument or idea, he or she relates it to his or her foundational knowledge. In other words, the audience member tries to compare and contrast the speaker's message with his or her own knowledge of the subject. Finally, an active listener tries to anticipate the rest of the speaker's message. Not only is this a good way to stay engaged with a speech, it provides an excellent measure of attention. When a listener is able to confidently predict the direction of a speech, he or she can be certain that his or her understanding of what has been said so far is sound.

How an audience member should consider the content of a speech

When considering the content of a speech, audience members should pay special attention to three basic areas: main ideas, organization, and supporting evidence. The main ideas of the speech are the fundamental arguments or concepts the speaker is trying to convey. If the speech is effective, the main ideas will be obvious. Audience members should be paying the most attention to the articulation and elaboration of these main ideas. The way in which the main ideas are expressed and supported is referred to as the organization of the speech. For a speech to be effective, the speaker needs to organize his or her ideas clearly and avoid long digressions that obscure the main points of the speech. Finally, the audience member must consider

what supporting materials the speaker is using to provide evidence for his or her ideas or arguments and must determine whether these supporting materials are appropriate and credible.

How a listener should assess the situation in which a speech is given

To get the most out of a speech, a listener needs to consider all of the various factors that contribute to the speaker's message. One of the factors that does not receive a great deal of attention is the situation in which the speech is delivered. Many times, the physical and interpersonal setting in which a speech is delivered has a great deal of influence on the message. For instance, an audience member might consider whether the speaker has been required to make his or her address more or less formal for the occasion. The audience member also might consider whether the occasion on which the speech is being delivered has influenced the quality of the speaker's message. Finally, the audience member should consider whether the physical environment in which the speech is delivered has been more or less conducive to understanding and appreciating the speaker's message.

How a listener should assess the characteristics of the speaker

As part of the overall critique of a speech, an audience member should consider the personal characteristics of the speaker. For instance, the audience member might consider what he or she knew about the speaker before the speech and then determines whether this information has had any influence on his or her interpretation of the speaker's message. The audience member might also consider whether the speaker's personal presentation indicated credibility or made his or her message difficult to believe. Many times, a speaker with a good message and solid supporting materials comes across as vague and disorganized because of his or her physical appearance and vocal mannerisms. Audience members should try to distinguish between weaknesses in the speaker's message and weaknesses in the speaker's personal presentation.

How a listener should analyze the message of the speech

When a member of an audience listens to a speech, he or she should be paying attention to three fundamental factors: ideas, organization, and support. The most important thing to consider is whether the speaker's main ideas are logical and clearly expressed. If the ideas are comprehensible, an audience member can then consider whether the speaker has expressed those ideas in a logical order or in a disorganized way. Finally, the audience member needs to consider whether the speaker has adequately supported his or her main ideas by argument or factual evidence. Does the speaker provide enough support for his or her arguments to remain credible? Is the evidence provided relevant to the main ideas of the speech?

Speech communication instructors often refer to public speaking as a "transaction," or a way of indicating the important active roles of both the speaker and audience. Too often, people consider speech-giving as a process in which one person actively provides information while another group of people passively receives information. Instead, the ideal public speaking relationship is one in which the speaker presents a message and the audience presents feedback. Even when the audience is not given an opportunity to speak, they provide feedback in the form of attention or inattention. By referring to public speaking as a transaction, instructors emphasize the roles and responsibilities of both speaker and audience. In general, speech communication instructors would define a transaction as any communication in which information passes from speaker to listener and vice versa.

Purpose of studying public speaking

There are a number of reasons for studying public speaking, but the most commonly cited are social, intellectual, and consumer motives. People need to learn to speak in public in order to function in society and to manage relationships, administrate social events, and minimize conflict. Intellectually, a study of public speaking gives insight into human thought, ethics, and persuasion. Public speeches can generate emotions and ideas in listeners as well as influence their existing thoughts and feelings. It is also important to study public speaking not only to improve one's own speaking skills, but to improve one's ability to analyze and interpret the speeches of others. Students need to be able to understand the forum of public expression, the rhetorical vocabulary, and the various methods of thinking critically about speech.

Basic methods for studying public speaking

An effective speech communication teacher will incorporate different pedagogical modalities into his or her instruction so that students receive exposure to a wide range of different methods. Students should practice giving different kinds of speeches in both formal and informal settings. Some of the different types of speeches include technical lectures, extemporaneous speeches, and entertaining monologues. Students should get some practice interpreting and analyzing different kinds of public speech, such as advertisements, political speeches, public service announcements, editorials, or other forms. It is also valuable for students to become familiar with acclaimed historical speeches.

Memorizing and reading a speech

When delivering a speech, the speaker may need to decide whether to memorize or read the text. There are advantages to each approach. When a speech is memorized, the speaker can make eye contact with the audience and use his or her hands to make illustrative gestures. Memorized speeches run the risk of sounding overly rehearsed, however, and the speaker may falter if he or she loses track of the speech. Some speakers prefer to read their speeches, often because they prefer to have a copy of the speech for reference. If the speaker plans to read his or her speech, he or she should become extremely familiar with the speech so it is not necessary to read every word from the paper. Regardless of whether a speech is memorized or read, the speaker should practice delivery to increase fluency.

Goals of public speaking

For most people, the obvious goals of public speaking are political victories and support for social movements. Both are common motives of public speech, but they are not the only recognized intention of public communication. Public speech is often used to define an individual or a community. For instance, people may use speeches to describe particular attributes of themselves or of the group to which they belong. People also use speeches simply to disseminate information. Speeches can be used to inspire other people to action. Famous addresses like the "I Have a Dream" speech of Martin Luther King, Jr. exemplify this kind of speech. Finally, public speaking can be used to introduce arguments and to debate controversial questions in a community. The presidential debates before the general election are a good example of this.

Speeches

Purpose of an informative speech

When one is delivering an informative speech, his or her primary goal is to instruct the audience on a particular subject. If the speech is effective, the audience members will leave with more knowledge and understanding. College lectures are a great example of an informative speech. Although informative speeches may be entertaining, the humor or "color" of the speech should not distract from the overall intention, which is to disseminate information. Informative speeches often contain specific statistical data and an organized set of arguments and supporting evidence. Many informative speeches contain mention of counter-arguments, including rebuttals.

Impromptu speech

An impromptu speech is one delivered "off-the-cuff"; that is, one delivered with a minimum amount of preparation and in an informal style. Not everyone is capable of delivering an effective impromptu speech. Most people can give a successful impromptu speech only if the topic is one on which they have discoursed before or if they are extremely familiar with their topic. Of course, we all make impromptu speeches as a matter of course in our daily lives. Every time you are asked to give your opinion on a subject or to explain an idea, you are in effect making an impromptu speech. By studying speech communication, however, people can learn the elements of effective impromptu speeches and improve their ability to deliver them.

Extemporaneous speech

An extemporaneous speech combines elements of preparation and improvisation. When one is delivering an extemporaneous speech, he or she is drawing on prepared research but not reading directly from a sheet of paper nor reciting the speech from memory. An extemporaneous speech is more conversational and informal than a written speech and is therefore more appropriate for casual gatherings. The colloquial and informal nature of an extemporaneous speech can be extremely helpful in cultivating a good rapport between speaker and audience. To deliver an effective extemporaneous speech, however, the speaker must be extremely familiar with his or her source material.

Eulogy

A eulogy is a speech that praises a particular individual and highlights his or her best qualities. Eulogies are often given at funerals as the speaker remembers the deceased in a positive light. Eulogies are not the appropriate form for criticism or objective analysis of a person's life. On the other hand, a eulogy may fail if the audience finds it so excessively laudatory that it is not believable. In some cases, a eulogy of sorts may be given in praise of a particular event, community, or culture. Typically, a eulogy is delivered to an audience that is already disposed to think favorably of the subject. The speaker is typically someone who has extensive personal experience with the subject of the eulogy.

Introductory speech

It is common for a speech of introduction to precede a keynote speech, a presentation, or a public performance of some kind. For instance, a symphony director will often give a brief speech of introduction before a concert. The best introductory speeches do not simply list the achievements or characteristics of the person or event that is to follow. Rather, they engage the interest of the audience and whet their appetite for what is to come. A good speech of introduction should not include any criticism of what is to follow. It is always a good rule of thumb for the introductory speaker to confer with those who are to follow so that his or her message can be as appropriate as possible.

Welcoming speech

A welcoming speech is often given at the beginning of a convention, meeting, or special event of some kind. Typically, the welcome will be delivered by a representative of the group or organization putting on the event. For instance, the chairman of a professional organization administering a business convention might deliver a speech of welcome to convention attendees. Welcoming speeches are typically light on substance and primarily provide an overview of the events to follow. Also, a welcoming speech typically includes a message of thanks to the organizers and administrators of the event. The speaker often indicates his or her personal goals for the event and may tell the audience how to make their questions and comments known to the event administrators.

Purpose of an entertaining speech

The only goal of some speeches is to entertain and amuse the audience. Standup comedy is a type of entertaining speech. Many speeches that also contain information or persuasive content are primarily entertaining. The keynote speakers at conferences and conventions often cloak their arguments in witty anecdotes and jokes. Obviously, serious subjects are not appropriate content for entertaining speeches. However, many speakers will introduce some elements of an entertaining speech to first capture the attention of the audience and then persuade them to engage seriously with the more weighty elements of the speech.

Importance of having specific purposes for a speech

The first step in preparing a speech is knowing the specific purpose of that speech. This enables the speaker to focus on what is important and to research efficiently for relevant material. Knowing the specific purpose of the speech allows the speaker to emphasize the most important points within the speech. The specific purpose of a speech might be informing the audience on a particular point, changing a few minds on a particular subject, raising some money, or simply entertaining the audience. It is a good idea to make the specific purpose of the speech explicit in the speech. Although you do not want to beat your audience over the head with your intentions, there should be no question as to what the speech is meant to accomplish. In general, the specific purpose of a speech is defined in terms of the desired reaction from the audience.

Persuasion

Persuasion is the art of changing the attitudes, beliefs, or actions of other people. It can be used for any number of purposes: to sell a product, to make a friend, to advance a cause, or simply to win an argument. To a certain degree, even primarily informative speeches contain an element of persuasion. The speaker is encouraging his or her audience to understand a given subject in the same way he or she does. To be persuasive, the speaker must have a clear idea of what he or she is trying to accomplish. Also, it is important to understand the best persuasive strategy for achieving the desired effect Persuasion can be styled as direct argument or as more indirect, even subversive, suggestion.

Purpose of a persuasive speech

Persuasive speeches are designed to change the minds of the audience or motivate the audience to action. The precise goals of a persuasive speech are dependent on the particular cause promoted by the speaker. Moreover, the methods employed in a persuasive speech will depend on the subject matter and the speaker's rhetorical style. Some speakers employ a dry, data-driven style when making a persuasive speech. They hope to overwhelm their audience with the strength and breadth of information. Other speakers seek to beguile their audience by amusing and entertaining them. This kind of speech is appropriate for general audiences and non-technical subjects. When a persuasive speech is being delivered to an audience of experts, or is centered on a complex issue, it must include cogent reasoning and supportive data.

Relationship between persuasion and likeability

Students of rhetoric have long noticed the correlation between a charismatic personality and persuasion. Basically, if a speaker is able to establish strong personal relationships with his or her audience, he or she is much more likely to be an effective persuasive communicator. The most important thing a persuasive speaker can do is to establish trust from the outset. If a speaker can convince the audience that he or she has their best interests at heart and is a competent source of information, the work of persuasion is largely done. Establishing trust and respect with the audience is as much a matter of one's credentials as one's appearance and presentation. Speakers who can demonstrate expertise and empathy are likely to find success with the audience.

Relationship between persuasion and competence

To be persuasive, an individual must be perceived as competent by the audience. Competence manifests itself in a number of characteristics, such as preparedness, poise, thoughtfulness, and clarity. A competent speaker should be able to answer questions from the audience on a specific subject, or should at least be able to explain where the answers could be found. A competent speaker must have supporting evidence for his or her arguments and must make this evidence clear to the audience. A competent speaker will also be able to organize his or her message effectively, giving the audience the best opportunity to educate themselves. Finally, a competent speaker will appear unhurried and calm.

Relationship between personal conviction and persuasion

Audiences seem to have a sixth sense for insincerity. They can tell when a speaker does not really believe his or her message. For this reason, effective persuasion is greatly benefited by the speaker's deep conviction in what he or she is saying. It is often said that before a speaker can persuade anyone else, he or she needs to be persuaded. When the strength of a speaker's convictions is evident in his or her delivery, the natural empathy of the audience will assist in persuasion. Historically, a survey of the great persuasive orators (Martin Luther King Jr., Abraham Lincoln, Pericles, etc.) confirms that strong belief is a boon to persuasive rhetoric.

Relationship between reputation and persuasion

Another factor that can greatly influence a speaker's power of persuasion is reputation. When a speaker has a reputation for upright behavior and responsibility to the truth, an audience is much more likely to believe his or her message. The credibility of the speaker is imperative, regardless of the topic. If the content of the speech is highly specialized, the audience will want to know that the speaker has some advanced training in the subject.

When an audience arrives for a speech already knowing the positive reputation of the speaker, the work of persuasion is almost complete. For many politicians and orators, building a reputation that encourages persuasion is the work of a lifetime.

Value of direct familiarity with sources in a persuasive speech

Having direct knowledge of sources can be extremely beneficial to a speaker's power of persuasion. For instance, imagine a motivational speaker on the subject of weight loss. If that speaker has had the experience of being overweight and then successfully losing weight and becoming healthier, the audience will be much more likely to take his or her words to heart. When a speaker can claim direct experience of the topic on which he or she speaks, the audience is unlikely to attribute the speaker's motives to personal gain or manipulation. The most effective speakers are able to present their personal experience as a model for the examination and consideration of the audience.

Relationship between mimicry and persuasion

Unconscious mimicry or imitation can be one of the most powerful forces for persuasion. Human beings have a natural tendency to imitate the behavior of those they perceive to be leaders or role models. People often adopt beliefs or act in ways uncharacteristic of who they really are in order to mirror the behavior of a leader. This phenomenon is due in part to the tendency of human beings to minimize differences between one another as a means of preventing conflict. Of course, to inspire imitation on the part of the audience, a speaker must appear competent and have a good reputation. The members of an audience should be particularly skeptical of speakers who encourage them to adopt a point of view simply because others are doing so.

Being persuaded with following directions

Human beings have a natural tendency to believe what designated authority figures tell them. In part, this is an inherited characteristic. Early humans, in order to survive in the wild, often had to rely on the advice and guidance of their peers. In many cases, people will follow directions from an authority figure without considering the ramifications of their actions. This phenomenon was evidenced during the Nuremberg trials after World War II, as numerous Nazi officials defended their actions as "just following orders." The educational system also encourages people to trust authority figures and follow directions. Audience members should be aware of this tendency and should guard against blindly accepting the recommendations of a speaker.

Persuaded with accepting a suggestion

A persuasive speaker may sometimes use a suggestion rather than a direct command to achieve his or her goal. A suggestion is simply a less forceful recommendation; it implies that the audience has the ability to decide for themselves whether or not to accept the guidance of the speaker. Suggestion is a good strategy for dealing with naturally skeptical audience members, who will resist any overt attempts to change their minds. Because it is an indirect form of persuasion, however, suggestion requires a bit more subtlety on the part of the speaker. , But because it gives the listener the impression that he or she has arrived independently at a conclusion, suggestion can be more effective than direction.

Relationship between persuasion and dramatization

A persuasive speaker often employs the language and techniques of drama to capture the interest of the audience. In other words, the speaker will frame his or her arguments as part of a larger narrative. The speaker may introduce certain representative characters and may spend a short time describing the human characteristics of these people. The speaker may then introduce some conflict against which these characters must struggle. This kind of generic dramatic scenario gives the audience a sort of "hook" on which to hang its attention. Instead of being required to pay attention to dry statistics and formal arguments, the audience can become absorbed in the stories of the characters. Many speakers find this captivation to be a spur to positive persuasion.

Relationship between persuasion and the motivation of the speaker
When an audience is considering the elements of a persuasive speech, they will likely give some thought to the motivations of the speaker. For instance, when approached by a salesperson, a customer is likely to assume that the salesperson has a vested personal interest in making a sale and does not necessarily have the best interests of the consumer at heart. In other contexts, however, the motivation of the speaker may be harder to discern. In an academic speech, for instance, the audience will be aware that the speaker is attempting to promote a certain viewpoint, but they may not be able to determine exactly why the speaker supports that point of view. To the extent that the audience can discern the motivation of the speaker, they will be able to intellectually consider the merits of the speech, and not be swayed by emotion.

Resistance to persuasion
Audiences will naturally be resistant to persuasive arguments that attempt to take them out of their normal routine. People of all ages have a tendency to fall into habitual behaviors that can be difficult and even painful to interrupt. A persuasive speaker, however, is by nature one who attempts to convert an audience to a new way of living or thinking. He or she will therefore encounter the listeners' resistance, based on their entrenched habits. Habitual behavior can be attacked in a number of ways. One is to persuade the audience that these habits are detrimental. Another is to suggest the advantages that can be gained from a new way of living or thinking. In all cases, however, the speaker should remember that most behavioral change is incremental and not the result of sudden conversion.

Unique qualities of a speech that persuades the audience to change
One of the most common kinds of persuasive speech is one in which the speaker attempts to persuade the audience to change something. The speaker may be asking the listeners to change their behavior, their opinion on some subject, or the way in which some issue is handled in their community. These kinds of speeches usually follow a similar arc: first, the speaker describes the disastrous state of affairs at present. Second, the speaker introduces his or her proposal for remedying the situation. Third, the speaker indicates the rewards that the audience will obtain by accepting the proposal of the speaker. If the speech is effective, by its conclusion the audience should be practically intoxicated with the expansive vision of a positive future the speaker has outlined.

Unique qualities of a speech that persuades the audience to not change
Another kind of persuasive speech is one in which the speaker attempts to persuade the audience to not change something. Like the speech in support of change, the speech against change has three classic components. First, the speaker argues that things are fine as they are. Second, the speaker argues against any proposals for change that have been made. Third, the speaker describes the negative consequences for the audience if changes are made. As with the speech in support of change, the speech against change begins by setting the general scene and only gradually works its way around to addressing the individual concerns of the audience members. In this way, the last impression the audience receives is that of the effects of change or stasis on their own lives.

Practicing speech delivery

Excellent speech delivery does not just happen. It is the result of extensive practice. After the speaker has outlined and drafted the speech, he or she needs to practice delivering it. Practicing a speech serves a number of purposes. For one thing, the speaker might not detect weak points in the speech until he or she actually speaks the words aloud. In addition, it is helpful to record oneself practicing the speech and then play back the tape to identify weaknesses in the delivery. It is often a good idea to practice delivering a speech in front of friends or family and then have them critique the performance. Perhaps the most important point is that practice delivering the speech allows the speaker to further familiarize him or herself with the material, thus increasing the level of comfort and fluency in delivery.

Methods for cultivating self-confidence while giving a speech

Most people struggle with some degree of anxiety when they are required to speak in public. One of the best things a person can do to reduce speech anxiety is to present a confident image. Naturally, one should always practice delivering a speech several times beforehand. Through repetition, the speaker becomes familiar with the appropriate gestures and rhythms of the speech, which gives rise to increasing confidence in his or her ability to deliver. Another good way to build confidence is to make eye contact with the audience during speech delivery. A forthright, steady gaze from the speaker connotes a feeling of confidence. Finally, confidence can be communicated through posture and body language. Standing up straight and emphasizing key points with hand gestures is a great way to communicate self-confidence.

Essential points of speech evaluation

There are a number of things to look for when evaluating the quality of a speech. All effective speeches share a few essential characteristics, such as a good introduction—one that engages the audience and introduces the main idea or argument of the speech. The introduction also establishes the tone of the rest of the speech. The body of the speech should include clear exposition of ideas and appropriate supporting material. The conclusion of the speech should reinforce the main idea or claim and solidify audience understanding. The presentation of the speech should be appropriate to the audience and setting and should be fluent in its delivery.

Basic elements of speechmaking

To master the speechmaking process one should clearly understand a few basic elements. The central figure is the speaker; that is, the one delivering the speech. The speaker brings a self-conception as well as a conception, or impression, of the audience's general identity. In the study of speechmaking, the audience is sometimes referred to as the "receiver." Like the speaker, the audience members will have a self-image as well as an impression of the speaker. The setting in which the speech is delivered is known as the "situation." The speaker uses various channels of communication, including words and gestures, to communicate his or her message. The audience members will deliver their responses to the speech both verbally and through body language. This response to the speech is called feedback.

Basic elements of the message of a speech

The message of a speech is communicated not only with the words being spoken but also through the speaker's self-presentation. In other words, the quality of the speaker's voice and his or her body language contribute to the message as well. The message of the speech is generally considered to have three basic components: structure, content, and presentation. The structure of the speech is the order in which information is delivered. To be effective, a speech must have a logical and coherent structure. The content of the speech is the information it contains; even an entertaining or persuasive speech must have good content. Finally, the presentation of a speech is the style in which it is delivered to the audience. Different kinds of speeches require different presentation styles. The most important thing is to match the presentation to the intention of the speech.

Most important attributes of a speaker

To be an effective speaker, one must have a clear intention, a good attitude, and extensive knowledge of the subject of the speech, as well as a degree of credibility with the audience. The speaker should fully understand the intention of the speech, even if that intention is not directly expressed in the speech. Sometimes a speaker will have a hidden motive or a long-term goal that cannot be expressed in the speech. To establish credibility, the speaker should possess a solid working knowledge of the subject of the speech. When the speaker is fluent in the subject he or she is discussing, the speech will flow more naturally and the speaker will be able to tailor his or her message to the audience's level of understanding. Referring to a speaker's "attitude" simply means his or her self-conception; that is, the image the speaker has of himself or herself. If a speaker has a positive self-image, he or she is more likely to deliver an effective speech.

Characteristics of the speech listener

The individual or groups of individuals who listen to a speech bring their own characteristics to bear on the quality of the speech. For one thing, listeners will always have their own intentions. That is, they will always be seeking to obtain something from the speech, whether it is information or entertainment. Listeners will also have varying degrees of skill, meaning that some groups will be better at understanding a complex message. Listeners will also bring their pre-existing attitudes toward the speaker and the speaker's subject. To deliver an effective message, a speaker needs to perform an audience analysis to determine the characteristics of his or her listeners.

Basic kinds of feedback
Feedback is the response of the audience to the message delivered by a speaker. Although feedback is typically thought of as verbal responses to the message, it also includes body language, attention or inattention, and participation in dialogue after the speech. To be effective, a speaker must be attuned to all these kinds of feedback. In other words, he or she must monitor the audience throughout the speech to identify signs of boredom or engagement. The feedback a speaker receives while delivering his speech is called immediate feedback. The feedback the speaker receives after delivering the speech is called delayed feedback. Delayed feedback usually takes the form of critical comments, praise, or questions. A practiced speaker will use feedback to improve subsequent speeches.

Importance of selecting a subject appropriate to the time limits of the speech

Many speakers handicap themselves from the start by selecting a subject that is either too expansive or too narrow for their needs. To be effective, a speech subject must be appropriate for the amount of time available for giving the speech. Obviously, a half-hour speech can go into much more detail and tackle a wider range of issues than can a five-minute speech. A very short speech should have only one main idea, whereas in a longer speech the speaker may have time to deliver several important points and give supporting information for each. Although the best way to determine the appropriate subject for the time limit is to gain experience as a public speaker, beginning speakers can nevertheless help themselves by considering the parameters of a speech as they begin to consider possible subjects.

Elements of a presentation

Over the last few years, the presentation has emerged as the most common speech form in the United States. Members of the business community frequently give presentations, but this form is also common to academic lectures, community discussions, and religious gatherings. One of the defining characteristics of a presentation is that it contains other media besides simply a speaker. It is common for a speaker to include

PowerPoint slides, photographs, brochures and handouts, short videos, audio samples, in a presentation. Because presentations are often designed to be given over and over again to different audiences, they may be complex, detailed, and highly coordinated.

Basic presentation aid
One of the defining characteristics of a presentation is the use of presentation aids. Speakers often include supplementary audio or visual materials that elaborate or reinforce their presentation points. Currently, the most popular presentation aid is PowerPoint, a software program that allows speakers to assemble a collection of slides to accompany their speech. Speakers also frequently include video samples in their presentations. In business, tables and charts are frequently used to illustrate the points of a presentation. In the classroom, a teacher might use handouts or overhead projector transparencies as presentation aids. Basically, any media used by the speaker to supplement his or her spoken message is considered a presentation aid.

Increasing importance of the presentation in the United States
Most speech communication experts believe that presentations will increasingly become the most popular form of public communication. In large part, this is because the citizenry of the United States has been raised on television and radio commercials. That is, they are well used to multimedia presentations. For many people, a simple speech is boring. Presentation aids such as audio and video are often necessary to hold the interest of modern-day audiences. In the future, the most successful persuasive speakers will undoubtedly be those who can apply the traditional elements of direction and suggestion to a presentation containing enough multimedia to engage the interest of the audience.

Fundamental qualities of a well-organized speech

All well-organized speeches have certain qualities in common. For instance, a well-organized speech is comprehensible, meaning it can be understood by all members of the audience. A well-organized speech also has a formal unity, which means all of its parts contribute to the main idea. A unified speech has no extraneous parts. A well-organized speech is also comprehensive—it covers all the issues an audience member would expect to be addressed by a speech on the given subject. Finally, a well-organized speech does not have any repetition. Every major point should be covered in its entirety, but no points need to be repeated once they have been clearly delivered.

Process of speech organization
The process of speech organization entails selecting the elements that will comprise the speech, placing them into a coherent order, and arranging the supporting material for each message unit. During the organization process, a speaker will often summarize each message unit in a simple sentence. This gives the speaker simple building blocks that can be easily rearranged. In general, a speech should include a coherent introduction, body, and conclusion. The introduction should engage the interest of the audience and summarize the main points to be made. The body should contain the central points of the speaker's argument, as well as the supporting evidence. The conclusion should summarize the argument and give the audience food for thought.

Outline for a proof speech

Speech communication instructors often refer to a "proof speech." This is a common type of speech, in which the speaker introduces his or her argument and then attempts to prove it. Proof speeches follow a consistent pattern. In brief, a proof speech has four components: introduction, argument, development, and conclusion. A speech that follows this pattern allows the audience to become acquainted with the thrust of the speaker's arguments before substantiation is offered. The lengths of the various components of a proof speech will vary, depending on the speaker's interests and the knowledge level of the audience. For instance, an audience already familiar with the subject matter may not require as much supporting material to be convinced.

Impromptu speech pattern

Any relatively informal speech on a light subject can be referred to as an impromptu speech. An impromptu speech may be given on very short notice and will therefore give evidence of much less preparation. Even so, impromptu speeches tend to follow a similar pattern. There are four basic steps in a typical impromptu speech: an engaging introduction, a brief overview, elaboration, and summary. Notice that the four components of an impromptu speech directly parallel the components of a proof speech. The only real difference is that the delivery will be looser and the style of delivery will endeavor to be more entertaining. An impromptu speech often begins with a humorous or intriguing anecdote and often ends with a light touch as well.

Problem-solving pattern of speech-making

In a problem-solving speech, the speaker outlines a particular problem, attempts to diagnose the cause, and then suggests a potential solution. Problem-solving speeches are at their heart persuasive speeches, since they attempt to convince the audience of the merits of adopting a particular strategy to solve a given problem. To be effective, however, a problem-solving speech needs to follow a logical pattern. These speeches typically begin with an introduction and a definition of the problem in question. The speaker will then summarize the possible causes of the problem and discuss some of the possible solutions. Following this, the speaker will make a case for one of the

solutions and provide supporting evidence and argumentation. Finally, the speaker will attempt to rebut some of the possible counterarguments to the proposed solution.

Appropriate outline for a call-to-action speech

When speech communication instructors describe a call-to-action speech, they are referring to a speech that intends to inspire the audience to follow some recommended course of action. A call-to-action speech has five typical components: engaging the audience, describing why the audience should want to change something, explaining the best way to change, describing the positive consequences of making the change, and directly indicating how change can be made. It is not really possible to rearrange the steps in a call-to-action speech. Unless the argument is delivered in this order, the speech will likely be ineffective. It is important to end by outlining the positive consequences of change and making an emotional plea, as this leaves the audience on a high note, which is most likely to translate into direct action.

Denotative meaning

Denotative meaning is the way in which a word indicates something else. The word "table," for instance, denotes a flat surface with three or more legs. A speaker must always be conscious of the denotative meaning of the words he or she uses. The denotative meaning is not decided on an individual basis. Rather, it is the product of unconscious agreements on meaning made by the members of a community. In other words, to ensure that he or she communicates effectively with the audience, the speaker must have a familiarity with the denotative meanings that will be known to the members of that audience. Effective speakers continually refer to a dictionary during speech composition in order to solidify their understanding of denotative meanings.

Connotative meaning

Connotative meaning is any implication or a suggestion connected to a word that extends beyond the denotative meaning of the word. The connotative meaning of the word, then, is not strictly the definition of the word. Connotative meanings are often quite emotional in character. For instance, the denotative meaning of the word "whale" is a large mammal that lives in the ocean. When the same word is used in a certain way, however, its connotative meaning may refer to someone who is overweight. Speakers need to be aware of both the connotative and the denotative meanings of the words they use. Otherwise, they run the risk of confusing or even offending the audience members. A detailed dictionary will often have explanations of the various connotative meanings of common words.

Role of definitions in communication

To be effective, a speaker must understand the basic definitions of the words he or she is using and make sure to share these definitions with the audience. If the audience members assume different definitions than those the speaker intends, there will be no possibility of communication. Speaker should always strive for clarity and precision in their choice of words. "Clarity" here means choosing words that directly convey the speaker's intended meanings. Clear language admits no confusion about the subject matter or intent. "Precise" in this context means words that do the best jobs of denoting the exact meaning intended by the speaker. When the language of a speech is precise, the audience should not have to guess what is denoted by each word.

Abstract terms in communication

It is easy to discover the denotative meanings of simple nouns like table, turkey, and television. It is more difficult to determine the denotative meanings of abstract nouns; that is, nouns that describe feelings, ideas, or concepts. Some examples of abstract terms

are "freedom," "jealousy," and "capitalism." For the definitions of these words, a speaker must rely on a dictionary and on his own sense of how the word is used in a given community. For the most part, speakers who wish to present themselves as objective will try to make the denotative meanings of their words precise and minimize the connotative meanings as much as possible. Not only are connotative meanings more subjective for an audience, but they tend to introduce some emotional response. In other words, they compromise the speaker's objectivity.

Effective naming in communication

As much as possible, an effective speaker will try to choose the right words to describe his or her subject. In some cases, there may be several names for the same thing. For instance, the same car might be referred to as a sedan, an auto, or a jalopy. These three names all carry with them different connotations. Furthermore, whereas a word like "auto" suggests a certain objectivity or seriousness on the part of the speaker, a word like "jalopy" is more appropriate for a humorous or colorful speech. To maintain the right tone, then, a speaker will need to be able to select the appropriate terms. The only way to do this consistently is to develop a keen ear for language by reading widely and listening to the ways that people talk.

An effective speaker will be able to compose descriptions that clarify and illuminate his or her subject matter. For instance, consider the difference between describing a person as a "good man" and describing him as a "heroic, courageous inspiration to his community." Obviously, the second description is more colorful and paints a more comprehensive picture of the person. Indeed, it includes the information that the described person was valued for his effect on his fellow citizens. As much as possible, a speaker wants to include descriptions that combine engaging detail and vivid language, without being so colorful as to distract from the main point of the speech. A facility for effective description can be encouraged by paying attention to the way description is handled by great authors and speakers.

Effects that cultural background can have on connotative meaning

Members of any particular cultural group often have special connotative meanings for words. Because connotative meanings can carry such emotional power, it is especially important for a speaker to understand the connotative meanings shared by his or her audience before delivering a speech. The best way to acquire such a sense of connotative meaning is to spend time with the members of the community. Developing a feeling for what is appropriate language for a given audience is as much a matter of intuition as the acquisition of particular definitions. When in doubt, a speaker should avoid using any language that may have unpleasant or hostile connotative meaning to his audience.

Effects of dialect on communication

A dialect is simply a unique way of speaking that is common to a particular segment of a community. All Americans have a dialect of one sort or another. Individuals who have spent their entire lives within a given community, however, may not be aware that their mode of speech or of understanding language is different from that of any other American. To some extent, the widespread availability of television and radio has minimized the differences among American dialects. Nevertheless, a speaker needs to be aware of the dialects spoken by the members of his or her audience. Within certain dialects, common words may have unique connotative meanings that can confuse or even pervert a speaker's message. At the same time, the effective use of local dialect is a great way to endear oneself to the audience and to establish a firm channel of communication.

Avoiding distractions while delivering a speech

As much as possible, an effective speaker will minimize distractions during a speech. Distractions can include things done by the audience as well as by the speaker him- or herself. Of course, it is not possible for a speaker to control the behavior of an audience, but he or she can exercise self-control. Too many speakers challenge the patience of the audience by hemming and hawing over their words, making distracting gestures, or engaging in frequent vocal tics. For many speakers, making noises like "uh" and "er" while searching for the right word is natural and unconscious. It can be very distracting to an audience, however, so a speaker would do well to practice delivering his or her message without incorporating these filler sounds.

Speaking in a manner appropriate to the topic and setting of the speech

Ideally, with experience a speaker develops the ability to deliver his or her message in a manner appropriate to the topic, the audience, and the setting. For instance, when speaking to a group of five or six people, it is inappropriate to use a booming voice and wild, dramatic gestures. Likewise, it takes a very sophisticated speaker to deliver an intimate, informal lecture to a group of two or three hundred. One of the best ways to develop a sense of what is appropriate for a given setting is to study effective speakers in various settings. Notice how they vary their vocal quality and nonverbal communication repertoire in different environments. To gain the attention and respect of the audience, the speaker needs to deliver his or her message in a manner that will meet their expectations.

Nonverbal communication in establishing the credibility of a speaker

Many speakers underestimate the positive effects that nonverbal communication can have on their success in delivering a message.

By making assertive and forceful gestures, a speaker can create an image of credibility and confidence. Similarly, by making easy gestures, a speaker can promote an image of relaxation and expansiveness. The trick is to know which gestures are appropriate in which situations. Furthermore, an effective speaker will be able to modulate the volume and pitch of his or her voice in accordance with the requirements of the speech. A bombastic tone is not appropriate to an academic discourse, nor is a dry delivery appropriate for a political rally. A speaker needs to be aware of the expectations of the audience, and only challenge them when such a challenge is necessary.

Methods of improving voice and articulation problems

For many people, delivering an effective public speech is an uphill battle because they have never mastered the basics of vocal presentation. For instance, many people have not learned the proper manner of articulating complex sounds in English. Also, many people have not received enough exposure to effective oratory and therefore do not understand the essential rhythms of speech delivery. There are a few common ways to improve voice and articulation problems. Some articulation problems are the result of physiological issues and can only be treated by a doctor. Other issues, however, are behavioral and can be resolved with therapy and training. Increasingly, schools are staffing speech clinicians to help students resolve problems with articulation.

Procedure for improving one's own public speech
The process of improving public speech technique will vary depending on the individual's particular challenges. A few common remedies can be generally helpful however. For one thing, a person can record themselves and listen to the way they speak. Speakers are frequently unaware of their articulation problems while giving a speech, but these problems become clear upon

review. With practice, speakers can train themselves to diagnose particular problems and can subsequently learn to self-correct them. Practice in producing the correct sound every day should result in almost immediate progress. After a while, the corrections will become habitual and will no longer need review or practice.

Body Language in public speaking

Posture in public speaking
Many speakers fail to recognize the significance of proper posture in the delivery of a speech. As much as words or gestures, a speaker's posture transmits information about his or her attitude, credibility, and confidence. To present a message effectively, a speaker should stand up as straight and tall as possible. Slouching forward or bending over one's notes indicates a lack of interest and preparation. This kind of advice may seem trivial, but an audience will subconsciously pay closer attention to anyone whose posture indicates command and authority. Effective speakers pay close attention to their own posture and make sure that poor posture does not disrupt the transmission of their message.

Facial expression in public speaking
The facial expressions made by a speaker can have a significant impact on the effectiveness of message delivery. The facial expressions of the speaker can either reinforce or contradict his or her words. If the words being spoken are amusing or colorful, it is appropriate for the speaker to be smiling and have a relaxed facial expression. If the speaker is addressing a serious subject while grinning, however, the audience will most likely discount what he or she is saying. A speaker needs to match his or her facial expressions to the subject matter and to the expectations of the audience. A large audience can expect the facial expressions of the speaker to be slightly exaggerated, while a small audience may be put off by what seems like a leering or grimacing speaker.

Eye contact in public speaking

Speakers should never underestimate the importance of eye contact during message delivery. For one thing, it is very difficult for an audience member who is making eye contact with the speaker to lose interest. An effective speaker will often shift his or her gaze around the room, making eye contact with as many people as possible. Under no circumstances should a speaker look up in the air, stare at his or her notes, or fix his or her eyes on some point in the distance. At the same time, the speaker should not constantly move his or her eyes around the room, as this may be perceived as anxious behavior. Eye movements should be calm, regular, and smooth.

Gestures in public speaking

A public speaker should make sure that his or her gestures are in harmony with the subject matter of the speech and the expectations of the audience. Many people are in the habit of either moving their hands frequently during speech or keeping their hands stationary. Both of these approaches are only appropriate in certain circumstances. When delivering a speech to a large audience, or delivering a speech with a high emotional content, a speaker may be advised to incorporate wide, energetic gestures. These kinds of motions are not appropriate for a more somber subject, however. And although gestures can amplify the meaning of the speaker's words, they should never become a distraction from the message of the speech.

Proper way to use notes during a speech

Many speakers will require notes, but they should rely on these notes as little as possible during delivery of the speech. For one thing, notes tend to prevent a speaker from making effective eye contact and using his or her hands expressively while speaking. Also, speakers who become reliant on notes may not be able to orient themselves in a speech if something goes wrong with the notes. Notes should only be used as a reference point of last resort. They should be kept down in front of the speaker, preferably out of view of the audience. They should not be held and should be on as few pieces of paper as possible, to prevent excessive shuffling during a speech. Finally, a speaker who requires notes should carefully look them over before a speech to make sure they are understandable and arranged properly.

Skills required for making a speech

To deliver a successful speech, an individual needs to have acquired certain skills. For one thing, the speaker must understand in depth the topic about which he or she is speaking. He or she must also be able to address the topic from a number of different points of view and to answer any questions the audience might have after the speech. More generally, a successful speaker must have an air of authority, so the audience will pay attention and trust his or her words. A speaker should also have what is known as rhetorical sensitivity, or the ability to adapt his or her message to different audiences. Successful speakers know that a given style of speaking may be very effective with one audience and ineffective with another. A successful speaker will be able to modulate his or her voice and gestures appropriately.

State apprehension as a component of speech anxiety

To some extent, everyone grapples with speech anxiety. The fear of embarrassment or public disclosure can be overcome only with significant practice at public speaking. There are a couple of different kinds of speech anxiety. "State apprehension" is defined as speech anxiety that is only felt in specific situations. For instance, an individual who is comfortable talking in class but becomes anxious when required to speak informally with peers is experiencing state apprehension. Many people experience state apprehension in relation to delivering formal speeches in front of a group. State apprehension has both physical and mental symptoms, including vocal tics, sweaty palms, and a trembling voice.

Trait apprehension as a component of speech anxiety

Some people experience speech anxiety to a greater degree than others. Those aspects of speech anxiety that are unique to an individual are known as trait apprehensions. For instance, someone might have an aversion to public speaking because of a past experience. People who have an unnaturally high level of trait apprehension tend to avoid situations in which they will be required to speak to a large group. The good news for these individuals is that trait apprehension can be overcome with experience. Unfortunately, however, this means practicing public speaking until it becomes natural.

Interpretation of speech anxiety
Speech anxiety is a common malady but not one that should cause a person to lose heart. Even the most successful speakers have a bit of anxiety when delivering a message. In a way, this anxiety is a positive thing, because it focuses the attention and encourages concentration. Speech anxiety is a natural response to confronting an uncertain and unfamiliar situation. Research suggests that those who suffer from severe speech anxiety are often the most effective public speakers. Also, most speakers report that the anxiety they feel before delivering a speech is much greater than the anxiety they feel when actually in the process of speaking.

Using speech anxiety productively
The abundance of nervous energy felt before delivering a speech can be used to the speaker's advantage. For one thing, many people find that speech anxiety sharpens their senses and focuses their concentration on the task at hand. Human beings are naturally inclined to focus their attention when they perceive a threat. The good thing about speech anxiety is that the attention is sharpened even though the threat is not significant. Many accomplished speakers use speech anxiety to increase their level of excitement and dynamism while delivering a

speech. Indeed, many speakers say that without speech anxiety, they would not be able to achieve the rhetorical effects that have made them successful speakers.

Oral assessments

Oral assessments are used for two reasons: when written assessments are not feasible, and to evaluate a student's mastery of such topics as verbal language proficiency, debating skills, and the ability to think and respond quickly. These types of assessments can be stressful and some students may have trouble responding and become tongue-tied; and therefore it is important to conduct the session in private or in an atmosphere of acceptance. As an interactive form of communication, the teacher needs to avoid filling in the blanks and providing body language clues that might influence the student's response. It is also important to avoid accentuating gender, race, or cultural differences in the content or delivery of the questions and/or tasks. The examination period should be long enough and the tasks required general enough in order to ensure that the student's knowledge and proficiency can be adequately presented and evaluated.

Evaluation of oral presentation

Oral presentations offer a wealth of possibilities to evaluate student growth and development in several areas, including:
- Understanding of the subject
- Planning and organizing abilities
- Communication skills

This flexible assessment tool can be assigned to an individual student or as a group project. If given to a group, additional skills can be evaluated including response to other opinions, listening behaviors, active participation in discussions, and contributions to the work product. Teachers need to recognize that some students may have difficulty with or little or no experience conceptualizing, organizing, and delivering a presentation. To address these issues as well as any performance anxieties, it is necessary to establish a classroom atmosphere of acceptance so that students feel confident when giving a presentation. Allowing students some control over the choice of topic also helps alleviate some of the stress involved in standing up in front of the group.

Rating scale for oral presentation

Student's Name: _____

Date & Class Period:_____

Performance test

A performance test is used to evaluate a particular skill that is one of the primary objectives of the class. Playing a musical instrument, using the backhand stroke in tennis, making a dress, doing a tune-up on a motor vehicle, and conducting a lab experiment are all skills that can be tested using this method. The teacher must ensure that the same criteria are used to evaluate each student and that every student has the same amount of time to demonstrate the skill. If it is an outdoor activity, climate conditions should be considered. Students need to be informed ahead of time on what they will be evaluated and when it will take place. In designing a performance task, teachers should be as specific as possible and consider the objective carefully. Students should be evaluated on both the process and the results. An observation checklist or rating scale is helpful in evaluating a performance test.

Performance assessments

Performance assessments are used to evaluate students' progress in specific tasks like demonstrating a skill, solving a complex problem with multiple parts, or participating in a general classroom discussion. The teacher is looking for what the student has learned and retained through what he does and not merely what he says. Information gathered through performance assessments is easy to communicate to students and parents because it describes observable, verifiable actions and offers concrete discussion points to use during conferences. There are four steps to successfully integrate performance assessments into a balanced, comprehensive view of student progress:

1. What is to be observed and assessed.
2. Develop the criteria to be used.
3. Decide which recording method to use between anecdotal records, an observation checklist, or a rating scale.
4. Inform the students that they are being evaluated, on what they are being evaluated, and the criteria being used.

Choruses

As used in Greek drama, the chorus is a group of actors that furnishes a commentary on the play as it unfolds. The chorus in Greek drama probably evolved from the choral tradition of musical productions. Traditionally, the chorus speaks for society rather than any character in the play. This means the chorus is the objective observer of the dramatic action.

Shakespeare occasionally used the chorus in some of his plays. *Henry V* and *Romeo and Juliet* are examples of this. In musical dramas, the term refers to a group of singers and dancers who play an important part of the production. Modern drama usually does not employ a chorus, although it was used in T. S. Eliot's play *Murder in the Cathedral* in 1935. The chorus in modern musical theatre often acts as a collective actor that adds to the spectacle of the production.

Dramatic stages

Most simply, a stage is the space where a dramatic production takes place. There are currently three major types of stages in use:

1. The theatre-in-the-round or the arena stage allows the audience to surround the stage, which provides a much different dramatic experience for both players and audiences alike.

Originally, this form of stage was used in classical theatre in Greece and Rome, and it is widely used today in smaller experimental theatres around the world.

2. The apron or thrust stage seats audiences on the sides of a platform. Less commonly used today, Shakespeare's Globe Theatre was an early form of the apron stage.
3. The most common stage in current use is the proscenium stage, where the audience sits in front of a stage framed by the acting space. This form is very common in drama, opera, and musical presentations.

The type of stage used affects the action of the dramatic work, and each offers a unique experience to the audience.

Reading drama

Using imagination

A play is written to be spoken aloud. The drama is in many ways inseparable from performance. Reading drama ideally involves using imagination to visualize and recreate the play with characters and settings. The reader stages the play in his imagination, watching characters interact and developments unfold. Sometimes this involves simulating a theatrical presentation, while some may imagine the events happening before them. In either case, the reader is imagining the unwritten in order to recreate the dramatic experience. Novels present some of the same problems, but a narrator will provide much more information about the setting, characters, inner dialogues and many other supporting details. In drama, much of this is missing and we are required to use our powers of projection and imagination to taste the full flavor of the dramatic work. There are many empty spaces in reading dramatic texts that must be supplied by the reader to fully appreciate the work.

Reading Drama as Text

An oft heard criticism of reading drama is that the experience pales when compared to watching a performance. There are however some advantages to reading drama as text:

1. Freedom from interpretation - a performance will have a bias, point-of-view, and perspective that the written text does not. Text is free of interpretations of actors, directors, producers, and technical staging.
2. Additional information - the text of a drama may be accompanied by notes or prefaces placing the work in a social or historical context. Stage directions may also provide relevant information about the authors' purpose. None of this is typically available at live or filmed performances.
3. Study and understanding - difficult or obscure passages may be studied at leisure and supplemented by explanatory works. This is particularly true of older plays with unfamiliar language which cannot be fully understood without an opportunity to study the material.

Dramatic dialogue

Dramatic dialogue can be difficult to interpret and changes depending upon what words are emphasized and the tone used. Where the stresses, or meters, of dramatic dialogue fall can determine meaning. Variations in emphasis are only one factor in the manipulability of dramatic speech. Tone is of equal or greater importance and expresses a range of possible emotions and feelings that cannot be readily discerned from the script of a play. The reader must add tone to the words to understand the full meaning of a passage. Recognizing tone is a cumulative process as the reader begins to understand the characters and situations in the play. Other elements that influence the interpretation of dialogue include the setting, possible reactions of the characters to the speech, and possible gestures or facial expressions of the actor. There are no firm rules to guide the interpretation of dramatic speech. An open and flexible attitude are essential in interpreting dramatic dialogue.

Dramatic action

Action is a crucial element in the production of a dramatic work. Many dramas contain little dialogue and much action. In these cases, it is essential for the reader to carefully study stage directions, and to visualize the action on the stage. Benefits of understanding stage directions include knowing which characters are on the stage at all times, who is speaking to whom, and following these patterns through changes of scene.

Stage directions also provide additional information, some of which is not available to a live audience. The nature of the physical space where the action occurs is vital, and stage directions help with this. The historical context of the period is important in understanding what the playwright was working with in terms of theaters and physical space. The type of staging possible for the author is a good guide to the spatial elements of a production.

Speech, dialogue soliloquies

Analysis of speech and dialogue is important in the critical study of drama. Some playwrights use speech to develop their characters. Speeches may be long or short, and written in as normal prose or blank verse. Some characters have a unique way of speaking which illuminates aspects of the drama. Emphasis and tone are both important, as well. Does the author make clear the tone in which lines are to be spoken, or is this open to interpretation? Sometimes there are various possibilities in tone with regard to delivering lines.

Asides and soliloquies can be important in plot and character development. Asides indicate that not all characters are privy to the lines. This may be a method of advancing or explaining the plot in a subtle manner. Soliloquies are opportunities for character

development, plot enhancement, and to give insight to characters motives, feelings, and emotions. Careful study of these elements provides a reader with an abundance of clues to the major themes and plot of the work.

Dialect

Dialect is any distinct variety of a language, especially one spoken in a region or part of a country. The criterion for distinguishing dialects from languages is that of mutual understanding. For example, people who speak Dutch cannot understand English unless they have learned it. But a speaker from Amsterdam can understand one from Antwerp; therefore, they speak different dialects of the same language. This is, however, a matter of degree; there are languages in which different dialects are unintelligible.

Dialect mixtures are the presence in one form of speech with elements from different neighboring dialects. The study of speech differences from one geographical area to another is called dialect geography. A dialect atlas is a map showing distribution of dialects in a given area. A dialect continuum shows a progressive shift in dialects across a territory, such that adjacent dialects are understandable, but those at the extremes are not.

Enhancing reading experience

Art and music contain many opportunities for interacting with literature for the enrichment of all. Students could apply their knowledge of art and music by creating illustrations for a work or creating a musical score for a text. Students could discuss the meanings of texts and decide on their illustrations, or a score could amplify the meaning of the text.

Understanding the art and music of a period can make the experience of literature a richer, more rewarding experience. Students should be encouraged to use the knowledge of art and music to illuminate the text. Examining examples of dress, architecture, music, and dance of a period may be helpful in a fuller engagement of the text. Much of period literature lends itself to the analysis of the prevailing taste in art and music of an era, which helps place the literary work in a more meaningful context.

Observation checklist

An observation checklist is a list of specific skills, behaviors, attitudes, and processes that are relevant to a student's development and contribute to his ability to successfully complete learning activities. To be effective, these checklists need to be used frequently and be collected over a period of time. One or two observations can be misleading and will not provide an accurate measurement to reach a fair evaluation. Before a using a checklist, a teacher must decide upon its purpose, how and when it will be used, and what the criteria will be. During the observation period, all occurrences of each item shown on the list need to be recorded. It is helpful for later evaluation if the teacher has a quick reference shorthand system to describe each appearance, e.g., ! equals excellent, @ equals adequate, ? equals iffy, X equals inappropriate. After the session, notes should be added to clarify or elaborate the shorthand ratings.

Developing an observation checklist takes time. It can be helpful to write down all the skills, behaviors, attitudes, and processes required to acquire mastery of the subject and that are appropriate for the particular age group. The language should be simple and easy to understand, so that the checklists can be used during student and parent conferences. Items needed for the specific task or activity to be evaluated can be chosen from the master list. There should be no more than twelve items on a checklist: any more than that becomes difficult to track, especially when observing several students at the same time. Individual checklists can be developed for specific functions, e.g., participation in a class discussion, proficiency at using a microscope, the mechanics of preparing a

term paper. Whatever the rating scale, it must be used consistently, applied fairly, and easy to use during the observation period.

Document design

Good document design promotes readability. Readability depends very much on the purpose and audience for the writing, as well as subject and length parameters. All design choices should be made based on the particular writing assignment. Using a computer gives a writer multiple options for design.

Margins should be between one and one and a half inches on all sides. Double spacing is advised to improve readability. A normal size font,(10 to 12 points), and a fairly standard typeface are recommended. Left justified text provides the best readability, and headings should be considered for longer texts. Brief and informative headings are best, and headings should be consistently formatted depending on the level of generalization. First, second, and third level headings should be clearly and consistently highlighted. It is usually wise to be conservative in highlighting headings, lest the text look too "busy", and lack impact.

Visual elements

Visual elements such as charts, graphs, tables, photographs, maps, and diagrams are useful in conveying information vividly and in a summary form.

Flow charts and pie charts are useful in helping readers follow a process. or showing numerical information in graphic style. Tables are less stimulating but offer devices for summarizing information. Diagrams are useful and sometimes necessary in scientific writing, to explain chemical formulas for example.

Visual elements may be placed in a document close to the textual discussion, or put in an appendix, labeled, and referred to in a text. Sometimes page layout makes it difficult to position visuals in optimum proximity to the corresponding text. In these cases visuals may be placed later in the text, and readers told where they can find it. Software may be used to help the text flow around the visual for maximum impact.

Electronic communication

<u>E-mail</u>
E-mail has become so common in personal and business communication that it deserves its own conventions. Electronic documents will continue to grow in use and importance and writers' must become skilled in this emerging format.
Some guidelines for effective E-mail include:
1. The subject should be meaningful and concise and immediately clear to the reader.
2. The most important part of the message should appear on the first screen.
3. Summarize long messages in the first paragraph.
4. Write concisely in short, relevant paragraphs.
5. Use a mixture of capital and lower case letters for ease in reading.
6. Include the text of the attachment in the body of the E-mail if possible.
7. Proofread after using spell-check and grammar check software.

<u>Website</u>
Academic and business web sites are aimed at audiences looking for specific information or ideas, rather than entertainment. Quick and easy access to important information is the hallmark or an effective website. A website consists of a homepage and related internal pages.

In creating an effective web site the purpose, audience, and format of the site is critical. The opening screen is most important, as many Web users will resist scrolling to locate information. The opening screen introduces visitors to the site, provide an overview of its contents, and include navigational links to other sections of the site. General pages are linked to more specific ones, and design elements should be consistent throughout. Put key information on each internal page. Each page should provide a brief overview that explains the contents of the page at a glance. Links should be provided for other sources that would provide valuable information for visitors.

Important Terms

Allegory - a type of narrative that uses a story to symbolize another meaning. Biblical stories use allegory extensively . A form of allegory is personification where abstract ideas are represented by literary characters. For example, morality plays performed in the middle ages had characters named Evil, Goodness, Greed and so forth. Many satirical works are allegories for social and political events or institutions. Allegory was largely replaced by symbolism in modern literary works.
Alliteration - a device that repeats stressed sounds in a sequence of words closely connected to one another. Old English and Middle English use alliteration extensively while it is only occasionally seen in modern literature.
Anaphora - refers to a figure of speech in which a word or words are repeated at the beginning of successive lines of verse in rhetoric.
Anticlimax - occurs in fiction or drama when a critical point in the work is resolved and the dramatic tension recedes. The term can be used negatively if it refers to a weakness in a drama or story. Sometimes an anticlimax is used to enhance a scene or serve as a respite from a period of action.
Assonance - a form of rhyme where vowels rhyme but not consonants.
Clichés - sayings or dialogue much overworked in common language. They are used in developing characters and sometimes in comical and farcical ways.
Climax - occurs when a state of tension in a literary work reaches its peak, usually with a resolution of some kind. There may be many

or only one climax in a work, depending on the plotting and length of the story. A climax is usually preceded by an increasing level of tension, usually between the protagonist and antagonist. The climax may take the form of action, speech, or symbolism.

Closure - the modification of the structure of a work which makes absence of further development unlikely. It creates the expectation of nothing and leaves the reader or audience satisfied that the plot development is over. Closure often has a dramatic force of its own and sometimes is the final climax.

Dialect continuum - shows a progressive shift in dialects across a territory, such that adjacent dialects are understandable, but those at the extremes are not.

Dialect geography - the study of speech differences from one geographical area to another.

Dialect mixtures - the presence in one form of speech with elements from different neighboring dialects.

Diction - is the choice of language in a literary work. Diction may be formal, colloquial, and slang. The use of diction to set a tone for the work meant to induce a mood in the audience. Slang is used commonly in modern fiction while formal and colloquial diction are used for specific effects.

Discourse - any coherent succession of sentences, spoken or written. Thus a novel, short story, essay, speech, or interview in which successive utterances or sentences hang together. The word is equivalent to text.

Discourse analysis - an attempt by linguists to extend the method of analysis for the description of words and sentences to the study of larger structures in the production of connected discourse. The term "text linguistics" is a similar process coined many years later.

Discourse Representation Theory - a formal account of the meaning of discourse, in which a semantic representation called a discourse representation structure is derived cumulatively, sentence by sentence, by rules operating on representations of their syntax. This structure was conceived as an idealized model of the way in which people in everyday life understand passages of connected speech.

Foreshadowing - uses hints in a narrative to let the audience anticipate future events in the plot. Foreshadowing can be indicated by a number of literary devices and figures of speech, as well as through dialogue between characters. In Ibsen's play Hedda Gabler, Hedda plays with a gun early in the play which foreshadows her eventual suicide. Shakespeare's Macbeth, the three witches in the opening scene foreshadow horrific events to come. Examples abound in all forms of literature, but are perhaps most evident in drama.

Hyperbole - a figure of speech that use extreme exaggeration for dramatic effect. It usually functions to compare and is used quite often in romantic works. Love poetry is an example of a subgenre that fosters the use of hyperbole. Hyperbole may also be used in a farcical manner for comic effect.

Personification - another figure of speech which attributes human qualities to an inanimate object or abstract entity. Personification helps us to use our self-knowledge and extrapolate it to understand abstract concepts, forces of nature, and common events. Personification is sometimes achieved by similes or analogies to strengthen the imagery.

Style - a particular manner of using language to narrate a story, develop a dramatic mood, or evoke a mood. Style can also refer to a period of literary history or to an individual writer.

Tone - refers to the attitude expressed about the subject through the author. This expression is communicated by language, character development, plotting, and the creation of attitudes about the subject. Mood is sometimes mistaken for tone, but the two have important differences. Mood is generally understood to be the feeling the work provokes in the audience. although this can sometimes be identical to tone , they are often quite different.

Writing

Choosing topics

Very often the choice of a subject may be assigned or determined by someone besides the writer. When the choice is left to the writer, it is sometimes wise to allow the topic itself to "select" the writer. That is to say those topics that interest, engage, puzzle, or stimulate someone may be good choices. Engaging the writer is the most important factor in choosing a topic. Engagement notes a strong interest and spirit of inquiry about the subject. It is a signal that the subject and author are interacting in some creative sense, which usually encourages good writing. Even with an assigned topic, a particular aspect of the subject may interest the writer more than others. The key to any writer's choice of topic is the ability of a subject to inspire the author to question, speculate, inquire and interact. From this natural interest and attraction, some of the most creative writing develops.

A common problem is limiting the scope of a writing assignment. Narrowing the scope is not always enough, because the new subject may itself be too broad. Focusing on an aspect of a topic often effectively results in a topic both interesting and manageable. For example narrowing a topic like the "Civil War" to the "Battle of Antietam" may still leave an unwieldy topic. To sharpen the focus, an aspect such as "The use of artillery by Confederates at the battle of Antietam" could be selected.

Understanding assignments

Many writing assignments address specific audiences (physicians, attorneys, and teachers) and have specific goals. These writers know for whom and why they are writing. This can clarify the writing significantly. Other assignments, particularly in academic settings, may appear with no specific subject, audience, or apparent purpose. Assignments may come with some variables; a specified audience, subject, or approach and leave the rest up to the writer. Because of these variables, it is useful to consider the following questions:

1. What specifically is the assignment asking the writer to do?
2. What information or knowledge in necessary to fulfill the assignment?
3. Can the topic be broadened or limited to more effectively complete the project?
4. Are there specific parameters or other requirements for the project?
5. What is the purpose of the assignment?
6. Who is the intended audience for the work?
7. What is the length of the assignment? Does it limit or require a certain number of pages? If so, what are the parameters?
8. What is the deadline for the assignment? Sometimes preliminary materials are to be submitted before the main assignment. Considering these factors will give a writer information needed to set a schedule for the project.

Length and document design

Writers seldom have control over length and document design. Usually a academic assignment has a specified length, while journalists work within tight word count parameters. Document design often follows the purpose of a writing project. Specific formats are required for lab reports, research papers, and abstracts. The business world operates within fairly narrow format styles, the business letter, memo, and report allowing only a small departure from the standard format.

There are some assignments that allow the writer to choose the specific format for the work. The increased flourishes provided by computers allow a great deal of creativity in designing an visually stimulating and functional document. Improving readability is always a worthwhile goal for any project, and this is becoming much easier with available software.

Deadlines

Deadlines are a critical element in any writing assignment. They help a writer budget their time to complete the assignment on schedule. For elaborate or complex writing projects, it is useful to create a working schedule that includes time for research, writing, revising, and editing. Breaking the process down into more workable parts with their own deadlines, helps keep a writer aware of the progress being made.

Purposes of writing = PIE

What is the main purpose of the proposed piece? This may be very clear and focused, or ambiguous. A writer should be clear about the purpose of his writing, as this will determine the direction and elements of the work. Generally purposes may be divided into three groups:
1. To entertain.
2. To persuade or convince.
3. To educate or inform.

Some or all of these purposes may be the goal in a given writing assignment. It is helpful to try and identify the major purpose of a writing piece, as well as any secondary purposes involved. Purpose in writing must be linked closely to the writer's goals in undertaking the assignment. In academic settings, it is usually more accurate to think in terms of several goals. A student may wish to convince the audience in an entertaining and informative fashion. However one goal should be paramount. Expectations of the instructor play an important role in an academic assignment.

Recursive nature

The process of writing is described as recursive; This means that the goals and parts of the writing process are often a seamless flow, constantly influencing each other without clear boundaries. The "steps' in the writing process occur organically, with planning, drafting and revising all taking place simultaneously, in no necessary or orderly fashion. The writer rarely pays attention to the recursive patterns. The process unfolds naturally, without attention or dependence on a predetermined sequence. The writing process is a series of recursive activities, which rarely occur in a linear fashion, rather moving back and forth between planning, drafting, revising, more planning, more drafting, polishing until the writing is complete. Forthcoming topics will cover many parts of the process individually, but they go on together as a seamless flow.

Considering an audience

The careful consideration of the anticipated audience is a requisite for any project. Although much of this work is intuitive, some guidelines are helpful in the analysis of an audience:
1. Specifically identify your audience. Are they eclectic or share common characteristics?
2. Determine qualities of the audience such as age, education, sex, culture, and special interests.
3. Understand what the audience values; brevity, humor, originality, honesty are examples.
4. What is the audience's attitude toward the topic; skeptical, knowledgeable, pro or con?
5. Understand the writer's relationship to the audience; peer, authority, advocate, or antagonist?

Understanding the qualities of an audience allows the writer to form an organizational plan tailored to achieve the objectives of the writing with the audience in mind. It is essential to effective writing.

Level of formality

In choosing a level of formality in writing, the subject and audience should be carefully considered. The subject may require a more dignified tone, or perhaps an informal style would be best. The relationship between writer and reader is important in choosing a level of formality. Is the audience one with which you can assume a close relationship, or should a more formal tone prevail?

Most student or business writing requires some degree of formality. Informal writing is appropriate for private letters, personal e-mails, and business correspondence between close associates. Vocabulary and language should be relatively simple.

It is important to be consistent in the level of formality in a piece of writing. Shifts in levels of formality can confuse readers and detract from the message of the writing.

Understanding the topic

Easily overlooked is the basic question of ascertaining how knowledgeable the writer is about the subject. A careful evaluation should be made to determine what is known about the topic, and what information must be acquired to undertake the writing assignment. Most people have a good sense of how to go about researching a subject, using the obvious available resources: libraries, the internet, journals, research papers and other sources. There are however some specific strategies that can help a writer learn more about a subject, and just as importantly, what is not known and must be learned. These strategies or techniques not only are useful in researching a subject, they can also be used when problems come up during the actual writing phase of the assignment. These strategies include brainstorming, free writing, looping, and questioning.

Brainstorming
Brainstorming is a technique used frequently in business, industry, science, and engineering. It is accomplished by tossing out ideas, usually with several other people, in order to find a fresh approach or a creative way to approach a subject. This can be accomplished by an individual by simply free-associating about a topic. Sitting with paper and pen, every thought about the subject is written down in a word or phrase. This is done without analytical thinking, just recording what arises in the mind about the topic. The list is then read over carefully several times. The writer looks for patterns, repetitions, clusters of ideas, or a recurring theme. Although brainstorming can be done individually, it works best when several people are involved. Three to five people is ideal. This allows an exchange of ideas, points of view, and often results in fresh ideas or approaches.

Free writing
Free writing is a form of brainstorming in a structured way. The method involves exploring a topic by writing about it for a certain period of time without stopping. A writer sets a time limit, and begins writing in complete sentences everything that comes to mind about the topic. Writing continues without interruption until the set period expires. When time expires, read carefully everything that has been written down. Much of it may make little or no sense, but insights and observations may emerge that the free writer did not know existed in his mind. Writing has a unique quality about it of jogging loose ideas, and seeing a word or idea appear may trigger others. Freewrtiting usually results in a fuller expression of ideas than brainstorming, because thoughts and associations are written in a more comprehensive manner. Both techniques can be used to complement one another and can yield much different results.

Looping

Looping is a variation of freewriting that focuses a topic in short five-minute stages, or loops. Looping is done as follows:

1. With a subject in mind, spend five minutes freewriting without stopping. The results are the first loop.
2. Evaluate what has been written in the first loop. Locate the strongest or most recurring thought which should be summarized in a single sentence. This is the "center of gravity", and is the starting point of the next loop.
3. Using the summary sentence as a starting point, another five minute cycle of freewriting takes place. Evaluate the writing and locate the "center of gravity" for the second loop, and summarize it in a single sentence. This will be the start of the third loop.
4. Continue this process until a clear new direction to the subject emerges. Usually this will yield a starting point for a whole new approach to a topic.

Looping can be very helpful when a writer is blocked or unable to generate new ideas on a subject.

Questioning

Asking and answering questions provides a more structured approach to investigating a subject. Several types of questions may be used to illuminate an issue.

1. Questions to describe a topic. Questions such as "What is It?", "What caused it?", "What is it like or unlike?", "What is it a part of"? What do people say about it?" help explore a topic systematically.
2. Questions to explain a topic. Examples include" Who, how, and what is it?", "Where does it end and begin?" What is at issue?", and "How is it done?".
3. Questions to persuade include "What claims can be made about it?", "What evidence supports the claims?", "Can the claims be refuted?", and "What assumptions support the claims?"

Questioning can be a very effective device as it leads the writer through a process in a systematic manner in order to gain more information about a subject.

Thesis

A thesis states the main idea of the essay. A working or tentative thesis should be established early on in the writing process. This working thesis is subject to change and modification as writing progresses. It will serve to keep the writer focused as ideas develop.

The working thesis has two parts: a topic and a comment. The comment makes an important point about the topic. A working thesis should be interesting to an anticipated audience; it should be specific and limit the topic to a manageable scope. Theses three criteria are useful tools to measure the effectiveness of any working thesis. The writer applies these tools to ascertain:

1. Is the topic of sufficient interest to hold an audience?
2. Is the topic specific enough to generate interest?
3. Is the topic manageable? Too broad? Too narrow? Can it be adequately researched?

Creating an effective thesis is an art. The thesis should be a generalization rather than a fact, and should be neither too broad or narrow in scope. A thesis prepares readers for facts and details, so it may not be a fact itself. It is a generalization that requires further proof or supporting points. Any thesis too broad may be an unwieldy topic and must be narrowed. The thesis should have a sharp focus, and avoid vague, ambivalent language. The process of bringing the thesis into sharp focus may help in outlining major sections of the work. This process is known as blueprinting, and helps the writer control the shape and sequence of the paper. Blueprinting outlines major points and supporting arguments that are used in elaborating on the thesis. A completed blueprint often leads to a development of an accurate first draft of a work. Once the thesis and opening are complete, it is time to address the body of the work.

Formal outlines

A formal outline may be useful if the subject is complex, and includes many elements. here is a guide to preparing formal outlines:

1. Always put the thesis at the top so it may be referred to as often as necessary during the outlining.
2. Make subjects similar in generality as parallel as possible in the formal outline.
3. Use complete sentences rather than phrases or sentence fragments in the outline.
4. Use the conventional system of letters and numbers to designate levels of generality.
5. There should be at least two subdivisions for each category in the formal outline.
6. Limit the number of major sections in the outline. If there are too many major sections, combine some of them and supplement with additional sub-categories.
7. Remember the formal outline is still subject to change; remain flexible throughout the process.

Research

Research is a means of critical inquiry, investigations based on sources of knowledge. Research is the basis of scientific knowledge, of inventions, scholarly inquiry, and many personal and general decisions. Much of work consists of research - finding something out and reporting on it. We can list five basic precepts about research:

1. Everyone does research. To buy an car, go to a film, to investigate anything is research. We all have experience in doing research.
2. Good research draws a person into a "conversation" about a topic. Results are more knowledge about a subject, understanding different sides to issues, and be able to discuss intelligently nuances of the topic.
3. Research is always driven by a purpose. Reasons may vary from solving a problem to advocating a position, but research is almost always goal oriented.
4. Research is shaped by purpose, and in turn the fruits of research refine the research further.
5. Research is usually not a linear process; it is modified and changed by the results it yields.

Many writing assignments require research. Research is basically the process of gathering information for the writer's use. There are two broad categories of research:

1. Library research should be started after a research plan is outlined. Topics that require research should be listed, and catalogues, bibliographies, periodical indexes checked for references. Librarians are usually an excellent source of ideas and information on researching a topic.
2. Field research is based on observations, interviews, and questionnaires. This can be done by an individual or a team, depending on the scope of the field research.

The specific type and amount of research will vary widely with the topic and the writing assignment. A simple essay or story may require only a few hours of research, while a major project can consume weeks or months.

Research material
- Primary sources are the raw material of research. This can include results of experiments, notes, and surveys or

interviews done by the researcher. Other primary sources are books, letters, diaries, eyewitness accounts, and performances attended by the researcher.

- Secondary sources consist of oral and written accounts prepared by others. This includes reports, summaries, critical reviews, and other sources not developed by the researcher.

Most research writing uses both primary and secondary sources. Primary sources from first-hand accounts and secondary sources for background and supporting documentation. The research process calls for active reading and writing throughout. As research yields information, it often calls for more reading and research, and the cycle continues.

Organizing information

Organizing information effectively is an important part of research. The data must be organized in a useful manner so that it can be effectively used. Three basic ways to organize information are:

1. Spatial organization - this is useful as it lets the user "see" the information, to fix it in space. This has benefits for those individuals who are visually adept at processing information.
2. Chronological organization is the most common presentation of information. This method places information in the sequence with which it occurs. Chronological organization is very useful in explaining a process that occurs in a step-by-step pattern.
3. Logical organization includes presenting material in a logical pattern that makes intuitive sense. Some patterns that are frequently used are illustrated, definition, compare/contrast, cause/effect, problem/solution, and division/classification. Each of these methods is discussed next.

Logical organization

There are six major types of logical organization that are frequently used:

1. Illustrations may be used to support the thesis. Examples are the most common form of this organization.
2. Definitions say what something is or is not is another way of organization. What are the characteristics of the topic?
3. Dividing or classifying information into separate items according to their similarities is a common and effective organizing method.
4. Comparing, focusing on the similarities of things, and contrasting, highlighting the differences between things is an excellent tool to use with certain kinds of information.
5. Cause and effect is a simple tool to logically understand relationships between things. A phenomena may be traced to its causes for organizing a subject logically.
6. Problem and solution is a simple and effective manner of logically organizing material. It is very commonly used and lucidly presents information.

Writing

An initial plan

After information gathering has been completed and the fruits of the research organized effectively, the writer now has a rough or initial plan for the work. A rough plan may be informal, consisting of a few elements such as "Introduction, Body, and Conclusions", or a more formal outline. The rough plan may include multiple organizational strategies within the over-all piece, or it may isolate one or two that can be used exclusively. At this stage the plan is just that, a rough plan subject to change as new ideas appear, and the organization takes a new approach. In these cases, the need for more research sometimes becomes apparent, or existing information should be considered in a new way. A more formal outline leads to an easier transition to a draft, but it can also limit the new possibilities that may arise as the plan unfolds. Until the outlines of the piece become clear, it is usually best to remain open to possible shifts in approaching the subject.

Supporting the thesis
It is most important that the thesis of the paper be clearly expounded and adequately supported by additional points. The thesis sentence should contain a clear statement of the major theme and a comment about the thesis. The writer has an opportunity here to state what is significant or noteworthy of this particular treatment of the subject. Each sentence and paragraph in turn, should build on the thesis and support it.

Particular attention should be paid to insuring the organization properly uses the thesis and supporting points. It can be useful to outline the draft after writing, to insure that each paragraph leads smoothly to the next, and that the thesis is continually supported. The outline may highlight a weakness in flow or ideation that can be repaired. It will also spatially illustrate the flow of the argument, and provide a visual representation of the thesis and its supporting points. Often things become clearer when outlined than with a block of writing.

First draft
Drafting is a mysterious art, and does not easily lend itself to rules. Generally, the more detailed the formal or informal outline, the easier is the transition to a first draft. The process of drafting is a learning one, and planning, organizing, and researching may be ongoing. Drafting is an evaluative process as well, and the whole project will be under scrutiny as the draft develops. The scope may be narrowed or widened, the approach may change, and different conclusions may emerge.

The process itself is shaped by the writer's preferences for atmosphere during the writing process. Time of day or night, physical location, ambient conditions, and any useful rituals can all play into the writer's comfort and productivity. The creation of an atmosphere conducive to the writer's best work is a subtle but important aspect of writing that is often overlooked. Although excellent writing has often been done in difficult situations, it is not the best prescription for success.

Evaluating the draft
Once a draft is finished, an evaluation is in order. This can often mean reviewing the entire process with a critical eye. There is no formal checklist that insures a complete and effective evaluation, but there are some elements that can be considered:
- It should be determined whether sufficient research was done to properly develop the assignment. Are there areas that call for additional information? If so, what type?
- What are the major strengths of the draft? Are there any obvious weaknesses? How can these be fixed?
- Who is the audience for this work and how well does the material appeal to them?
- Does the material actually accomplish the goals of the assignment? If not, what needs to be done?

This is a stage for stepping back from the project and giving it an objective evaluation. Changes made now can improve the material significantly. Take time here to formulate a final approach to the subject.

Objective criticism
Now is the time to obtain objective criticisms of the draft. It is helpful to provide readers with a list of questions to be answered about the draft. Some examples of effective questions are:
- Does the introduction catch the reader's attention? How can it be improved?

- Is the thesis clearly stated and supported by additional points?
- What type of organizational plan is used? Is it appropriate for the subject?
- Are paragraphs well developed and is there a smooth transition between them?
- Are the sentences well written and convey the appropriate meaning?
- Are words used effectively and colorfully in the text?
- What is the tone of the writing? Is it appropriate to the audience and subject?
- Is the conclusion satisfactory? Is there a sense of completion that the work is finished?
- What are main strengths and weaknesses of the writing? Are there specific suggestions for improvement?

Title, introduction, and conclusion
- A good title can identify the subject, describe it in a colorful manner, and give clues to the approach and sometimes conclusion of the writing. It usually defines the work in the mind of the reader.
- A strong introduction follows the lead of the title; it draws the readers into the work, and clearly states the topic with a clarifying comment. A common style is to state the topic, and then provide additional details, finally leading to a statement of the thesis at the end. An introduction can also begin with an arresting quote, question, or strong opinion, which grabs the reader's attention.
- A good conclusion should leave readers satisfied and provide a sense of closure. Many conclusions restate the thesis and formulate general statements that grow out of it. Writers often find ways to conclude in a dramatic fashion, through a vivid image, quotation, or a warning. This

in an effort to give the ending the "punch" to tie up any existing points.

An introduction announces the main point of the work. It will usually be a paragraph of 50 to 150 words, opening with a few sentences to engage the reader, and conclude with the essay's main point. The sentence stating the main point is called the thesis. If possible, the sentences leading to the thesis should attract the reader's attention with a provocative question, vivid image, description, paradoxical statement, quotation, anecdote, or a question. The thesis could also appear at the beginning of the introduction. There are some types of writing that do not lend themselves to stating a thesis in one sentence. Personal narratives and some types of business writing may be better served by conveying an overriding purpose of the text, which may or may not be stated directly. The important point is to impress the audience with the rationale for the writing.

The body of the essay should fulfill the promise of the introduction and thesis. If an informal outline has not been done, now is the time for a more formal one. Constructing the formal outline will create a "skeleton" of the paper. Using this skeleton, it is much easier to fill out the body of an essay. It is useful to block out paragraphs based on the outline, to insure they contain all the supporting points, and are in the appropriate sequence.

The conclusion of the essay should remind readers of the main point, without belaboring it. It may be relatively short, as the body of the text has already "made the case" for the thesis. A conclusion can summarize the main points, and offer advice or ask a question. Never introduce new ideas in a conclusion. Avoid vague and desultory endings, instead closing with a crisp, often positive, note. A dramatic or rhetorical flourish can end a piece colorfully.

Examining paragraphs

Paragraphs are a key structural unit of prose utilized to break up long stretches of words into more manageable subsets, and to indicate a shift in topics or focus. Each paragraph may be examined by identifying the main point of the section, and insuring that every sentence supports or relates to the main theme. Paragraphs may be checked to make sure the organization used in each is appropriate, and that the number of sentences are adequate to develop the topic.

Examining sentences

Sentences are the building blocks of the written word, and they can be varied by paying attention to sentence length, sentence structure, and sentence openings. These elements should be varied so that writing does not seem boring, repetitive, or choppy. A careful analysis of a piece of writing will expose these stylistic problems, and they can be corrected before the final draft is written. Varying sentence structure and length can make writing more inviting and appealing to a reader.

Examining words

A writer's choice of words is a signature of their style. A careful analysis of the use of words can improve a piece of writing. Attention to the use of specific nouns rather than general ones can enliven language. Verbs should be active whenever possible to keep the writing stronger and energetic, and there should be an appropriate balance between numbers of nouns and verbs. Too many nouns can result in heavy, boring sentences.

Examining tone

Tone may be defined as the writer's attitude toward the topic, and to the audience. This attitude is reflected in the language used in the writing. If the language is ambiguous, tone becomes very difficult to ascertain. The tone of a work should be appropriate to the topic and to the intended audience. Some writing should avoid slang and jargon, while it may be fine in a different piece. Tone can range from humorous, to serious, and all levels in between. It may be more or less formal depending on the purpose of the writing, and its intended audience. All these nuances in tone can flavor the entire writing and should be kept in mind as the work evolves.

Tone is distinguished from mood, which is the feeling the writing evokes. Tone and mood may often be similar, but can also be significantly different. Mood often depends on the manner in which words and language are employed by the writer. In a sense tone and mood are two sides of a coin which color and language enliven the total approach of a writer to his subject. Mood and tone add richness and texture to words, bringing them alive in a deliberate strategy by the writer.

Examining point-of-view

Point-of-view is the perspective from which writing occurs. There are several possibilities:

1. First Person - Is written so that the "I" of the story is a participant or observer.
2. Second Person - Is a device to draw the reader in more closely. It is really a variation or refinement of the first person narrative.
3. Third Person - The most traditional form of third-person point-of-view is the "omniscient narrator", in which the narrative voice, (presumed to be the writer), is presumed to know everything about the characters, plot, and action. Most novels use this point-of-view.
4. A Multiple Point-Of-View - The narration is delivered from the perspective of several characters.

In modern writing, the "stream-of consciousness" technique developed fully by James Joyce where the interior monologue provides the narration through the thoughts, impressions, and fantasies of the narrator.

Voice

Writers should find an appropriate voice that is appropriate for the subject, appeals to the intended audience, and conforms to the conventions of the genre in which the writing is done. If there is doubt about the conventions of the genre, lab reports, informal essays, research papers, business memos, and so on - a writer may examine models of these works written by experts in the field. These models can serve as examples for form and style for a particular type of writing.

Voice can also include the writer's attitude toward the subject and audience. Care should be taken that the language and tone of the writing is considered in terms of the purpose of the writing and it intended audience.

Gauging the appropriate voice for a piece is part art, and part science. It can be a crucial element in the ultimate effectiveness of the writing.

Writing conventions

Conventions in writing are traditional assumptions or practices used by authors of all types of text. Some basic conventions have survived through the centuries - for example the assumption that a first person narrator in a work is telling the truth - others such as having characters in melodramas speak in asides to the audience have become outmoded. Conventions are particularly important in specialized types of writing which demand specific formats and styles. This is true of scientific and research papers, as well as much of academic and business writing. This formality has relaxed somewhat in several areas but still holds true for many fields of technical writing. Conventions are particularly useful for writers working in various types of nonfiction writing, where guidelines help the writer conform to the rules expected for that field. Conventions are part of the unspoken contract between writer and audience, and should be respected.

Writing preparation

Effective writing requires preparation. The planning process includes everything done prior to drafting. Depending on the project, this could take a few minutes or several months. Elements in planning, and include considering the purpose of the writing, exploring a topic, developing a working thesis, gathering necessary materials, and developing a plan for organizing the writing. The organizational plan may vary in length and components, from a detailed outline or a stack of research cards. The organizational plan is a guide to help draft a writing project, and may change as writing progresses, but having a guide to refer to can keep a project on track. Planning is usually an ongoing process throughout the writing, but it is essential to begin with a structure.

Editing

Time must always be allowed for thorough and careful editing in order to insure clean and error-free work. It is helpful to create a checklist of editing to use as the manuscript is proofed. Patterns of editing problems often become apparent and understanding these patterns can eliminate them. Examples of patterns of errors include misuse of commas, difficulty in shifting tenses, and spelling problems. Once these patterns are seen, it is much easier to avoid them in the original writing. A checklist should be prepared based on every piece of writing, and should be cumulative. In this manner. progress may be checked regularly and the quantity and type of errors should be reduced over time. It is often helpful to have peer proof a manuscript, to get a fresh set of eyes on the material. Editing should be treated as an opportunity to polish and perfect a written work, rather than a chore that must be done. A good editor usually turns into a better writer over time.

Proofreading

As a proofreader, the goal is always to eliminate all errors. This includes typographical errors as well as any inconsistencies in spelling and punctuation. Begin by reading the prose aloud, calling out all punctuation marks and insuring that all sentences are complete and no words are left out. It is helpful to read the material again, backwards, so the focus is on each individual word, and the tendency to skip ahead is avoided.

A computer is a blessing to writers who have trouble proofreading their work. Spelling and grammar check programs may be utilized to reduce errors significantly. However it is still important for a writer to do the manual proofing necessary to insure errors of pattern are not repeated. Computers are a wonderful tool for writers but they must be employed by the writer, rather than as the writer. Skillful use of computers should result in a finely polished manuscript free of errors.

Evaluating student writing

The evaluation of student writing should be structured to include three basic goals:
1. To provide students a description of what they are doing when they respond.
2. To provide a pathway for potential improvement.
3. To help students learn to evaluate themselves.

To fulfill these goals it is necessary for the concept of evaluation be broadened beyond correcting or judging students. Any teacher response to a student's response should be considered part of the evaluation. In responding to student's responses, a teacher may use written or taped comments, dialogue with students, or conferencing between teachers and students to discuss classroom performance. Students may be asked to evaluate themselves and a teacher and student can review past progress and plan directions for potential improvement.

Teacher's response
There are seven basic components of teacher's responses to be considered:
1. Praise - To provide positive reinforcement for the student. Praise should be specific enough to bolster student's confidence.
2. Describing - Providing feedback on teacher's responses to student responses. This is best done in a conversational, non-judgmental mode.
3. Diagnosing - Determining the student's unique set of strengths, attitudes, needs, and abilities. This evaluation should take into consideration all elements of the student.
4. Judging - Evaluating the level, depth, insightfulness, completeness, and validity of a student's responses. This evaluation will depend on the criteria implied in the instructional approach.
5. Predicting - Predicting the potential improvement of student's responses based on specific criteria.
6. Record-keeping - The process of recording a student's reading interests, attitudes, and use of literary strategies, in order to chart student progress across time. Both qualitative and quantitative assessments may be used.
7. Recognition - Giving students recognition for growth and progress.

Assessments

Preparing for literary tests
Literary tests are measures of a student's individual performance. Literary assessments are measures of performance of a group of students without reference to individuals. Tests take into consideration what the teachers have taught the students, while assessments do not.

For either tests or assessments, the teacher needs a clear purpose on which to base their questions or activities. Students should be told of the purpose of the tests or assessments so they will know what to expect. Tests should be used sparingly as a one tool among many that can be used to evaluate students. Tests should encourage students on formulation of responses rather than rote answers. They should evaluate students on the basis of their responses rather than 'correct answers". Improvement over time may be noted and the student given praise for specific responses.

Standardized achievement tests
These multiple choice tests measure student's ability to understand text passages or apply literary concepts to texts. Although these tests are widely used, they have many limitations. They tend to be based on a simplistic model that ignores the complex nature of a reader's engagement with a text. These tests also do not measure student's articulation of responses. The purpose of these tests is to rank students in group norms, so that half the students are below the norm.

To accurately measure a student's abilities teachers should employ open ended written or oral response activities. In developing such tests, teachers must know what specific response patterns they wish to measure. The steps involved in measuring these response patterns must be clearly outlined. Teachers may wish to design questions that encourage personal expressions of responses. This would obviate the pitfall of testing primarily facts about literature rather than how students relate and use this information to engage texts.

Assessing attitudes toward literature
An important element in teaching literature is to understand the attitudes of students about reading and studying text. This may be done by group or individual interviews encouraging students to discuss their feelings about literature. Another way to measure attitudes is with a paper and pencil rating scale using six or eight point Liker scales.

This type of assessment can be refined to explore preferences in form and genre.

Another type of assessment is done by using semantic scales to indicate students interest (or lack thereof) in reading in general and favored forms and genres.

Questionnaires can be developed to learn more about student's habits regarding literature. Do they use the library regularly, read books or periodicals, and what types of reading is done. Comparisons before and after instruction can indicate the effect of the instruction on habits and attitudes about literature.

Assessing instructional methods
Assessing instructional methods within a school, district, or state can help determine instructional goals and techniques relative to overall system goals. Results can indicate needed changes in the curriculum and can help an accreditation process measure the quality of an English or literature program.

An effective assessment usually includes interviews, questionnaires, and class-room observation. Trained observers rate the general type of instruction being provided, (lectures, modeling, small groups, and so on), the focus of instruction (novels, poetry, drama, and so on), the critical approach used, the response strategies used, and the response activities employed. Observers may also analyze the statements of goals and objectives in a curriculum, as well as the scope and sequence of the curriculum.

Interviews of both students and teachers are helpful in getting first hand accounts of instruction and results.

Classroom based research

Teacher's can conduct their own informal descriptive research to assess the effects of their teaching on student's responses. This allows teachers an opportunity to review and reflect on their instructional methods and results. This research can take many forms including:

- An analysis of student's perception of guided response- activities to determine which were most effective.
- An analysis of student's small and large group discussions.
- A teacher self analysis of their own taped, written, or conference feedback to students writing.
- Interviews with students about their responses and background experiences and attitudes.
- Evaluating student's responses to texts commonly used in their instruction.

These are only a few possibilities for effective classroom based research. Any research that provides insight into student needs and preferences can be a valuable tool.

Conducting classroom research
1. Create a research question related to literature instruction or responses.
2. Summarize the theory and research related to the topic.
3. Describe the participants, setting, tasks, and methods of analysis.
4. Summarize the results of the research in a graph, table, or report.
5. Interpret or give reasons for the results.
6. Draw conclusions from the results that suggest ways to improve instruction and evaluation of students.

Teachers must always keep in mind the purposes driving the research. Evaluation itself is relatively easy, the challenge is using the evaluations to help both students and teachers to grow, and become better at what they are doing.

Reviewers

Many professional and business writers work with editors who provide advice and support throughout the writing process. In academic situations, the use of reviewers is increasing, either by instructors or perhaps at an academic writing center. Peer review sessions are sometimes scheduled for class, and afford an opportunity to hear what other students feel about a piece of writing. This gives a writer a chance to serve as a reviewer.

Textual perspective

A textual knowledge of literature implies readers are taking a perspective or stance on the text. They are examining ways in which separate parts of the text relate to its overall form or structure. Textual perspectives must be used as a part of overall learning, not as an isolated feature. Textual perspective alone excludes both the author's life and the emotional experiences and attitudes of the reader. it fails to account for the readers' prior knowledge in their engagement with the work. A textual approach may include the ways in which the text shapes students' experience and emotional engagement. Based on previous reading, social acculturation, attitudes, and a host of other factors, students bring a wealth of information into any encounter with a text. Students may compare and contrast elements of their text with other works they have read or seen to form a more rounded engagement with a work.

Social perspective
A rich resource for students' of literature is their own developing social knowledge. For adolescent students', social relationships are of primary importance. It is common for younger students' to impose their own social attitudes on a text, which is fertile ground for exploring how the understanding of texts is colored by social attitudes and experiences. Student's attitudes can help them reflect on the characters in a work, and can determine their relationship with the text itself.

Social perspectives can shed light on a number of important ways which can effect a reader's engagement with the text. A skillful teacher may probe these attitudes and experiences and make students' more aware of the impact of social attitudes to reading and studying a work of literature. This knowledge can become cumulative and promote more careful understanding of a literature over a period of time.

Cultural and historical context
The cultural knowledge and background of readers effects their response to texts. They can relate the works in a context of subcultures such as peer group, mass media, school, religion, and politics, social and historical communities. Engaging with the texts, readers can better understand how characters and authors are shaped by cultural influences. Cultural elements influence reader's reactions to events, including their responses to literature.

Cultural and historical context is important in understanding the roles of women and minorities in literature. Placing works of literature in their proper cultural setting can make a work more understandable and provoke reader interest in the milieu of the day. These factors can stimulate a reader's interest in how their own cultural background impacts the engagement with the text. Thus, the cultural aspects of literature become an opportunity for the reader to gain insight into their own attitudes.

Topical perspective
In using a topical perspective, students apply their background in a variety of different fields, for instance sports, science, politics or cooking, to the literary work they are studying. Students may then engage the text in a holistic manner, bringing all their knowledge to bear on a work. It is useful to encourage students to determine how their own information pool relates to the work. There are an infinite number of fields or topics that relate to literature.

Students are most likely to integrate topics they are currently studying into their engagement with a text. These topics would

include history, science, art, and music among others. Thinking about literature from these other topical point-of-view can help students ' understand that what they are learning in other courses enhances their experience of both literature and life.

Effects of prior knowledge

History
When students employ topical knowledge of history in their study of literature, they may do much more than remember date, events, and historical figures in relation to a text. They may well apply what they know about a historical period to better understand the attitudes and relationships in a work of literature. Students learn to think historically, considering different explanations for events, or cause and effect relationships in tracing a sequence of events. For example in reading Steinbeck's novels, students may draw on what they know about the historical period of the depression. Hemingway's "Farewell To Arms" may evoke a historical picture of Europe embroiled in World War I.

Literature offers an opportunity to apply historical knowledge in the context of a work. Students understand that both literary and historical accounts of an event or character may differ significantly, and that one may illuminate the other.

Scientific knowledge
Students can apply their knowledge of science when reading literature. Their description of carefully observed phenomena can be used to describe a piece of writing. after reading essays by science writers, students' may be encouraged to transpose this knowledge into reading other texts. Understanding the scientific method gives readers' an opportunity to impose this process on events narrated in literature. The validity of events may be tested in the students' mind to assess the "reality" of the text.

- 124 -

There are many texts that take as their subject the role of the scientist in society. In reading "Frankenstein" or "Dr. Faustus", many issues can be raised about the responsibilities of scientists in conducting experiments.

The blending of science and literature is particularly compelling to some students' when they read science fiction or futuristic texts. An example would be "1984" which posits a authoritarian government controlling the lives of people.

Research papers

Hypothesis

The result of a focusing process is a research question, a question or problem that can be solved by through research data. A hypothesis is a tentative answer to the research question that must be supported by the research. A research question must be manageable, specific, and interesting. Additionally, it must be argumentative, capable of being proved or disproved by research.

It is helpful to explore a topic with background reading and notes before formulating a research question and a hypothesis. Create a data base where all the knowledge of a topic is written down to be utilized in approaching the task of identifying the research question. This background work will allow a narrowing to a specific question, and formulate a tentative answer, the hypothesis. The process of exploring a topic can include brainstorming, freewriting, and scanning your memory and experience for information.

Observing data

Collecting data in the field begins with direct observation, noting phenomena in a totally objective manner, and recording it. This requires a systematic approach to observation and recording information. Prior to beginning the observation process, certain steps must be accomplished:

1. Determine the purpose of the observation and review the research question and hypothesis to see that they relate to each other.
2. Set a limited time period for the observations.
3. Develop a system for recording information in a useful manner.
4. Obtain proper materials for taking notes.
5. Consider the use of cameras, video recorders, or audio tape recorders.
6. Use the journalistic technique of asking "who, what, where, when, and why" to garner information.

Research interviews

After determining the exact purpose of the interview, check it against the research question and hypothesis. Set up the interview in advance, specifying the amount of time needed. Prepare a written list of questions for the interview, and try out questions on peers before the interview. Prepare a copy of your questions leaving room for notes. Insure that all the necessary equipment is on hand, and record the date, time, and subject of the interview.

The interview should be businesslike, and take only the allotted time. A flexible attitude will allow for questions or comments that have not been planned for, but may prove helpful to the process. Follow-up questions should be asked whenever appropriate. A follow-up thank you note is always appreciated and may pave the way for further interviews. Be mindful at all times of the research question and hypothesis under consideration.

Surveys

Surveys are usually in the form of questionnaires which have the advantage of speed and rapid compilation of data. Preparation of the questionnaire is of critical importance. Tie the questionnaire to the research question as closely as possible, and include questions which will bear on the hypothesis. Questions that can be answered "yes" or "no" can be easily tabulated. The following checklist may be helpful:

1. Determine the audience for the questionnaire and how best to reach them.
2. Draft questions that will provide short, specific answers.
3. Test the questions on friends or peers.
4. Remember to include a deadline for return of the questionnaire.
5. Format the questionnaire so that it is clear and easily completed.
6. Carefully proofread the questionnaire and insure that it is neatly reproduced.

Library research

After reviewing personal resources for information, the library is the next stop. Use index cards or notepads for documentation. Create a system for reviewing data. It is helpful to create "key words" to trigger responses from sources. Some valuable guidelines for conducting library research include:

1. Consult the reference librarian for sources and ideas.
2. Select appropriate general and specific reference books for examination. Encyclopedias are a good place to start. There are numerous specialized encyclopedias to assist in research.
3. Survey biographical dictionaries and indexes for information.
4. Review almanacs, yearbooks, and statistical data.
5. Scan periodical indexes for articles on the research topic.
6. Determine if there are specialized indexes and abstracts that may be helpful.
7. Review the computer or card catalog for relevant references.

Drafting the research essay

Before beginning the research essay, revisit the purpose, audience, and scope of the essay.

An explicit thesis statement should summarize major arguments and approaches to the subject. After determining the special format of the essay, a survey of the literature on the subject is helpful. If original or first-hand research is involved, a summary of the methods and conclusions should be prepared.

A clustering strategy assembles all pertinent information on a topic in one physical place. The preparation of an outline may be based on the clusters, or a first draft may be developed without an outline. Formal outlines use a format of "Thesis statement", "Main topic", and "Supporting ideas" to shape the information. Drafting the essay can vary considerably among researchers, but it is useful to use an outline or information clusters to get started. Drafts are usually done on a point-to-point basis.

Introduction

The introduction to a research essay is particularly important as it sets the context for the essay. It needs to draw the reader into the subject, and also provide necessary background to understand the subject. It is sometimes helpful to open with the research question, and explain how the question will be answered. The major points of the essay may be forecast or previewed to prepare readers for the coming arguments.

In a research essay it is a good idea to establish the writer's credibility by reviewing credentials and experience with the subject. Another useful opening involves quoting several sources that support the points of the essay, again to establish credibility. The tone should be appropriate to the audience and subject, maintaining a sense of careful authority while building the arguments. Jargon should be kept to a minimum, and language carefully chosen to reflect the appropriate tone.

Conclusion

The conclusion to a research essay helps readers' summarize what they have learned. Conclusions are not meant to convince, as this has been done in the body of the essay. It can be useful to leave the reader with a memorable phrase or example that supports the argument. Conclusions should be both memorable but logical restatements of the arguments in the body of the essay.

A specific-to-general pattern can be helpful, opening with the thesis statement and expanding to more general observations. A good idea is to restate the main points in the body of the essay, leading to the conclusion. An ending that evokes a vivid image or asks a provocative question makes the essay memorable. The same effect can be achieved by a call for action, or a warning. Conclusions may be tailored to the audience's background, both in terms of language, tone, and style.

Reviewing the draft
A quick checklist for reviewing a draft of a research essay includes:
1. Introduction - Is the reader's attention gained and held by the introduction?
2. Thesis - Does the essay fulfill the promise of the thesis? Is it strong enough?
3. Main Points - List the main points and rank them in order of importance.
4. Organization - What is the organizing principle of the essay? Does it work?
5. Supporting Information - Is the thesis adequately supported? Is the thesis convincing?
6. Source Material - Are there adequate sources and are they smoothly integrated into the essay?
7. Conclusion - Does the conclusion have sufficient power? Does it summarize the essay well?
8. Paragraphs, Sentences, and Words - Review all these for effectiveness in promoting the thesis.
9. Overall Review - Evaluate the essay's strengths and weaknesses. What revisions are needed?

Modern Language Association style

The Modern Language Association style is widely used in literature and languages as well as other fields. The MLA style calls for noting brief references to sources in parentheses in the text of an essay, and adding an alphabetical list of sources, called "Works Cited", at the end. Specific recommendations of the MLA include:
1. Works Cited - Includes only works actually cited. List on a separate page with the author's name, title, and publication information, which must list the location of the publisher, the publishers' name, and the date of publication.
2. Parenthetical Citations - MLA style uses parenthetical citations following each quotation, reference, paraphrase, or summary to a source. Each citation is made up of the author's last name and page reference, keyed to a reference in "Works Cited".
3. Explanatory Notes - Explanatory notes are numbered consecutively, and identified by superscript numbers in the text. The full notes may appear as endnotes or as footnotes at the bottom of the page.

American Psychological Association style

The American Psychological Association style is widely followed in the social sciences. The APA parenthetical citations within the text directs readers to a list of sources. In APA style this list is called "References". References are listed on a separate page, and each line includes the author's name, publication date, title, and publication information. Publication information includes the city where the publisher is located, and the publisher's name. Underline the titles of books and periodicals, but not articles.

APA parenthetical expressions citations include the author's last name, the date of publication, and the page number. APA style allows for content footnotes for information needed to be expanded or supplemented, marked in the text by superscript numbers in consecutive order. Footnotes are listed under a separate page, headed "Footnotes" after the last page of text. All entries should be double-spaced.

Revisions

Revising sentences

Revising sentences is done to make writing more effective. Editing sentences is done to correct any errors. Revising sentences is usually best done on a computer, where it is possible to try several versions easily. Some writers prefer to print out a hard copy and work with this for revisions. Each works equally well and depends on the individual preference.

Spelling and grammar checks on software are a great aid to a writer but not a panacea. Many grammatical problems, such as faulty parallelism, mixed constructions, and misplaced modifiers can slip past the programs. Even if errors are caught, the writing still must be evaluated for effectiveness. A combination of software programs and writer awareness is necessary to insure an error free manuscript.

Global revisions

Global revisions address the larger elements of writing. They usually affect paragraphs or sections, and may involve condensing or merging sections of text to improve meaning and flow. Sometimes material may be rearranged to better present the arguments of the essay. It is usually better for the writer to get some distance from the work before starting a global revision. Reviewers and editors can be usefully employed to make suggestions for revision. If reviewers are utilized, it is helpful to emphasize the focus on the larger themes of the work, rather than the finer points. When undertaking a global review, the writer might wish to position himself as the audience, rather than the writer. This provides some additional

objectivity, and can result in a more honest appraisal of the writing and revisions that should be made. Global revisions are the last major changes a writer will make in the text. seal to persuade, inform, or entertain them. Answering these questions as objectively as possible will allow for a useful global revision.

1. Purpose - Does the draft accomplish its purpose? Is the material and tone appropriate for the intended audience? Does it account for the audience's knowledge of the subject? Does it seek to persuade, inform, or entertain them?
2. Focus - Does the introduction and the conclusion focus on the main point? Are all supporting arguments focused on the thesis?
3. Organization and Paragraphing - Are there enough organizational cues to guide the reader? Are any paragraphs too long or too short?
4. Content - Is the supporting material persuasive? Are all ideas adequately developed? Is there any material that could be deleted?
5. Point -of-view - Is the draft free of distracting sifts in point-of-view? Is the point-of-view appropriate for the subject and intended audience?

Paragraphs

A paragraph should be unified around a main point. A good topic sentence summarizing the paragraphs main point. A topic sentence is more general than subsequent supporting sentences. Sometime the topic sentence will be used to close the paragraph if earlier sentences give a clear indication of the direction of the paragraph. Sticking to the main point means deleting or omitting unnecessary sentences that do not advance the main point.

The main point of a paragraph deserves adequate development, which usually means a substantial paragraph. A paragraph of two or three sentences often does not develop a point well enough, particularly if the point is a strong supporting argument of the thesis. An occasional short paragraph is fine, particularly it is used as a transitional device. A choppy appearance should be avoided.

Methods of development
- Examples are a common method of development and may be effectively used when a reader may ask "For Example?" Examples are selected instances, not an inclusive catalog. They may be used to suggest the validity of topic sentences.
- Illustrations are extended examples, sometimes presented in story form for interest. They usually require several sentences each, so they are used sparingly. Well selected illustrations can be a colorful and vivid way of developing a point.
- Stories that command reader interest, developed in a story form, can be powerful methods of emphasizing key points in a essay. Stories and illustrations should be very specific and relate directly to a point or points being made in the text. They allow more colorful language and instill a sense of human interest in a subject. Used judiciously, illustrations and stories are an excellent device.
- Analogies draw comparisons between items that appear to have nothing in common. Analogies are employed by writers to attempt to provoke fresh thoughts and changed feelings about a subject. They may be used to make the unfamiliar more familiar, to clarify an abstract point, or to argue a point. Although analogies are effective literary devices, they should be used thoughtfully in arguments. Two things may be alike in some respects but completely different in others.
- Cause and effect is a excellent device and are best used when the cause and effect are generally accepted as true. As a matter of argument, cause and effect is usually too complex and

subject to other interpretations to be used effectively. A valid way of using cause and effect is to state the effect in the topic sentence of a paragraph, and add the causes in the body of the paragraph. This adds logic and form to a paragraph, and usually makes it more effective.

Types of paragraphs
- A paragraph of narration tells a story or part of a story. They are usually arranged in chronological order, but sometimes include flashbacks, taking the story back to an earlier time.
- A descriptive paragraph paints a verbal portrait of a person, place, or thing, using specific details that appeal to one or more of our senses - sight, sound, smell, taste, and touch. It conveys a real sense of being present and observing phenomena.
- A process paragraphs is related in time order, generally chronological. It usually describes a process or teaches readers how to perform the process.
- Comparing two subjects draws attention to their similarities but can also indicate a consideration of differences. To contrast is to focus only on differences. Both comparisons and contrasts may be examined point-by-point, or in succeeding paragraphs.

Organizing information
- A grouping of items into categories based on some consistent criteria is called classification. The principle of classification a writer chooses will depend on the purpose of the classification. Most items can be classified by a number of criteria, and the selection of the specific classification will depend on the writer's aims in using this device.
- Division, on the other hand, takes one item and divides it into parts. Just as with classification, the division must

be based on a valid and consistent principle. For example a body may be divided into various body systems easily, but not as easily divided into body functions, because the categories overlap

- Definition classifies a concept or word in a general group, then distinguishes it from other members of the class. Usually simple definitions can be provided in a sentence or two, while more complex ones may need a paragraph or two to adequately define them.

Coherence

A smooth flow of sentences and paragraphs without gaps, shifts, or bumps leads to paragraph coherence. Ties between old information and new, can be smoothed by several strategies.

1. Linking ideas clearly, from the topic sentence to the body of the paragraph is essential for a smooth transition. The topic sentence states the main point, and this should be followed by specific details, examples, and illustrations that support the topic sentence. The support may be direct or indirect. In indirect support the illustrations and examples may support a sentence that in turn supports the topic directly.
2. The repetition of key words adds coherence to a paragraph. To avoid dull language, variations of the key words may be used.
3. Parallel structures are often used within sentences to emphasize the similarity of ideas and connect sentences giving similar information.
4. Minimize shifting sentences from one verb tense to another. These shifts affect the smooth flows of words and can disrupt the coherence of the paragraph.

Transitions

Transitions are bridges between what has been read and what is about to be read. Transitions smooth the reader's path between sentences, and inform readers of major connections to new ideas forthcoming in the text. Transitional phrases should be used with care, selecting the appropriate phrase for a transition. Tone is another important consideration in using transitional phrases, varying the tone for different audiences. For example in a scholarly essay, "in summary" would be preferable to the more informal "in short".

When working with transitional words and phrases, writers usually find a natural flow that indicates when a transition is needed. In reading a draft of the text, it should become apparent where the flow is uneven or rough. At this point, the writer can add transitional elements during the revision process. Revising can also afford an opportunity to delete transitional devices that seem heavy-handed or unnecessary.

Lengths of paragraphs

The comfort level for readers is paragraphs of between 100 and 200 words. Shorter paragraphs cause too much starting and stopping, and give a "choppy" effect. Paragraphs that are too long often test the attention span of the reader. Two notable exceptions to this rule exist. In scientific or scholarly papers, longer paragraphs suggest seriousness and depth. In journalistic writing, constraints are placed on paragraph size by the narrow columns in a newspaper format.

The first and last paragraphs of a text will usually be the introduction and conclusion. These special purpose paragraphs are likely to be shorter than paragraphs in the body of the work. Paragraphs in the body of the essay follow the subject's outline; one paragraph per point in short essays, and a group of paragraphs per point in longer works. Some ideas require more development than others, so it is good for a writer to remain flexible. A too long paragraph may be divided, while shorter ones may be combined.

Paragraph breaks are used for many reasons, usually as devices to improve the flow or content of the text. Some examples for beginning new paragraphs include:
1. To mark off the introduction and concluding paragraphs.
2. To signal a shift to a new idea or topic.
3. To indicate an important shift in time or place.
4. To emphasize a point by repositioning a major sentence.
5. To highlight a comparison, contrast, or cause and effect relationship.
6. To signal a change in speakers, voice, or tense.

Argumentative writing

Constructing a reasonable argument, the goal is not to "win" or have the last word, but rather to reveal current understanding of the question, and propose a solution to the perceived problem. The purpose of argument in a free society or a research field is to reach the best conclusion possible at the time.

Conventions of arguments vary from culture to culture. In America arguments tend to be direct rather than subtle, carefully organized rather than discursive, spoken plainly rather than poetically. Evidence presented is usually specific and factual, while appeals to intuition or communal wisdom are rare.

Argumentative writing takes a stand on a debatable issue , and seeks to explore all sides of the issue and reach the best possible solution. Argumentative writing should not be combative, at it's strongest it is assertive.

A prelude to argumentative writing is an examination of the issue's social and intellectual contexts.

Introducion
The introduction of an essay arguing an issue should end with a thesis sentence that states a position on the issue. A good strategy is to establish credibility with readers by showing both expert knowledge and fair-mindedness. Building common ground with undecided or neutral readers is helpful.

The thesis should be supported by strong arguments that support the stated position. The main lines of argument should have a cumulative effect of convincing readers that the thesis has merit. The sum of the main lines of argument will outline the overall argumentative essay. The outline will clearly illustrate the central thesis, and subordinate claims that support it.

Evidence must be provided that support both the thesis and supporting arguments. Evidence based on reading should be documented, to show the sources. Readers must know how to check sources for accuracy and validity.

Supporting evidence
Most arguments must be supported by facts and statistics. Facts are something that is known with certainty, and have been objectively verified. Statistics may be used in selective ways to for partisan purposes. It is good to check statistics by reading authors writing on both sides of an issue. This will give a more accurate idea of how valid are the statistics cited.

Examples and illustrations add an emotional component to arguments, reaching readers in ways that facts and figures cannot. They are most effective when used in combination with objective information that can be verified.

Expert opinion can contribute to a position on a question. The source should be an authority whose credentials are beyond dispute. Sometimes it is necessary to provide the credentials of the expert. Expert testimony can be quoted directly, or may be summarized by the writer. Sources must be well documented to insure their validity.

Counter arguments

In addition to arguing a position, it is a good practice to review opposing arguments and attempt to counter them. This process can take place anywhere in the essay, but is perhaps best placed after the thesis is stated. Objections can be countered on a point-by-point analysis, or in a summary paragraph. Pointing out flaws in counter arguments is important, as is showing the counter arguments to have less weight than the supported thesis.

Building common ground with neutral or opposed readers can make a strong case. Sharing values with undecided readers can allow people to switch positions without giving up what they feel is important. People who may oppose a position need to feel they can change their minds without compromising their intelligence or their integrity. This appeal to open-mindedness can be a powerful tool in arguing a position without antagonizing opposing views.

Fallacious arguments

A number of unreasonable argumentative tactics are known as logical fallacies. Most fallacies are misguided uses of legitimate argumentative arguments.

Generalizing is drawing a conclusion from an array of facts using inductive reasoning. These conclusions are a probability, not a certainty. The fallacy known as a "hasty generalization" is a conclusion based on insufficient or unrepresentative evidence. Stereotyping is a hasty generalization about a group. This is common because of the human tendency to perceive selectively. Observations are made through a filter of preconceptions, prejudices, and attitudes.

Analogies point out similarities between disparate things. When an analogy is unreasonable, it is called a "false analogy". This usually consists of assuming if two things are alike in one respect, they must be alike in others. This, of course, may or may not be true. Each comparison must be independently verified to make the argument valid.

Post Hoc Fallacy

Tracing cause and effect can be a complicated matter. Because of the complexity involved, writers often over-simplify it. A common error is to assume that because one event follows another, the first is the cause of the second. This common fallacy is known as "post hoc", from the Latin meaning "after this, therefore because of this".

A post hoc fallacy could run like this: "Since Abner Jones returned to the Giants lineup, the team has much better morale". The fact that Jones returned to the lineup may or may not have had an effect on team morale. The writer must show there is a cause and effect relationship between Jones' return and team morale. It is not enough to note that one event followed another. It must be proved beyond a reasonable doubt that morale was improved by the return of Jones to the lineup. The two may be true but do not necessarily follow a cause and effect pattern.

Assumptions

When considering problems and solutions, the full range of possible options should be mentioned before recommending one solution above others. It is unfair to state there are only two alternatives, when in fact there are more options. Writers who set up a choice between their preferred option and a clearly inferior one are committing the "either...or" fallacy. All reasonable alternatives should be included in the possible solutions.

Assumptions are claims that are taken to be true without proof. If a claim is controversial, proof should be provided to verify the assumption. When a claim is made that few would agree with, the writer is guilty of a "non sequitur" (Latin for "does not follow") fallacy. Thus any assumption that is subject to debate cannot be accepted without supporting evidence is suspect.

Syllogism

Deductive reasoning is constructed in a three-step method called a syllogism. The three steps are the major premise, the minor premise, and the conclusion. The major premise is a generalization, and the minor premise is a specific case. The conclusion is deduced from applying the generalization to the specific case. Deductive arguments fail if either the major or minor premise is not true, or if the conclusion does not logically follow from the premises. This means a deductive argument must stand on valid, verifiable premises, and the conclusion is a logical result of the premises.

"Straw man" fallacy

The "straw man" fallacy consists of an oversimplification or distortion of opposing views. This fallacy is one of the most obvious and easily uncovered since it relies on gross distortions. The name comes from a side setting up a position so weak (the straw man) that is easily refuted.

Composition

Composition refers to a range of activities which include the achievement of literacy, transmission of culture, preparation for writing skills in the workplace, and writing as a mode of personal expression and identity. Composition has evolved into an interdisciplinary study and an eclectic practice. Writing is a always a process, performing a critical role in education.

Composition studies, like its companion, rhetoric, is a practical and theoretical study Originally it was limited to teaching and correction of student's grammar. Composition has come of age as a writing process, a complex network of interweaving social, political, and individual components.

The field now includes collaborative writing, two or more students writing together, each assuming specific responsibilities with a heavy emphasis on joint revisions. Continued innovations and experimentation are an ongoing part of composition studies.

Literary devices

Allusions

An allusion is a reference within a text to some person, place, or event outside the text. Allusions that refer to events more or less contemporary with the text are called topical allusions. Those referring to specific persons are called personal allusions. An example of personal allusion is William Butler Yeat's reference to "golden thighed Pythagoras" in his poem " Among School Children".

Allusions may be used to summarize an important idea or point out a contrast between contemporary life and a heroic past. An example of this would be James Joyce's classical parallels in "Ulysses" in which heroic deeds in the "Odyssey" are implicitly compared to the banal aspects of everyday life in Dublin.

Allusions may also be used to summarize an important idea such as the concluding line from "King Kong", "It was beauty killed the beast".

Jargon

Jargon is a specialized language used among members of a trade, profession, or group. Jargon should be avoided and used only when the audience will be familiar with the language. Jargon includes exaggerated language usually designed to impress rather than inform. Sentences filled with jargon are both wordy and difficult to understand. Jargon is commonly used in such institutions as the military, politics, sports, and art.

Clichés

Clichés are sentences and phrases that have been overused to the point of triviality. They have no creativity or originality and add very little to modern writing. Writers should avoid clichés whenever possible. When editing writing, the best solution for clichés is to delete them. If this does not seem easily accomplished, a cliché can be modified so that it is not dully predictable and trite. This often means adding phrases or sentences to change the cliché.

Slang

Slang is an informal and sometimes private language that connotes the solidarity and exclusivity of a group such as teenagers, sports fans, ethnic groups, or rock musicians. Slang has a certain vitality, but it is not always widely understood and should be avoided in most writing. An exception could be when the audience is a specialized group who understand the jargon and slang commonly used by the members.

Sexist language

Sexist language is language that stereotypes or demeans women or men, usually women. Such language is derived from stereotypical thinking, traditional pronoun use, and from words used to refer indefinitely to both sexes. Writers should avoid referring to a profession as being basically male or female, and using different conventions when referring to men and women. Pronouns "he,him,and his"should be avoided by using a pair of pronouns or revising the sentence to obviate the sexist language.

Pretentious language

In an attempt to sound elegant, profound, poetic, or impressive, some writers embroider their thoughts with flowery phrases, inflated language, and generally pretentious wordage. Pretentious language is often so ornate and wordy that it obscures the true meaning of the writing.

Euphemisms

Euphemisms are pleasant sounding words that replace language that seems overly harsh or ugly. Euphemisms are wordy and indirect, clouding meaning through "pretty" words. However euphemisms are sometimes uses as conventions, when speaking about subjects such as death, bodily functions and sex.

Doublespeak

The term "doublespeak" was coined by George Orwell in his futuristic novel "1984". It applies to any evasive or deceptive language, particularly favored by politicians. Doublespeak is evident in advertising, journalism, and in political polemics. it should be avoided by serious writers.

Figures of speech

A figure of speech is an expression that uses words imaginatively rather than literally to make abstract ideas concrete. Figures of speech compare unlike things to reveal surprising similarities. The pitfalls of using figures of speech is the failure of writers to think through the images they evoke. The result can be a mixed metaphor, a combination of two or more images that do not make sense together.

In a simile the writer makes an explicit comparison, usually by introducing it with "like" or "as". An example would be " white as a sheet" or "my love is like a red, red, rose". Effective use of similes can add color and vivid imagery to language. Used carefully and sparingly, they provide a writer with an effective device to enhance meaning and style.

Figures of speech are particularly effective when used with discretion and selectively. Examples of figures of speech can be found in all genres of writing.

Allegories

Allegories are a type of narrative in which the story reflects at least one other meaning. Traditional allegory often employs personification, the use of human characters to represent abstract ideas. Early examples of the use of allegory were the medieval mystery plays in which abstractions such as Good, Evil, Penance, and Death appeared as characters.

Another type of allegory uses a surface story to refer to historical or political events. Jonathan swift was a mater at using allegory in this manner, particularly in his "Tale of a Tub" (1704), a satirical allegory of the reformation.

Allegory has been largely replaced by symbolism by modern writers. Although they are sometimes confused, symbolism bears a natural relationship to the events in a story, while in allegory the surface story is only an excuse for the secondary and more important meaning. Allegory has had a revival in postmodern writing, and is seen in much contemporary literature.

Ambiguity

In writing historically, ambiguity is generally viewed as an error or flaw. The word now means a literary technique in which a word or phrase conveys two or more different meanings. William Empson defines ambiguity as " any verbal nuance, however slight, which gives room for alternative reactions to the same piece of language." Empons chief purpose in defining ambiguity was to note how this device affects the interpretation of poetry. Empson identified seven types of ambiguity including the traditional meaning. These seven types of ambiguity each provided a different view of possible interpretation of text in writing. Empsons's "Seven Types of Ambiguity" was the first detailed analysis of the phenomena of multiple meanings, sometimes called plurisignation. Ambiguity can be a useful device for some types of writing but does lend itself to informative or persuasive text.

30/100

Practice Test

Practice Questions

1. Which of the following students may need extra instruction and evaluation with respect to oral language skills?
    a. Rosa: whose first language is Spanish. Rosa speaks with a distinct accent and can be difficult to understand when speaking about a new or unfamiliar topic.
    b. Greer: who avoids oral assignments when possible. He avoids speaking up in class and only responds when called upon.
    c. Ashley: who often has trouble answering questions in class. Her responses are often off-topic. She also struggles with oral presentations, seeming to present a string of unrelated facts.
    d. Brett: who frequently becomes loud and disruptive whenever group work is assigned. He often becomes involved in heated discussions with classmates when discussing ideas.

2. Mr. Callas is introducing a unit on oral traditions from around the world. He wants his seventh-grade students to gain a better understanding of the relationship between written text and oral language, as well as increase their multi-cultural understanding. Which of the following assignments would be the most relevant?
    a. "Read Chapter 12 on Oral Traditions and complete the end-of-chapter review."
    b. "Select a poem or song from a culture around the world and recite it for the class."
    c. "Conduct a poll of twenty fellow students, asking about their family's country of origin. Present a graph or diagram of your results in class."
    d. "Choose a country to research and write a first-person narrative about a typical day in the life of one of its citizens. The narratives will be read in class."

3. Which of the following exercises would be the most appropriate tool for helping students evaluate the effectiveness of their own spoken messages?
    a. Discuss written and oral assignments in class before completing them. Once the assignments are completed, the teacher meets individually with each student to discuss the content and effectiveness of each student's work.
    b. Instruct students to present oral reports in class, which are then "graded" by classmates. A score of 1-10 is assigned based on students' perception of the reports' clarity. The student's average score determines his report's effectiveness.
    c. Ask each student to prepare an oral report and a content quiz that highlights the report's main idea. The student then uses classmates' scores on the reviews to determine his report's effectiveness.
    d. Put students into groups of three. Two students complete a role-playing assignment based on prompts provided by the teacher. The third student gives constructive feedback on how the other two can refine and clarify their speech.

Use the following information to answer the next two questions.

Mr. Gilbert teaches fourth graders whose reading skills range from emergent to advanced. He introduces an activity called "Book Buddies" in which his students are paired with emerging Kindergarten readers to practice reading beginner-level short books. He hopes they will gain confidence and increase their own reading skills through these visits. Mr. Gilbert's students pick their Book Buddies up once a week and read together for about half an hour.

4. What aspect of this program is most likely to increase all of the fourth-graders' oral language skills?
    a. Finding opportunities to explain unfamiliar ideas or sound out new words with the younger students.
    b. Spending time with younger students and being reminded of how much they have learned in the past three years.
    c. Being exposed to different kinds of reading texts.
    d. Practicing their decoding skills and increasing their vocabulary.

5. What might be the best way to adapt the Book Buddy program for fourth grade students who are still learning English?
    a. Exempt ESOL students from the program altogether so that they can practice reading with their primary teacher.
    b. Create some groups that have three Book Buddies: a skilled reader, an ESOL student, and a Kindergartener; this will allow the English language learner to listen, learn, and give guidance when he is able.
    c. Make no changes to the program and simply allow the younger students and the English language learner to help each other decode and compare ideas in their own way.
    d. Allow English language learners to listen to books on tape read by native English speakers with their Kindergarten partners.

6. Mr. Campbell begins each Language Arts lesson with the "Phrase of the Day." This phrase ranges from analogies to idioms to snippets of figurative language. His students use their journals to explain what they think the phrase means and to draw a picture, also. Mr. Campbell then reveals the phrase's true meaning, which the children record on the same page as their own interpretations. When he reviews these pages in the students' journals, Mr. Campbell is most likely to:
    a. Check to ensure that each student is diligently recording both their own interpretations and the correct interpretations.
    b. Use the mechanics and spelling errors within to help him design test questions and worksheets.
    c. Grade the pages for originality and humor.
    d. Use them to informally assess students' oral language skills.

7. Which of the following activities would incorporate the best use of technology to increase students' oral language skills?

    a. Students visit the school computer lab to work on math and science activities with software that utilizes voice-recognition technology in an interactive process.

    b. Students use an internet program and computer camera to converse with English-speaking students in other countries.

    c. Students can visit the classroom's Language Lab, in which there are tape recorders and CD players. Students can use these players to listen to novels, poetry, and other literary works on tape.

    d. A teacher videotapes a class discussion about a story and replays it for the students to watch and discuss.

8. Every year, students prepare with excitement for Historical Characters Day. Each student is expected to choose a character who was influential in years past and compose a report on why he was important. The students are permitted to dress up as their respective characters on the day on which the reports are turned in. This year, the teachers want to incorporate an aspect of this anticipated event that will more directly increase their students' oral communication skills. Of the options they have brainstormed, which of the following would be most helpful?

    a. Ask the students to read their reports aloud to the class.

    b. Require that the reports be memorized so that students can make better use of voice modulation and eye contact while presenting.

    c. Require the students to write why they chose their character and three interesting things they learned on a set note cards, and present what they have written to the class.

    d. Hold an election for the student with the most realistic costume and require students to give supporting evidence for their votes.

Use the information below to answer the questions 9 and 10:

A middle school teacher consistently includes "the Daily Chat" in her lesson plans, several times a week. Students are placed into pairs, with the occasional group of three. The teacher chooses one student during each chat with whom she will partner. During these conversations, students can pick a topic and discuss it for five to ten minutes. They are asked to use the following log sheet:

Date:
Name:
Partner's Name:

☐ My partner looked at me most of the time while we were speaking.
☐ My partner listened while I was speaking.
☐ My partner waited until I finished before taking his turn to speak.
☐ My partner enunciated while speaking (I understood the words he was saying).
☐ My partner explained himself well (I understood the ideas behind what he was saying).

9. Which skill is least likely to be improved by this activity?

a. Active listening; students listen for the purpose of understanding and responding appropriately.

b. Speaking clearly; students practice speaking in ways that can be easily heard and understood.

c. Nonverbal communication skills; students communicate engagement in conversation through body language, etc.

d. Oral conflict resolution; students can resolve disagreements using their verbal skills.

10. What is the most likely purpose for the teacher to partner with a new student during each Daily Chat?

a. She wants to make sure that the students get positive feedback on a regular basis during skill-building exercises.

b. She has found that there are almost always absent students, creating a space for her to function as a partner during days where one student lacks a partner.

c. She recognizes the value of building oral communication skills with adults as well as peers.

d. She wants to demonstrate how to resolve conflicts or common problems that students often face when attempting to communicate effectively.

11. The eighth-grade class will be holding class elections in the fall as part of an integrated Social Studies and English unit. The students will be studying government elections and modeling their process based on their studies. The candidates for Vice President and President will debate pre-determined issues in front of their class using modified rules found in formal debates (i.e. they are timed and will use a moderator). Which of the following exercises would be most beneficial to introduce in English class to help prepare each student for the debates?

a. Watch recordings of Presidential and Vice Presidential debates from years past and model their speech from what they have heard.

b. Create multiple opportunities for students to discuss the pre-determined issues in class, allowing for free-flowing dialogue and differing opinions.

c. Students write their thoughts in short-essay format so that each section can be read aloud during the appropriate part of the debate.

d. Students determine a position on each selected issue and assign it to a note card or small piece of paper. On each card, they record two to three reasons or supporting ideas for the opinion.

12. A teacher wants to work on her students' listening comprehension in addition to their reading comprehension, since she understands that the skills are interrelated. She has a series of short stories that she thinks the students will enjoy. Which of the following would be the best supplement to typical written comprehension exercises?

a. Preview content and then read the stories aloud to the students. Assess listening comprehension through verbal and written questions.

b. Ask the students to choose one story each to read aloud to a small group. Encourage the students to discuss what they have learned afterward.

c. Assign each student a story to read and require them to write a report on it. Each student should then present his report based on what he has learned to the class.

d. Have the students read stories aloud to the class, and create mock tests based upon the main ideas which they identify.

13. Ms. Walters wants to help her brand-new group of still-emergent fourth-grade students build comprehension skills. Which of the following exercises would be the best way to quickly gauge the students' current comprehension levels during the first week of class?
    a. Provide the students with instruction-level text to be read independently. Hold an in-class discussion about what happened in the story.
    b. Read a story aloud to the class and then ask each student to draw three pictures representing the beginning, middle and end of the story.
    c. Put students into group or pairs to read the story aloud. Each group then collaborates to answer the story review questions.
    d. Have each student re-tell the story to the class in his own words.

14. Which of the following strategies would not be helpful in building the word-identification skills of emergent readers?
    a. Allowing for invented spelling in written assignments or in class work.
    b. Reinforcing phonemic awareness while reading aloud.
    c. Using dictionaries to look up unfamiliar words.
    d. Studying and reviewing commonly-used sight words at the students' ability level.

15. Mrs. Harris is pleased that her fifth-graders are showing progress in their reading comprehension and writing skills. The students are performing very well on their written tests, evaluations, and homework. After the holiday break, she wants to design lessons that increase the students' literacy skills by incorporating multiple contexts. Which of the following might be the best way to do this?
    a. Read their next book aloud and discuss it in class.
    b. Have the students quiz one another in small groups on the content of their textbooks and other reading assignments.
    c. Read a play in class and allow the students to act it out for their peers following their unit test.
    d. Administer spelling and vocabulary tests orally to determine students' verbal skills.

16. Which of the following would be most useful in assessing and documenting students' language progress throughout a school year?
    a. An audio/video recording of each student reading the same text at the beginning of the year and again at the end of the year
    b. A portfolio including pre-tests, post-tests, vocabulary work, journal entries, writing assignments, group projects and other relevant work from throughout the year
    c. Score composites and details from state- and national-referenced exams or other standardized tests.
    d. A detailed narrative composed by the student's teacher, detailing strengths, weaknesses, and descriptions of the student's work.

17. Valeria is a bright sixth-grader who struggles with reading fluency. She comes from a predominantly Spanish-speaking home and has only lived in the United States for two years. Her teacher plans to use the guided oral reading strategy to help increase Valeria's reading skills. Which of the following would not be a part of this strategy?
    a. Valeria is partnered with another student who is also struggling with language fluency in class.
    b. Valeria's partner reads a given text aloud and then gives her a chance to read the text silently several times.
    c. Valeria reads the text aloud three to four times.
    d. Valeria's partner gives encouragement and feedback.

18. Mr. Waleran requires his students of all ability levels to write freely in their journals twice a week. While students are encouraged to use proper spelling and mechanics as much as possible, the purpose behind this activity is to encourage students to express themselves through writing without concern for grading parameters. How should he adapt this activity for Dimitri, who has several academic delays that keep him from reading and writing in legible or coherent ways?

    a. Allow Dimitri to dictate his thoughts to another student or teacher who will then record them into his journal in writing.

    b. Encourage Dimitri to draw pictures in his journal that represent his thoughts, and encourage him to use the words he knows to label or describe the pictures.

    c. Tell Dimitri to keep an audio journal at home, using a personal tape recorder.

    d. Require Dimitri to attempt to write in complete sentences as much as he can, and then edit the journal together for spelling and mechanical errors.

19. A teacher reads to her students at least once a week. This month, she plans to read poetry to her class. The students will then discuss what they have heard for the rest of each class period. What is this teacher's most likely purpose in designing these lessons?

    a. To give students a break from extensive reading requirements.

    b. To build phonological awareness, specifically of rhyming words.

    c. To teach students that there is more to literature than prose.

    d. To increase students' listening skills while exposing them to new kinds of literature.

20. Mrs. Taylor is working with a diverse group of fifth-graders. She introduces a lesson and project that students can work on once they have finished their regular class work. Students may visit a section of the classroom where they can listen to a lesson via headphones on ancient Egyptian hieroglyphics and look at various library books on the subject. Students are then expected to create their own hieroglyphics that they can use to tell a short story. Which of the following skills is not built with this project?

    a. Understanding of various kinds of written expression, including non-alphabetic languages.

    b. Building multi-cultural awareness that will increase understanding between students of different backgrounds.

    c. Reading for purposes of information or new knowledge (i.e. 'reading to learn').

    d. Exposure to various media to build literacy skills across all levels of reading ability.

21. Each week, a teacher asks one student to bring in a recording of his favorite song and a written version of the lyrics. The students listen to the song and receive a copy of the lyrics. They discuss these words as either one large group or in small groups. What are these students probably learning from this exercise?

    a. Students are learning about the lives of their peers indirectly by listening to each student's favorite song; they can begin to understand each other by the meaning behind the song lyrics.

    b. Students are learning that they are very diverse in many ways: they have different musical tastes and prefer many different styles of music and expression.

    c. Students are learning that it is very difficult to communicate freely when bound by various musical traits such as rhyming, rhythm, and phrasing.

    d. Students are learning that literacy skills do not just pertain to schoolwork. These skills allow students to understand and communicate meanings through a variety of ways, including music and lyrics.

22. A teacher notices that one of her students is inconsistent with recalling his letter-sounds. He may remember a particular sound or blend one day and read it correctly; however, the next day, he may not be able to produce the same sound. What should she do?

a. Immediately refer the student to the appropriate professional for educational testing since it is likely that he is exhibiting early signs of a learning difference or disability.

b. Recognize that children all learn at different rates and that learning and producing letter-sounds involve multiple mental processes. Give the student as much time as he needs to internalize the sounds and produce them correctly.

c. Provide the student with targeted instruction in letter-sound correspondence, using a schema such as Alphabet Action, in which letter-sounds are associated with physical actions (e.g., C is for Catch). Set a time frame after which, if the student does not improve, to begin the procedure for special-needs testing.

d. Hold a conference with the child's parents and encourage them to seek outside tutoring or professional assistance with his reading skills.

23. Mrs. Bundy has three groups of students in her fifth-grade English class: those who want to answer every question, those who only speak when spoken to, and those who never speak at all. She is making plans for upcoming lessons and thinks about the last group of children who never speak up in class. What is important for Mrs. Bundy to know and do with respect to these students?

a. Know that some students are simply quiet and do not feel comfortable speaking up in class. As long as the children are completing their work accurately, do not be concerned about them.

b. Speak with those students after or before class. Let them know how important it is to express themselves in class, because that is part of what building literacy is all about.

c. Make a point to speak directly to those students who talk less in class. Limit the amount of time the more verbal students can speak in class and require the quieter students to answer more direct questions and prompts.

d. Place students who don't speak up in class together for group work. Make a point to spend time with those groups to give guidance and encouragement as they express their ideas verbally.

24. Some of the students in Mr. Smith's fourth-grade class cannot <u>decode</u> words well enough to read fluently in class. He knows they are well behind grade level and that he needs to provide them with activities that will allow them to be successful, building skills and confidence at the same time. Which activity would be best for this purpose?

a. Enlist the parents' help by sending home a weekly list of sight words that the students can practice and memorize, decreasing the need to decode when they read.

b. Show the students how to create words out of movable alphabet tiles or magnetic letters, building (encoding) words as they sound them out.

c. Provide the children with early childhood readers that contain only very simple words so that the children will not feel badly as they read.

d. Allow those children having trouble to stop each time they reach a challenging word and sound it out carefully, recording it to a list that will be studied for homework.

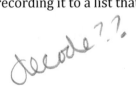

25. Which of the following statements is true regarding the relationship of reading fluency to reading comprehension?
    a. Reading fluency and reading comprehension should be considered separate, equally valuable skills that can be taught independently of one another.
    b. Reading comprehension is an important component of achieving a level of overall reading fluency.
    c. Reading fluency refers to a set of skills that should be continually improved upon, so that students can consistently comprehend that which they read.
    d. Reading comprehension and reading fluency are so intertwined that a child struggling in one area is often incapable of making progress in the other.

26. Abi, a fifth-grader, is reading aloud to his teacher during one-on-one reading time. His teacher uses this time to evaluate ongoing fluency and comprehension skills. Following today's reading, Abi's teacher determines that he needs practice with words that begin with digraphs. Which of the following sets of words would most likely be part of this assignment?
    a. Chicken, Shells, That
    b. Were, Frame, Click
    c. Sponge, Think, Blank
    d. Packed, Blistered, Smoothed

27. Which of the following generally would not be expected of an eighth-grader?
    a. Identify grade-level vocabulary words and be able to decode their roots, prefixes, and suffixes, as well as non-English words that are commonly used in English writing (e.g. phenomenon, charisma, etc.).
    b. Analyze literary works and identify common themes in various pieces of literature.
    c. Understand different points of view in literature (e.g. omniscient, subjective)
    d. Explain how media messages are reflective of the literature in cultures from which they originate.

Use the following information to answer question 28:

    Susannah wrote the following journal entry on her happiest memory during journal time:

    I lov going on picnics with my mom and dad. We et sandwitches and lemanad and somtyms mom and dad drink coffee. we play gams and haf fun.

28. Which of the following reading skills might be most helpful for Susannah?
    a. Decoding work focusing on silent ending phonemes.
    b. Sight word drills and practice.
    c. Reading aloud to a partner who gives constructive feedback.
    d. More spelling practice using original sentences.

29. A teacher writes four sentences on the board and instructs his students to copy the sentences from the board into their notebooks. They must underline words with prefixes and capitalize those with suffixes. Words with prefixes and suffixes though be underlined and capitalized. Which sentence is correct?

    a. The PRINCE declared his undying love for the PRINCESS.
    b. Add two cups of PRECOOKED chicken to the soup.
    c. This loud, loud noise is very DISPLEASING.
    d. The bookkeeper examined every page of the rare play.

30. Which of the following computer activities/games would be most beneficial during media time for students who are working on reading fluency?

    a. Students can select from a variety of high-interest texts and read aloud what they see on the screen.
    b. Students hear high-frequency sight and vocabulary words in their headphones and get points for "zapping" (clicking) the correct matching word on their screen.
    c. Students practice typing in a keyboarding program to build their speed and accuracy in writing reports and papers.
    d. Students can surf a limited and pre-approved number of internet sites to read on subjects of their choosing.

31. A teacher is fortunate to have many parent volunteers for the current school year, giving him parental help at least three times a week. He wants to utilize these volunteers in a way that will not only take into account their limited training, but will most benefit students. Which option should he choose?

    a. Ask each parent to speak to the class about what kinds of literacy skills they use each day in their careers.
    b. Enlist parents to help grade papers and presentations using a rubric.
    c. Ask parents to listen to his students read challenging but manageable texts, one at a time, helping students identify and sound out unfamiliar words.
    d. Primarily utilize parents' for non-instructional tasks, such as making copies, organizing the class library, monitoring the classroom during test time, etc.

32. Which of the following aspects of oral reading is the most important accompaniment to speed and accuracy?

    a. Vocal expression based on punctuation and content.
    b. Volume of the reader's/speaker's voice.
    c. Interest level of the text to be read aloud.
    d. Consistently increasing the number of words read aloud per minute.

33. Which of the following activities is widely used in building students' reading fluency?

    a. Sole focus on phonetic instruction.
    b. Repeated oral readings combined with feedback.
    c. Participation in vocabulary-building activities.
    d. Utilizing speed-reading techniques often used in adult literacy courses.

34. In monitoring a group of elementary-age students' reading fluency, which of the following students may need extra or specialized instruction?

a. A student who reads an unfamiliar text more slowly than he reads a familiar text.

b. A student reading an independent-level text, finding approximately 1 in 25 words difficult to read.

c. A student reading an instructional-level text, finding approximately 1 in 5 words difficult to read.

d. A student who scores a 70% on a comprehension test.

35. Which of the following reading assignments would be most appropriate as a context for teaching students how to preview information to improve comprehension?

a. A written version of a popular movie that most of the students have seen outside of class.

b. A reading assignment from the students' science class that they will be tested on next month.

c. A novel the students read in English class last year.

d. A set of poems that will be studied next month during Poetry Week.

36. A sixth-grade teacher is preparing to begin a unit in which students will be reading a novel in class. She plans to use the novel to teach her students specific strategies to improve and monitor their reading comprehension. Which of the following techniques would likely be taught during class?

a. Discuss story elements such as exposition, climax and resolution.

b. Demonstrate the practice of stopping at the end of chapters to summarize and review the content.

c. Ask students to complete a review sheet before taking the unit test.

d. Practice decoding unfamiliar words throughout the book by using knowledge of frequently-used root words.

37. A teacher notices that her new student, Carl, has a hard time answering questions related to comprehension during class and has scored low on comprehension quizzes and worksheets. What would be the most logical first step in determining how to help Carl?

a. Encourage Carl to read all assigned texts at least twice before class to help him understand what he has read.

b. Provide Carl with story maps of what he will be reading to assist his comprehension visually.

c. Ask Carl to read aloud with his teacher individually so that she can ensure that he is reading with expected accuracy and speed (i.e., fluently).

d. Modify Carl's class work so that he is able to work on easier comprehension material until his skills are brought up to speed.

38. Which of the following would be the best strategy for helping eighth-grade students choose books that they will read independently and use to write book reports?

a. Provide two choices from which the students can pick that you know everybody can understand.

b. Allow students to freely pick their books, but require that they read a few pages aloud to you in order to ensure that the reading level is neither too easy nor too difficult based on their abilities.

c. Encourage the students to read a book that contains unfamiliar words and idioms so that they will be challenged to use context clues, dictionaries and other sources to build comprehension.

d. Establish no parameters on book selection to encourage free choice and promote students' excitement about the project.

39. Which of the following students is not performing "at grade level" and may warrant academic support or testing?

a. Karishma, seventh grade, looks panicked and becomes very quiet when asked to state her opinion about a particular subject in class discussions and rarely raises her hand when a question about text comprehension is posed.

b. Lynne, fifth grade, is able to comprehend most of what she reads in plays and in fiction, but sometimes has trouble understanding poetry.

c. Barron, sixth grade, can read fluently aloud and often recall concrete facts, but is rarely able to draw conclusions, make inferences, or understand figurative language.

d. Sebastien, eighth grade, lacks motivation to read much of what is assigned in class and frequently fails to complete his homework; he often contributes intelligently to class discussions.

Use the following information to answer questions 40 and 41:

> Autumn must be the most enchanting season of all. The wind takes on a _____ chill that, when inhaled, _____ with the scent of _____ wood to lightly and_____singe your throat! Statuesque _____ seem to erupt into _____ blooms of colors seen _____ no other time, except _____ inside boxes of children's _____. For many people, the _____of camping, cookouts, sports, _____school creates warm, tingling _____ of security as the _____ slowly turns from Summer _____Fall. There is no other day in the year like the first day of Autumn.

40. The passage above is an example of what kind of reading comprehension assessment?

a. Vocabulary Memorization Test
b. Cloze Individual Assessment
c. Student Response Form
d. Figurative Language Assessment

41. In determining his students' reading comprehension levels, a teacher uses the above passage. He finds that about half of Anne's answers make sense in the blanks. Which answer choice describes the level at which Anne is reading the text?

a. instructional level
b. independent level
c. frustration level
d. novice level

42. Which of the following practices would assist students in constructing meaning from a fictional text written long before the students were born?

a. After the text is read for homework, students discuss any aspects of the story that they did not understand or that were unfamiliar to them.

b. Students individually visualize scenery and events in the text as they read.

c. The class makes a list of unfamiliar words in the text and looks them up in the dictionary as the text is read.

d. Before the text is assigned, students learn about pertinent historical events or aspects of culture that informed the writing of the text.

43. Which of the following strategies would be most appropriate for increasing comprehension before reading a chapter book without pictures?
    a. Previewing the chapter titles and identifying questions that would be answered by reading.
    b. Predicting the ending of the story after reading the introduction and first chapter of the book.
    c. Discussing what the students have heard from other individuals about the story.
    d. Researching and reading book reviews to get an idea of what experts have said about the story.

44. Which of these sets of factors would most greatly affect a student's reading comprehension in class and on tests?
    a. Oral language development, written language development and eating a healthy breakfast.
    b. Word analysis skills, sight word knowledge and ability to monitor understanding.
    c. Vocabulary development, sight word knowledge and reference skills.
    d. Prior knowledge, good classroom participation and academic performance in other subjects.

45. A teacher assigns a project in which students must compare excerpts from the Charles Dickens novel they are reading in class and an article from the week's newspaper. The teacher has chosen a specific passage from the novel. The students can choose the newspaper excerpts, as long as they are of similar lengths. The students must then write a short essay comparing the two. What is this teacher hoping to show her students?
    a. That Dickens' writing style is journalistic and that he informed much of what is considered to be current journalistic philosophy.
    b. That there are links between the students' lives and what they read in class; the relationships are there if they make an effort to see them.
    c. That you can compare even two unlike things.
    d. That there are distinct differences between the way meaning is constructed in daily life and in literature; different processes must be applied.

46. A seventh-grade teacher wants to encourage her students to read more for pleasure. She knows that the students' comprehension, vocabulary and writing skills will also be improved by reading more frequently. What is the best way to increase the amount of time students spend reading for pleasure?
    a. Assign "extra-credit" in which students can write a book report on a favorite book they read as a child.
    b. Increase the number of books and poems included in each unit of study.
    c. Ask the students to read a text of their choosing (e.g., a magazine, comic book, internet source, novel) each week and present to the class what they enjoyed about it.
    d. Have each student make a list of books they would like to read someday and then create a timeline for when they want to complete each one.

47. Students in Mr. Carmen's class receive a list of words each month that make up their spelling and vocabulary work. They are expected to write the words in original sentences to help them remember spellings and meanings of each one. Mr. Carmen also, however, wants to build the students' vocabulary using indirect learning styles. Which of the following would not contribute to learning vocabulary indirectly?
    a. Assigning more complex "bonus words" each month that can be written and defined for extra credit.
    b. Expecting students to read a weekly newspaper.
    c. Watching an instructional-level video in class and discussing any unknown words.
    d. Asking students to complete a series of short interviews with adults in their lives.

- 147 -

48. Which of the following vocabulary activities would best prepare students for a unit on imagery and figurative language?
a. A class discussion on the difference between literal and inferential comprehension.
b. A worksheet on synonyms and antonyms.
c. A set of word games (e.g., crosswords, word searches) involving adjectives and adverbs.
d. A vocabulary quiz

Use the following information to answer questions 49 and 50:
A class considers the paragraph below:

Sarah and Kelly grinned at one another conspiratorially as they approached Dad, who was quietly reading his paper in the living room. "Dad, we'd like to ride our bikes down to Emil's house today," giggled Kelly. She glanced at her sister and shifted her weight from foot to foot. Dad appeared to think this over for a moment and replied, "Sure, that's fine with me!" The girls scampered to get their bikes and were soon on their way. With the children gone, Dad noticed how peaceful and quiet the house sounded. His reverie was quickly interrupted as he heard Mom calling from upstairs, "okay, everybody, I told you at breakfast that I need as much help as I can get to help me give the dog a bath, clean the house and finish the laundry today!" Dad groaned, knowing that he had been conned!

49. Which method would be best for helping students determine the meaning of the word "reverie" in the next to last sentence?
a. Using context clues
b. Making an educated guess
c. Decoding the prefix, root, and suffix of the word
d. Previewing and reviewing

50. Which of the following questions, when assigned as an in-class writing topic, would allow the teacher to monitor the children's inferential comprehension?
a. What do you think the girls plan to do at Emil's once they arrive?
b. What does it mean to say that Dad had been "conned?"
c. Why is it important for everyone to help Mom with the chores?
d. What did Dad enjoy so much while he was reading?

51. Which of the following choices shows the correct type of text matched with an appropriate strategy for increasing reading comprehension?
a. Popular magazine: critical analysis/deconstruction
b. Literary novel: key concept synthesis
c. Persuasive essay: journaling over time, recording personal thoughts about the reading
d. Chapter from science textbook: text outlining with vocabulary and main ideas

52. Students in an eighth grade class examine this vocabulary list on Monday. Which literary genre is likely to be introduced this week?

Vocabulary:
Narrative
Heroism
Ancient
Martyr
Duality
Supernatural
Deity
Culture

    a. Historical Fiction
    b. Poetry
    c. Mythology
    d. Drama

53. Which question below applies most closely to data analysis skills for Mrs. Layton's fifth-graders?

Our Hobbies	
Reading	8
Soccer	4
Dance	3
Art	10
Music	9
Video Games	2

    a. How many students in all reported their hobbies in this chart?
    b. Which of these hobbies is the best use of time for students?
    c. What kind of activities do the students enjoy most: physical or artistic?
    d. What is the numeric difference between the most popular and least popular hobby?

54. Which of the following practices is the best use of technology to increase reading comprehension and literacy skills?
    a. Encourage the use of tape recorders in class, by which students can record classroom conversations and lessons to be reviewed during homework and study time.
    b. Accessing a specific website online that shows children how to use graphic organizers for the stories and texts which they are reading in class.
    c. Allowing students who have completed their class work to play games or spend monitored time online.
    d. Asking students to read articles on various comprehension skills and provide a post-test to measure how well they can apply specific skills.

55. Which of the following approaches would be best for scaffolding students' peer interactions regarding classroom and independent reading?

    a. Incorporating debates into class time in which students are assigned an argument and must debate its merits with another student.

    b. Encourage students to form book groups outside of the classroom in which they select and discuss books of interest.

    c. Free discussion across the entire classroom in which students raise their hands to share thoughts and are called upon by the teacher.

    d. Dividing students into small groups of three or four and discussing comprehension/opinion questions, monitored by the teacher.

Use the following information to answer question 56:
Look at an excerpt from the worksheet assigned to a group of sixth graders.

    Match the numbers to the corresponding letter.

    1. Victor spends about an hour every day helping his grandmother around the house.
    2. Stella is always quick to smile and talk with new students at school.
    3. Jorge did not read the directions that came with his brand new telescope.
    4. Faye has been enjoying the weekend art classes she just began.

    ___ a. He does not see or learn as much as he could.
    ___ b. They have grown much closer and have a stronger relationship.
    ___ c. She has begun to teach her little sister some of the things she has learned.
    ___ d. She is well-respected among all the students.

56. What particular skill does this set of questions address?

    a. Distinguishing fact from opinion

    b. Relationship of main and supporting ideas

    c. Understanding cause and effect

    d. Sequencing in a story

57. Mr. Garson's sixth-grade class is working on a creative writing assignment in which they imagine themselves living a "day in the life" of a person from another country. This project is intended to help his students understand different points of view. Mr. Garson is surprised that Kim, who moved to Houston from China last year, is struggling to complete the assignment. She is composing very slowly compared to her classmates. How should he help Kim?

    a. Allow Kim to write freely in her first language and then ask her English as a Second Language teacher help her translate the assignment into English.

    b. Suggest that Kim simply write about a day in her own life, since she probably understands the lives of those different from her.

    c. Allow Kim to choose another topic that she is more comfortable with to write creatively about.

    d. Pair Kim with another English-language learner to assist her with completing the assignment.

58. Ms. Carroll teaches Social Studies to sixth- and seventh-grade students. She recently assigned a written report for homework. Many of the students turned in reports that were difficult to read due to phonetic and incorrect spelling. When Ms. Carroll speaks with the Language Arts teachers on her team, they tell her that the same students typically achieve very high scores on their spelling tests. Students are given a word list at the beginning of each week to be studied, and then tested on some of the words each week (the teacher reads words aloud to be recorded on an answer sheet). Which of the following is most likely to be the reason for discrepancy in spelling skills between tests and assignments?

    a. When they must concentrate on other grammar and writing skills, the students forget what they have learned for their spelling tests.

    b. The students' handwriting skills are poor, leading to unclear words and inadvertent spelling mistakes.

    c. The students have determined a way to cheat on spelling tests, knowing exactly which words to study beforehand, and do not learn the entire list.

    d. The students memorize only specific words for the week; they have not had the opportunity to develop their spelling skills within the context of writing assignments.

59. What might be the best method for informally assessing students' writing development and skills?

    a. Create a rule that mistakes on class work can always be corrected for extra credit.

    b. Make time for journaling in class during which students can write freely without being graded on mechanics, spelling, or structure.

    c. Create a class website upon which students can write content and post comments to one another.

    d. Occasionally ask the students' other teachers how they are doing with writing assignments.

Use the following information to answer questions 60 and 61:

    Dear Grandma,

    Hello, how are you doing? How are grandpa and Daisy? Daisy is such a cute Dog she is growing up really fast. I just started Middle School last month, I stay late on Tusdays and Thursdays so I can practice with the Team and go to meetings. I wasn't too sure how it would work out for me when I started. there is a lot more homework and lots of new, older kids. but I am starting to get used to the homework and have met some cool, new friends. I am really looking forward to visting you and grandpa during Thanksgiving. I also joined the soccer team and the drama club. thank you so much for the art set you sent me for my birthday. I have already used it to do some skeches and some sculpting! Please make the Pumpkin Pie that I like so much! Okay, that's about all I have to say right now. Write me back if you can I'll see you soon!

    Love, Chris

60. A sixth-grade class is instructed to write letters to family members describing daily life that will be sent out via the post office. The teacher notices several writing errors that are common across the writing samples. If this letter is a primary example of these writing errors, which set is most salient?

    a. Organization of ideas, capitalization and punctuation

    b. Contractions, punctuation, and writing style

    c. Capitalization, spelling and use of passive voice

    d. Writing style, organization of ideas, and use of active voice

61. Which lesson would not be helpful in addressing the primary issues in the students' writing?
    a. Direct instruction on organizing ideas.
    b. Practice with peer-editing for punctuation and capitalization errors.
    c. Correcting sentences that incorrectly use passive voice.
    d. Review of commonly-made spelling and capitalization mistakes.

62. Ms. Trent plans to create a rubric that will help her grade her middle-schoolers' writing samples. She wants to make sure that she is consistent across time and between various students who write with different styles. Which of the following would be most important for her to do in order to help build her students' writing skills?
    a. Be sure to include every possible aspect of the writing process so that no detail is left out, as different students have different strengths.
    b. Share the rubric with students so that they can monitor their own understanding of the writing process as they complete their assignments.
    c. Use clear, simple language so that there is no confusion at a later date about what was intended.
    d. Divide each segment of the rubric into its own category and assign equal point values—the purpose of which will be to help students understand that each aspect of the writing process is of equal value.

63. All of the following approaches are important for building students' writing skills in conjunction with one another, except:
    a. Discussing the various purposes for writing, including self-expression, narration, story-telling, persuasion and explanation.
    b. Exercises and activities that isolate and build students' writing skills, including grammar, spelling, mechanics, etc.
    c. Creating multiple and various opportunities for students to feel more at ease with the process, diminishing fear or discomfort with it.
    d. Maintaining a sequential approach to teaching writing, allowing all students to excel at one level or in one context before moving on to another.

64. What is the primary grammatical problem with this student's paragraph?

> Each of the kids in our class love to play games. Our favorite game, Hide and Go Seek, are fun and easy to play anywhere you go. The people in our class really enjoys getting to spend time with friends.

    a. punctuation
    b. subject-verb agreement
    c. word choice
    d. split infinitives

Consider the following scenario to answer question 65:

> A teacher provides some guidelines for her students who are having trouble with the Revision step of the writing process:
>
> Take your time
> Read very carefully, line by line
> Use the proper symbols for specific revisions

65. What should she add to this list for students who are struggling with writing?
    a. If you find a mistake, re-write the whole sentence again.
    b. Ask a family member or friend to read your writing and suggest any revisions you ought to make.
    c. Read the paper once to correct only one convention at a time; re-reading multiple times helps eliminate mistakes.
    d. Write your paper carefully the first time around so that you do not have to spend much time in revision.

66. What activity would be most helpful to the students in the Revision step of the writing process?
    a. Provide extra direct instruction or lectures in the specific areas with which the students are struggling.
    b. Correct the students' writing and then require them to re-write their original pieces using proper grammar, spelling, etc.
    c. Place the students into pairs and have them correct each other's essays or papers to vary instruction and alleviate aversion to revision.
    d. Pull sentences from older students' writing and project it on the overhead. Use these samples to guide students in correcting them as a group.

67. All of the following are standard expectations of a child upon entering sixth grade (middle school), except for one. Which one is not a standard expectation of a child entering sixth grade?
    a. Identify and correctly spell words that are known as "commonly misspelled words," such as their/they're/there. ← 7 – 8th
    b. Identify various points of view in a text, including first-person, third-person, etc.
    c. Compose poetry employing techniques such as figurative language, alliteration, onomatopoeia, etc.
    d. Understands the meanings and uses of various parts of speech in reading and writing: verbs, nouns, adjectives, pronouns, conjunctions, adverbs, prepositions, etc.

68. For students who have access to word processors in class, which phase of the writing process would be most appropriate to require the use of pencil and paper?
    a. Prewriting
    b. Drafting
    c. Publishing
    d. Presenting

Use the following information to answer questions 69 and 70:

> The following conversation took place after class as a sixth-grade teacher handed Alex his most recent book report.
>
> Mrs. Blaine: "Alex, I think you did an excellent job on the first part of your book report. You really picked up on a lot of the details in the plot—what a great memory you have! But what about the second part of the assignment? I didn't see anything about whether or not you liked the book with reasons for your opinion?"
> Alex: "Yea…I just wasn't really sure what to write on that part, so I left it blank."
> Mrs. Blaine: "Can you tell me now how you felt about the book?"
> Alex: "It was alright, I guess. It was pretty good. It was boring at first, but I liked the way it ended."
> Mrs. Blaine: "And why is that?"

Alex: "It was cool how the burglar was someone you knew all along; the author gave you clues and stuff throughout the story and you could try to solve the mystery while you were reading it."

Mrs. Blaine: "I understand. I liked that part of the story, too. Getting started on work like this can be challenging at first. But it is important that you begin to learn this skill because you will use it over and over again in school and in your eventual career. Let's talk about some ways to help you get going."

Alex: "Okay...sounds good."

69. What skill is Mrs. Blaine referring to in the underlined sentence?
    a. Understanding his feelings.
    b. Completing assignments thoroughly without leaving any information out.
    c. Stating an opinion or thesis and supplying supporting evidence.
    d. Writing even when you are unsure about the topic or instructions.

70. What would be the best way for Mrs. Blaine to help Alex build his skills in this area?
    a. Have Alex write his opinions and each supporting idea on paper plates or pieces of cardstock and show him how to move them around and arrange them in logical order on a large table or the floor.
    b. Have Alex explain his opinions and supporting ideas to her while she writes them down for him; he can then re-write them into the body of his report.
    c. Have Alex participate in extra lessons that let him explore his feelings about or reactions to various media, including books.
    d. Have Alex review each assignment with her before he turns it in to ensure that he has not left anything out.

71. Mr. Benton is in the process of grading the first writing assignments of the year for his eighth-grade students. He is a bit overwhelmed at the volume of errors in grammar, usage and overall composition he finds in almost every student's writing. Mr. Benton wants to use a systematic approach to building his students' writing skills, beginning by giving the students a clear and simple method to apply to their work. His goal is that the students can take part in analyzing and monitoring their own progress. What should he do?
    a. Show his students an outline of the six common writing traits and ask the students to evaluate their own skills within each trait. Teacher and student can use this evaluation to establish a plan for working on the skills that need the most help.
    b. Assign each student a writing buddy. The students can meet during writing assignments to edit one another's work. They can then separate to make the suggested revisions.
    c. Encourage the students to grade their own work using a rubric provided to them. Meet with the student to determine where they believe they need the most help and focus class work around those areas.
    d. Teach the students that most writing assignments can be composed using the five-paragraph essay model. Invest class time and homework in perfecting the model that includes thesis, evidence, and conclusions.

The following scenario is used to answer question 72:

Mrs. Matson's 6th graders are chatting during snack time and she overhears the following conversation:

Ellie: I hate how my mom always asks me how my day was, every single day! And then she gets mad when I say it's fine. But it really IS fine almost every day!

Brynn: Oh, I know! My dad always wants to know what my reading is about, but sometimes I just don't feel like talking about it. It takes long enough to read it without talking about it.

Jon: You have it easy. My mom AND dad help me with my homework every night, and then they give me extra work to do!

72. Mrs. Matson would like to not only give students a chance to voice their feelings about the changing communications with their parents, but also help them find a way to channel those feelings into something positive. Which project would be best for allowing students a positive way to communicate with their parents about what is happening in school?

   a. Encourage the students to talk to their parents about everything that is happening in school; after all, their parents only want to help them.
   b. After talking about this issue, ask the students to write short pieces about their schoolwork and experiences during the day and compile them into a newsletter to be sent home every two weeks.
   c. Help the students write letters to their parents, telling them how they feel about the issue
   d. Tell students to keep a log of their activities in the classroom and throughout the day to be shown to parents on a daily or weekly basis.

Use the following scenario to answer question 73:

A middle-school teacher has written several questions on the chalk board to assist students in revising their most recent essays.

   Do you know the meanings of all the vocabulary in your essay?
   Did you use any major words (besides articles like a, an, and, the) more than three times?
   Do you like the way your writing sounds when you read it aloud?
   Does all the language used make sense?

73. Judging by the questions above, which writing trait is this teacher encouraging her students to work on today?

   a. sentence fluency
   b. ideas and development
   c. writing conventions
   d. word choice

Read the persuasive writing excerpt below to answer question 74:

"Why Peace is Important"

Peace is important to our lives. We have to have peace because we can't be fighting all the time. When people fight, they can't do anything else. It also makes everybody else feel upset and angry because they have to listen to the fighting. If you want to have peace you can talk to the person and try to get them to agree with you and say you are sorry if you do something wrong.

74. How could a teacher help this student develop his persuasive writing skills, based on this initial attempt?

a. Continue to give positive reinforcement; this student has a good understanding of the persuasive structure.

b. Introduce the use of a graphic organizer or flow chart to help the student organize his main idea and supporting evidence in a logical way.

c. Encourage the student to include more details in his writing to make it more interesting and more personal.

d. Focus primarily on the editing and revising processes to correct writing conventions, usage, and grammar.

75. A Language teacher is introducing a new writing topic to her class. She asks them to pretend that the person they are writing to or for is "an alien from outer space." What type of writing is she probably introducing?

a. Fantasy/fiction
b. Poetry
c. Persuasive essay
d. How-to article

76. Ms. Burns' fourth-graders are working very hard at building writing skills on many levels. They have come a long way with their knowledge of the six traits of writing, as well as their confidence in their own abilities. Some of the students have trouble finding their own unique "voices" when writing, probably because they are working so hard to maintain accurate grammar, spelling, organization, and continuity of ideas. How can Ms. Burns help the students inject their own personalities and voices into their writing without sacrificing correctness?

a. Explain that they should always be sure to include personal opinions and insights to make the writing interesting.

b. Project overhead examples of good writing that appropriately utilizes personal voice and lead a discussion about them in class.

c. Guide students to select only topics with which they are very knowledgeable and explain that it is never a good idea to write about something that is unfamiliar to them.

d. Teach students to imagine themselves as a new character every time they write--they should write from the point of view of that individual, phrasing things the way that person or character would if they were speaking.

Read the excerpt below to answer question 77:

I like sweets. Cookies, cake and ice cream are very sweet and good. I like to eat these things after school or after I eat. Sweet tastes are the best for me and I do not like salty food. When I eat dessert, I feel so good and happy. My mom says that I should not eat too many sweets or I will get cavities, so I have to brush my teeth after eating them.

77. Which activity would benefit this student's writing skills the most?
   a. Make "word bulletin boards" with the student to help her build vocabulary to make her writing more interesting.
   b. Practice with editing other students' writing to familiarize her with writing conventions.
   c. Grammar exercises, specifically subject-verb agreement.
   d. Encouraging her to select a more challenging writing topic to stretch her skill level.

78. Mr. Talbot's class has an opportunity to begin writing letters to students in France who are learning English, just as Mr. Talbot's class is learning French. He knows that this will be an excellent opportunity for the students to work on letter-writing as well as build their language skills. What other writing skill can he use this opportunity to strengthen in his students?
   a. He can help them work through the five-step writing process and the six traits of writing; letter-writing is an excellent exercise for bringing all of those traits and steps together.
   b. He can teach them the proper formatting of letters and the etiquette of writing a good letter.
   c. He can teach them to consider their audience when writing by talking about what they know of their pen pals' lives, what they would find interesting, and how to communicate effectively with others who are not like themselves.
   d. He can teach his students about the importance of proper writing conventions like punctuation, grammar, and spelling, because their pen pals are still learning English.

79. An eighth-grade teacher assigns an end-of-the-year project for her English students. The students are placed into groups and instructed to make an "ad campaign" that includes a print ad, a television/radio commercial, and a persuasive essay. What is the teacher's most likely primary objective?
   a. To equip students with practical, real-life job experience in a competitive world.
   b. To allow students to apply concepts they have learned about audience, point of view, media messages, etc.
   c. To incorporate the use of technology into a unit of study.
   d. To encourage students to work cooperatively in groups.

80. A sixth-grade teacher begins class by showing a series of inkblot images, one by one, on pieces of cardstock. She asks her students to number their papers from 1-20 and write down what they think each image depicts. After the exercise, she asks for a few volunteers to explain what they saw in each inkblot. What do you think this teacher is attempting to convey?
   a. That visual images can be interpreted differently, depending on the individual viewer.
   b. That cultural symbols are typically universal and are inherent in our cultural mindset.
   c. That psychological differences are often misconstrued as mental illness.
   d. That it is important not to confirm understandings of visual images with peers before determining their meaning.

81. After reading Shakespeare's Romeo and Juliet in class, students watch the most recent Hollywood film version, starring Leonardo DiCaprio. Their teacher leads a class discussion after the film. Which of the following essay topics would be most helpful in challenging students to analyze how visual media affects their perceptions of a piece of literature?

    a. Discuss your favorite character in the film version of Romeo and Juliet, and give at least three reasons to back up your opinion.

    b. Which version of Romeo and Juliet did you like better, and why?

    c. Compare the film with the play and point out at least four instances in which portions of the play were left out of the film version.

    d. Describe the setting of the film and discuss why you think the film's director chose to portray the play in modern times.

Consider the picture below for answering question 82:

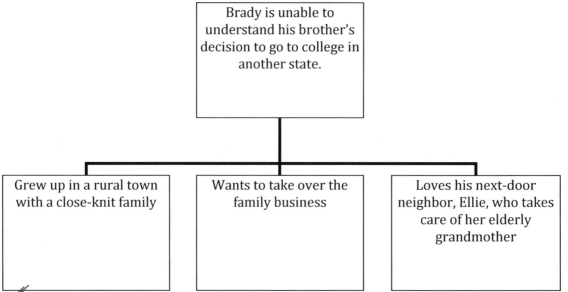

82. Mr. James created a poster featuring this chart to accompany his class instruction for the day. He will be showing students how to organize information into text organizers to help themselves understand what they have read. What other skill might this kind of organizer build as well?

    a. Constructing a paragraph

    b. Answering literature-based multiple-choice questions

    c. Character analysis

    d. Writing conventions

83. Mr. Ank has a game he plans to play with his middle school English students today. He has recorded several commercials from television and will play them without sound for the students. After each silent commercial, the students will share their ideas about what product the commercial is advertising. Following this game, the class will participate in a follow-up discussion and exercise. What is the likely purpose of Mr. Ank's game?

    a. To turn his students into savvy consumers.

    b. To help students understand how visual images affect meaning and understanding.

    c. To demonstrate how students can use visual images in their own schoolwork.

    d. To introduce variation into his instruction and give the kids a fun activity.

Use the drawing below to answer question 84.

84. A teacher plans to use the drawing above to explain story elements. Each point on the line represents an element of the story. Which choice matches the point on the chart with the smiling face above it?
   a. Rising Action
   b. Exposition
   c. Resolution
   d. Climax

85. Mrs. Gilbert, an English teacher, and Ms. Dudley, an Art teacher, are working together to create an integrated unit of study for their common students. The students will be studying King Tut, reading various accounts of his life, both fiction and non-fiction. Ms. Dudley will be guiding the students through various art projects related to the time period in which King Tut lived (e.g., making papyrus). Which choice provides an example of an additional project or lesson that will address visual interpretation and decoding skills?
   a. The students participate in Ancient Egypt Day and can dress up as characters or historical figures from the appropriate time period.
   b. The students visit a local museum exhibit on Ancient Egypt and keep a log of visual images and representations they see. The class discusses those images and their meanings during both classes.
   c. The students write stories about the lives of Ancient Egyptians and draw illustrations to go along with their writing.
   d. The students watch a movie about King Tut and create free-writing pieces based on what they have seen.

86. Mrs. Canas has had a parent offer to visit her fifth-grade class and provide a sign language seminar. The parent is fluent in American Sign Language and would like to offer her skills to benefit the students. Mrs. Canas thinks the seminar will be very interesting and provide a unique way to hone her students' listening and expressive skills. Which choice identifies another language skill set that would indirectly benefit from this seminar?

    a. Students' understanding of how visual messages, including body language, facial expression, and signs inform verbal communication and ideas.
    b. Students' fine motor skills and hand-eye coordination.
    c. Students' respect for other cultures, specifically the non-hearing community.
    d. Students' ability to communicate with other peers and adults in their community.

87. An eighth-grade class will be watching a mystery film in English class over the next two days. Throughout the story, the camera will often focus on objects or clothing that are colored bright red. These objects are always related to clues that lead the character toward solving the mystery. What literary device is the students' teacher planning to introduce in this context?

    a. Media deconstruction
    b. Color imagery
    c. Alliteration
    d. Symbolism

88. Middle school students at Ms. Kelso's school are expected to complete a large independent study project to be presented at the end of the second term. The project is the culmination of reading research, writing a paper, and the final element of publishing, or presentation. The students can choose how they present their work and are instructed to use visual aids. Which of the following would be a helpful guideline for Ms. Kelso to offer her students?

    a. Whenever possible, use pictures, video, music, charts and graphs to supplement your presentation for the purpose of keeping your audience's interest.
    b. Think about any parts of your paper that might be hard to explain. Choose a visual aid to help you show your audience the concept, and then use your words to explain it.
    c. Select the most interesting photographs from your research, create color photocopies, and pass them throughout the class during your presentation.
    d. Use your main ideas and supporting evidence to create a Power-point slideshow, making note-taking and organization simple and clear.

89. Which of the following visual images would be most appropriate for teaching students about how media images influence their perceptions and attitudes?

    a. a photograph found in a journalistic magazine, such as Time
    b. an illustration or diagram found in the students' own Social Studies textbook
    c. a political cartoon found in the newspaper
    d. a non-political cartoon found in another section of the newspaper

Use the following information to answer questions 90 and 91:

A middle school class is working through the process of creating a research project. Since this kind of assignment is completely new, their teacher provides direct instruction and practice assignments to help the students approach the large project.

90. Which of the following approaches would increase a middle-school student's preliminary research skills?
    a. Assign and analyze a research paper on a topic of the student's choosing.
    b. Require students to submit a separate outline before completing a research paper.
    c. Require students to turn in note cards containing relevant information on each source they will use in an upcoming research project. 3D Planner - Note cards 1st
    d. Pre-test on several subjects to determine which area or discipline to explore.

91. What is the first point at which the teacher should meet individually to talk with the student?
    a. After the student first chooses a topic
    b. After the student turns in research note cards
    c. After the student completes the initial outline
    d. After the rough draft has been turned in

92. An eighth-grade teacher notices that her students perform very well on scheduled tests in class, but struggle with pop quizzes or other in-class assignments that involve recalling information. In discussing this issue with other teachers on her team, she finds that this is a pattern across all disciplines. What would be the best way to help students retain information on a daily or weekly basis in the absence of the motivation of an upcoming test?
    a. Devote the first few minutes of class on previewing information and tasks and the last few minutes of each class summarizing highlights from class work and homework reading.
    b. Increase the frequency of pop quizzes in hopes that the students will begin to study at home more often.
    c. Give the students a study guide before each quiz so they know what will be tested.
    d. Allow the students to work on the quizzes in groups so that they can help each other with memory and recall.

Use the following scenario to answer question 93:

Mr. Katz draws these diagrams on the board at the beginning of English class. Janie and Katherine are the two main characters in the book which his class is currently reading.

Janie's Character Traits	Katherine's Character Traits
1. Bossy	1. Kind to others
2.	2.
3.	3.

	Same	Different
Janie	1. 2. 3.	1. 2. 3.
Katherine	1. 2. 3.	1. 2. 3.

93. Based on the above diagram, what concept do you think Mr. Katz plans to teach?
   a. Structural Text Analysis
   b. Compare/Contrast
   c. Inferential Comprehension
   d. Use of Graphic/Text Organizers

94. Mrs. Costanza's eighth-grade students bring up some concerns during class time. They complain that their teachers are assigning too much reading for homework and that they are worried that they will never be able to retain the information for tests. Some students say that they don't know how to predict what information is important and what is not. What can Mrs. Costanza do to help them?
   a. Encourage students to allow enough time when studying to effectively memorize all the necessary information in the texts and assigned readings.
   b. Teach the students the SQ3R (Survey, Question, Read, Recite/Write, and Review) method.
   c. Ask other eighth-grade teachers to provide study guides that will outline exactly what will be on each test.
   d. Discuss the importance of taking detailed notes in class and asking relevant questions during class discussions.

95. Ana Velasquez's eighth-grade class at Jones Middle School is beginning a unit in which they will be expected to complete a research project. They will choose from a list of topics and then write a report. Each student is required to have a bibliography that includes at least one entry each from the following sources: the internet, library books, newspaper articles, and magazine articles. Which of the following topics would be the best choice for Ana?
   a. Day in the Life of the Velasquez family
   b. Hurricane Katrina
   c. The History of Jones High School
   d. How to get your homework done faster!

Use the following information to answer questions 96 and 97:

   A teacher is talking with her students about the best way to retain information learned during a unit or course of study. She wants them to be prepared for high school and college, during which they will rely primarily on their class notes to study for tests and prepare papers. She describes these steps:

   1. Read all assigned material before class. Make notes on any new vocabulary, questions or ideas you have as you read.
   2. Take notes in class based on discussions and lectures.
   3. Before the test, review your notes and assigned readings, spending more time on those segments which you remember the least.

96. In step #2, the teacher shows her students how to divide their note pages in half, using one side of the paper for main ideas or questions, and the other side for details relating to those larger concepts. What is the likely purpose of her demonstration?

    a. To help students understand cause and effect relationships, which will assist them in other disciplines such as History and Science.

    b. To emphasize the difference between main ideas and details. This emphasis will support an upcoming lesson on constructing a five-paragraph essay with a main idea and supporting evidence.

    c. To help students be more orderly and write neatly when it comes to taking notes, which will in turn make studying for tests and papers much easier.

    d. To show students how they can begin to organize their information and understanding about a subject as they take notes, constructing meaning from a large amount of information.

97. What step should be included at #3 to supplement her instruction?

    a. Meet with a partner for any information you failed to write down during class.

    b. Take an audio recorder with you in order to record everything discussed in lectures and class.

    c. Review your notes periodically; at least once a week.

    d. Read all assigned material at least once more in its entirety.

98. An eighth-grade teacher plans to deliver a test on a book recently read and discussed in class. He plans to include some short answers, multiple choice, fill-in-the-blanks, and 2-3 essay questions. The students are familiar with multiple-choice and fill-ins, but are not accustomed to short answers and essays. He wants to scaffold their attempts to study the large amount of material. What should he do?

    a. Make the test "open-notes."

    b. Provide a copy of the questions ahead of time so that the students can formulate their answers.

    c. Provide several sessions of written practice and instruction with similar short-answer and essay questions, and discuss the students' answers afterward.

    d. Allow the students to re-take the test if they struggle the first time around.

99. Sully is struggling to write his eighth-grade research report. His writing is full of great ideas and generalizations, but few supporting details and little evidence. When his teacher suggests that he needs to provide more supporting information, he looks blankly at her. How can she help him understand this concept and improve his paper?

 a. Tell Sully that his writing topic is too broad, and ask him some guiding questions to narrow it down. These questions could include: "what is most important to you about this subject?" and "what do you most want your readers to learn about?"

 b. As much as it will be frustrating for Sully, explain to him that sometimes it is easiest to start from scratch when a paper does not fit the appropriate format. Instruct him to use his previous paper to make a new outline for a new paper. Help him make the outline in great detail and then encourage him to simply use his previous paper as a source for details when writing the newer version.

 c. Use a graphic organizer that contains two columns: "ideas" and "details/evidence." Guide Sully to pick his top three or four main ideas and fill in the right hand side with appropriate details and information. Encourage him to use this exercise to revise his paper by adding in his evidence and eliminating any information that is not listed on his graphic organizer.

 d. Help him brainstorm a list of facts about his topic from memory and his research. Show Sully how to take his ideas one by one, adding at least two facts or details after each idea. Instruct him to make sure that each idea has supporting evidence and details.

100. Mrs. Bray's students have been performing poorly on in-class quizzes, lately. She gives them notice that there will be quizzes in class, although she does not tell them when they will take place. How can she help improve the students' performance without giving them direct insight about the quiz dates or material?

 a. Provide more opportunities for taking tests and quizzes in order to lower anxiety and increase familiarity with the format.

 b. Talk with the students about how they are preparing for quizzes and suggest alternatives that match the intended outcomes of the quiz.

 c. When covering potential quiz information emphasize and indirectly communicate that students should pay close attention.

 d. Send a note home to parents asking them to study with their children in anticipation of the quizzes.

Answers and Explanations

1. C: Oral language skills can be distinguished from specific speech characteristics exhibited by some children. Many students like Rosa, whose first language is not English, will speak with an accent and may be less clear when speaking about a topic that is unfamiliar. In fact, even those who are not English Language Learners may exhibit difficulty speaking on new topics. Greer may avoid oral assignments or speaking in class for a number of reasons, such as self-consciousness. This student could be helped by evaluating oral language skills in a one-on-one environment or by introducing peer scaffolding to help reduce anxiety. Brett's demeanor in group assignments may also be due to social characteristics rather than oral skills; it would be important to evaluate his skills in various contexts. Ashley, however, shows marked problems communicating orally both in class discussion and in prepared assignments. She would benefit from specific instruction related to presenting ideas orally.

2. D: Choice "a" would be appropriate for class work or homework, but is less likely than other choices to provide a deep understanding of the relationships between oral and spoken word. Choice "b" would address multicultural interest, but would not require interpretation since only recitation is assigned. Choice "c" could allow students to learn more about their classmates' backgrounds, but would require more specific parameters to ensure that both the multicultural and oral learning outcomes were achieved. Choice "c" also does not address the assumption that the classmates' family backgrounds are diverse, which may not be the case. Choice "d" requires students to use their research skills to learn more about another culture. By assigning a first-person narrative, Mr. Callas encourages the students to imagine life from the perspective of another person. This assignment also requires the student to make the transition from research to written assignment to spoken word.

3. C: Each answer can be an effective tool in teaching students to build oral language skills. The question makes clear that the objective is to help students evaluate their own oral language skills, which will assist them in both spoken and written assignments. The only answer choice that involves the student himself evaluating his message is answer "c." When the student prepares a review/quiz based upon important information, he or she will be more able to speak specifically to that information. When classmates complete the review, the student can identify any patterns in the questions' answers that give clues as to how well those main ideas were communicated. In this way, the student can evaluate how effective the oral presentation was, without relying on classmates or the teacher.

4. A: Even for the older students who are a bit behind grade level, having a chance to help a younger student can increase their confidence and oral skills. Students are challenged to explain and give feedback to the Kindergarteners and will have to think about how best to explain ideas to another person. By pairing the older students with younger ones, they have a chance to be the "teachers," and must consider their purpose and audience when speaking. Regardless of the older student's reading abilities, he or she can build their confidence and skill in oral language by helping a younger student with basic reading skills.

5. B: The purpose of this exercise is for the older students to build their confidence and oral language skills by helping to teach younger students. By doing this, older students build their skills by thinking critically about how to help a new reader understand basic reading skills. In Choice "a",

the English language learner may build reading skills, but will not have a chance to build confidence or oral skills, which are just as important to their language development. In Choice "c", the English language learner may lose confidence in attempting to meet program standards without the necessary language skills. In Choice "d", students practice listening skills, which would only indirectly build oral skills. Choice "b" allows students to learn not only by listening, but by having a chance to explain or assist when he or she has the requisite skills to do so. A skilled student is also there to assist when needed.

6. D: The "Phrase of the Day" appears from the question prompt to be dedicated to certain types of oral language, including analogies and idioms. By asking the students to record interpretations in an informal way (through pictures or the students' own words), he will have insight as to their perceptions about common language. He also directly builds the students' oral language skills by giving them the correct meaning of the phrase with which the students can compare their original answers. In this way, Mr. Campbell assesses and builds skills without the use of a formal test or quiz.

7. B: Oral language skills incorporate speaking, listening, and knowledge of conventional language. In Choice "a", students would be limited to a very specific vocabulary in order to work with the science and math programs, and would not have opportunities to increase their knowledge of language. In Choice "c", students are practicing their listening skills, but are not required to speak or think critically about what they have heard. Choice "d" does involve technology and class discussions; however, the benefit of watching the discussion on tape is relatively unclear. In Choice "b", students not only have a chance to build their speaking and listening skills, but also increase their knowledge of other cultures and ways of speaking.

8. C: In choices "a" and "b," students are primarily using written language in order to present to the class. They are required to use what they have composed as the text for their oral presentations. In Choice "c", students have the chance to learn how to prioritize information they have read and written, and also learn to modify the written word to create an oral presentation based upon specific parameters. This exercise highlights the differences between the written and spoken word. Choice "d" does not necessarily involve all of the students and less directly increases the students' oral skills in a relevant way.

9. D: In this activity, students are practicing a variety of skills related to communication. By analyzing the log sheet, it is apparent that students are expected to work on their conversational skills, including listening and speaking. Choice "a" refers to those points on the log sheet that relate to listening while another person is speaking. Choice "c" also pertains to listening skills, specifically with eye contact and other behaviors that let the student know that his partner was listening and making an effort to understand. Choice "b" refers to the ability to speak clearly (each word can be clearly understood) and effectively (the ideas behind the words make sense to the listener). Choice "d" could potentially come to fruition; however, conflict resolution is not specifically addressed in this activity.

10. C: Oral language skills are almost un-quantifiable because they cover a multitude of competencies. Vocabulary, enunciation, listening, body language, comprehension and many other skills directly affect a student's communicative ability. This particular activity primarily focuses on peer interactions. However, conversing with adults provides opportunities for students to learn new vocabulary and ways of speaking. Choices "a," " b" and "d" are possible outcomes or functions of the teacher's partnering with a new student during each conversation. However, teachers must

keep in mind that it is just as important for students to converse with adults in a context that allows them to learn from observation as well as participation.

11. D: In the debate process, it is important for students to take a position and support it with evidence or arguments in order to make their claims effective. Choice "d" requires students to formulate their opinions and supporting arguments, and helps them reduce extraneous information and create "reminders" for their talking points on notecards. Choice "c" requires students to prepare their arguments but encourages reading aloud during the debate rather than actually speaking directly to their opponent or to the crowd. Choice "c" fails to help students distinguish between written language and oral language and their occasionally separate purposes. Choice "b" creates opportunities for informal debate, but does not teach students the parameters for formal debating. Choice "a" is similarly informal and does not familiarize students with the preparation process with respect to formulating arguments, opinions, or preparing to speak in front of a large audience.

12. A: In Choice "a", the teacher guides previewing of information to show students how to put themselves in the right frame of mind to listen carefully for meaning. Students are then able to listen in a guided way based upon the previewing. By varying the type of comprehension assessment, the teacher will get a better understanding of what the students learned. Choice "b" is a good exercise, but does not provide for direct instruction by the teacher or a particularly skilled student. In Choice "c", students are focusing more upon reading comprehension than listening since they must read the story to themselves and then write a report. There is then no way to gauge what they have learned. The final choice would be useful, but does not include teacher-guided previewing, which is very helpful in building comprehension.

13. B: At the start of a new school year, a teacher will likely choose to engage in a series of exercises to help her understand her students' current ability levels. These exercises must provide opportunities for evaluation of the whole class, rather than a select few students. In Choice "a", the teacher is not likely to get a lot of information from each student during class discussion, since not all children may participate. An instruction-level text may also prove too difficult for some students to read without guidance from a fluent reader. Choice "c", while a good exercise for peer-assisted reading, would not provide the teacher chances to evaluate each student's comprehension at once. Choice "d" would be very time-consuming; it would also cause students to influence each other's comprehension (e.g. the students going first may influence the comprehension of those re-telling the story later). Choice "b" allows the teacher to evaluate the students' independent comprehension levels with one assignment.

14. B: Emergent readers are those who are not yet reading fluently (with appropriate speed and accuracy). Choice "b" refers to the practice of reviewing relationships between letters and sounds, which is vital to building reading skills. Choice "c" would help students build vocabulary retention by requiring them to find unfamiliar words in the dictionary. This practice causes the student to analyze and retain spelling of unfamiliar words, as well as reinforces dictionary/reference skills. Choice "d" addresses the fact that many words in the English language are irregularly spelled and cannot be decoded with conventional phonetic instruction. While invented spelling described in Choice "a" may be permitted in emergent readers, this practice is not likely to build specific reading skills.

15. C: Literacy skills encompass a variety of contexts: written, verbal, comprehension, vocabulary, grammar, spelling, etc. Designing class work that touches on these multiple contexts must allow the children to increase not only skills that can be measured on tests or written work. Reading a play gives students a chance to touch on comprehension, vocabulary, and grammar; acting the play out creates the opportunity for increased comprehension and oral interpretation. Each of the alternate answers focuses on one specific aspect of literacy skills, without incorporating multiple contexts.

16. B: Assessment is an ongoing process that involves formal testing and a host of other methods. Students are working at any given time in the school year on a multitude of skills sets, and all of these skills are interrelated and developing simultaneously at different rates. It is impossible to ever provide a "snapshot" of a student's abilities, because each student develops in a unique and complex manner. Choice "a" would only offer insight into a student's reading fluency. Choice "c" would show how a student could perform on standardized tests; however, many factors such as anxiety and test-taking speed affect those scores. Choice "d" relies on the teacher to interpret the student's strengths and weaknesses and would require an almost impossible attention to detail. Choice "b" includes both formal and informal assessments as well as giving insight into writing, vocabulary and other skill sets in a comprehensive portfolio.

17. A: Those who are familiar with the guided oral reading strategy will note that the struggling student must be paired with a fluent and skilled partner. If you are not familiar with this strategy, all of the answer choices could conceivably be a part of the oral reading strategy and appear to be related to one another. However, one choice does not make sense after reading all four options. In answer choices "b" and "d," Valeria's partner is required to read the text aloud and offer correction or feedback when Valeria reads aloud. If Valeria is paired with another struggling student (as suggested in Choice "a", neither "b" nor "d" would prove effective in building her reading fluency.

18. B: Mr. Waleran's purpose is to encourage students to express themselves in written words, interpreting their thoughts into writing. However, there are often children who cannot write well enough to create coherent or legible works. In these cases, it is still possible for students to express themselves in writing. Choice "b" allows Dimitri to express himself by drawing, which will likely make him feel more comfortable with the activity. He will also have the chance to use words he does know and incorporate them into his work. As his skills grow, he can gradually transition into more formal writing. Choices "a" and "c" allow Dimitri to explore his thoughts, but do not build his writing skills. Choice "d" will, in all likelihood, become a chore for Dimitri and reinforce his struggles with reading and writing.

19. D: Part of building literacy skills is showing students how to listen effectively to various types of texts: narrative, poetry, informative, etc. In order to become competent in a variety of literacy skills, students must be able to listen for information and for pleasure/experience. This teacher is not only exposing them to poetry, but creating a forum in which they can actively listen and then discuss what they have experienced or learned. The scenario given in Choice "a" could possibly be true, as could Choice "c". But it is less likely that the teacher would devote an entire month of reading and listening to a specific type of text simply to give her students a break or to make a point about poetry versus prose. Choice "b" assumes that the poetry she reads will rhyme, which is not always the case.

20. B: Mrs. Taylor's project introduces students to an ancient form of expression that was written, but not based upon alphabetic principles, like English. This project is applicable to all levels of readers, as it incorporates various kinds of media to assist comprehension. Students are required to listen and read for information so that they can apply what they have learned to creating their own hieroglyphics. In Choice "b", the answer suggests that what is learned about hieroglyphics will assist students in understanding those with different backgrounds. However, hieroglyphics are not used in any widespread way today, and are much less helpful in building multicultural awareness than perhaps a lesson on modern Egyptian culture or writing.

21. D: Teachers should try to avoid shallow notions of what it means to provide cultural or multi-cultural education; in Choice "a", we cannot presume to understand another person by listening to his favorite music or watching a favorite movie. In Choice "b", there is also the assumption that there is a variety of musical tastes in the class, which may not be the case. In fact, if many students pick the same song, it is possible to use that choice to open up dialogue about what they lyrics mean and why they are so popular with the class. Choice "c" is posed in direct opposition to Choice "d". However, Choice "d" suggests what most teachers know to be true: literacy skills are not just important for schoolwork and class work; students must be able to take meaning from a variety of different sources in order to grow into educated adults. Music is an important medium through which students can express themselves and learn about the world around them through comprehension and listening skills.

22. C: All children learn their letter-sound correspondences at different rates. This particular child may simply be showing his teacher that he has not quite mastered this skill set yet. However, the inconsistence with producing the sounds could possibly be a signal that he needs specialized instruction. It is impossible, however, to know exactly what is going on without providing specialized instruction and giving that instruction time to improve skills. Choice "a" suggests an immediate referral for special-needs testing, which may be unnecessary and too soon in this scenario. Choice "b" states that all children learn differently which is certainly true, but does not provide a plan for helping the child improve. In the final choice, the parents may become needlessly alarmed and spend extra money in a situation where the intervention may not be necessary or even helpful. Choice "c" provides specific instruction in the deficient skill and acknowledges that the child may improve on his own; but if he needs it, extra help can be found.

23. D: Students are expected to be able to express themselves verbally and build upon one another's ideas in class as they complete fourth and fifth grades. However, many students lack the confidence or skills to participate in class discussions or conversations. Rather than leave those students to their own devices, as suggested in choices "a" and "b" a teacher must help instruct the students on how to communicate orally in situations where they can be successful. Choice "c" would require the students to speak out more, but might not alleviate issues with preparedness or confidence as would Choice "d" which allows students to feel more comfortable and get the teacher's guidance.

24. B: This prompt focuses not only on reading fluency skills, but also on the issue of the young reader's confidence. It is very common for students who feel unsuccessful at reading to avoid the skill altogether. The teacher in this question realizes something important: it is vital to build a student's confidence with reading as he or she builds skill. In choice "a" there is a faulty assumption that a student could ever memorize enough words to eliminate the need to decode. While some students with processing disorders or different learning styles do rely more heavily on sight words, this practice should not be solely relied upon. In choice "c" the students will likely feel negatively about being asked to read young children's books; their lack of confidence may be reinforced by this plan. In choice "d" students may also be frustrated by the extra work they are required to do

without any evidence of success with this practice. In Choice "b", students can build their fluency skills by creating words with various sounds, which is often easier for students than decoding as they are learning to read. As their knowledge of letter-sound relationships grows, they will become better at decoding words they see on the page. Allowing students to encode will also provide them with more chances to feel successful as they learn.

25. C: Reading fluency is defined as a set of skills including speed, accuracy and inflection when reading words on a page. Reading comprehension generally refers to the ability to understand what is being read. Both sets of skills are important, and reading fluency is vital to comprehension, which is the ultimate goal of the practice of reading. It is possible, even common, to isolate skills for the purpose of skill-building or to compensate for areas in which a student is struggling; however, all skills are inter-related. Children can make progress in some aspects of reading while still working on more difficult areas. Based on these ideas, choices "a" and "d" can be ruled out as possible answers. Comprehension is typically not classified as being part of fluency skills, which eliminates Choice "b". Reading fluency should be considered a vital part of overall reading skills: fluency must be improved so that, ultimately, the student can comprehend what is being read more fully.

26. A: It is important to evaluate specific reading skills, such as phonemic awareness, in a variety of contexts. Reading aloud with Abi allowed his teacher to notice that he consistently misread words beginning with digraphs. Digraphs are sounds in which two distinct letters, when combined, produce a single third sound (e.g. when "s" and "h" produce the "-sh" sound). Blends are words in which two letters produce a third sound which is a combination of both sounds put together (e.g. "b" and "l" combined to make "b"). The only set of words consisting only of digraphs is choice set "a."

27. D: The first three choices are all required standards to be met by eighth-graders. Students at this grade level should, of course, be able to identify grade-level words and understand the phonemes and elements within them. Students at this level should also be familiar with words that cannot necessarily be decoded with typical approaches, but that they will encounter on a regular basis (such as phenomenon or charisma). Eighth-graders should also be able to identify and explain similarities in different kinds of texts, as stated in Choice "b", and differences in points of view, as described in Choice "c". However, an extensive knowledge of cultural literature and its effect on media is required to meet the standard in Choice "d". This type of knowledge base, in addition to advanced deconstruction skills mentioned in Choice "d", is more typical of work done in grades 9-12.

28. A: In the passage, Susannah misspells seven words. Six of these misspelled words, when spelled correctly, have silent letter-sounds (phonemes). If Susannah misspells a particular pattern of words in her writing, she may have difficulty reading the same kinds of words independently. While sight word practice Choice "a" would certainly be helpful, teaching Susannah the concept of a "silent e" would be more effective than instructing her to learn similar words by memorizing them out of context. Choices "c" and "d" are also helpful in building reading skills; however, neither of them targets the specific type of word with which Susannah is struggling.

29. C: In Choice "a", the word prince is capitalized, though it does not have a suffix. The word undying is underlined, but should also be capitalized since it has both a prefix and a suffix. If you continue to apply the instructions given by the teacher, you will find that each sentence contains at least one mistake. Choice "c" contains a word with the root "please," which also has both a prefix and a suffix. Therefore, it is correctly underlined and capitalized.

30. B: Reading fluency refers to the speed, inflection and accuracy with which students read, either orally or silently. In order to read fluently, students must be able to decode, or break down into segments, words that adhere to the common rules of the English alphabet. For those words that are not easily decoded, students must build their vocabulary of "sight words," which are recognized without the need to decode. In Choice "a", students may or may not be reading fluently or accurately, since the computer program does not monitor how the student reads. In Choice "c", keyboarding practice bears no direct relationship to reading fluency. In Choice "d", again, the computer is simply a source for text, but does not build any specific fluency skill. In Choice "b", students are exposed to sight words and vocabulary in a fun way. Using a computer program allows for an unlimited supply of relevant words and for accurate scoring.

31. C: In Choice "a", parents would take up an inordinate amount of class time discussing literacy, without necessarily building any skills. This choice would also rely on the assumption that parents could speak effectively about this topic. Choice "b" would create inconsistency in grading, since there is interpretation and expertise required even in using a grading rubric. Choice "d" would certainly make the teacher's job easier to manage. However, Choice "c" allows parents with limited training to help students build reading fluency by reading challenging texts and building accuracy and speed. This choice satisfies both of the teacher's needs: taking into account the parents' limited training and helping the students most directly.

32. A: True fluency not only involves reading accurately and with appropriate speed, but using vocal inflection to communicate punctuation and emotion. Many students possess fluency with respect to accuracy or speed, but do not reflect interest or comprehension in their vocal modulation. Choice "b" suggests that volume is most important; however, volume can be considered a part of vocal expression. Choice "c" does not guarantee that the student will read with appropriate inflection or accuracy since interest level does not dictate fluency. At a certain point, students should not continue to increase their reading speed, as reading too quickly negatively affects comprehension. Therefore, Choice "d" is incorrect.

33. B: Much research points to the fact that students can increase their speed, accuracy and inflection when they engage in repeated readings of various texts. By reading assigned pieces more than once, they have a chance to apply feedback which they have received so that they make fewer mistakes and read more quickly. Students will struggle if they are only exposed to phonetic rules, without working on automatic word recognition or practice activities, as is suggested in Choice "a". Applying the same logic to vocabulary, it is necessary to rule out Choice "c". Choice "d" is not a widely accepted method for building reading fluency for student readers in traditional schools.

34. C: Generally speaking, students will read more slowly when introduced to texts and material that is new; speed increases with each subsequent reading. Hence, answer A) describes a normal child's reading pattern. When reading material independently, a student should not find more than approximately 1 in 20 words to be "difficult to read." Therefore, answer "b" is incorrect. Answer "d" refers to a comprehension test, which is not specifically related to the monitoring of fluency skills. This answer can be ruled out based upon its irrelevance. However, a student reading instructional-level material should find no more than 1 in 10 words difficult to read. Therefore, a student finding 1 in 5 questions difficult on an instructional-level test may need extra help or a text more appropriate for his age level.

35. B: Previewing information is a method by which students can work to improve their own unguided reading comprehension. During the previewing process, students consider the topic at hand, what they already know about it, and what they would like to learn or believe they will learn. Previewing helps students to approach reading for the purpose of comprehension ("reading to learn") and retention. In Choice "a", students will already be familiar with the text if they have already seen the movie; therefore, their previewing will be affected by familiarity with the text. The same is true for Choice "c", as the students have already read the novel. In Choice "d", previewing the poetry will indeed increase familiarity with the poems. However, reading poetry is typically not a process that involves "reading to learn." Instead, poetry is more often approached as a pleasure-reading activity or an opportunity for literary analysis. Allowing students to preview science material helps them actively learn to read for information and will aid them in other subjects.

36. B: The object of this unit is to teach students to monitor their own comprehension as they read longer and longer texts. The only choice that involves students analyzing their own understanding is Choice "b". This practice shows students logical points in the text to pause and ask themselves whether or not they understand that which they have read. Summarizing will help them identify main points in the story. Choice "b" is also the only choice that allows the teacher to directly instruct her students on comprehension while reading the book in class.

37. C: Many factors can affect a student's ability to understand what he or she is reading. Building comprehension skills is an ongoing process and can be made difficult if a student lacks the appropriate level of reading fluency. If he or she cannot read accurately or with enough speed, he or she will have much more trouble with comprehension than the average student. It is important to identify any decoding or vocabulary problems that might be affecting comprehension first; if those can be solved, comprehension skills may naturally increase as reading fluency increases.

38. B: The key word in this question is "independently." Students will be required to read a book on their own, synthesize the information they have found, pick out relevant main ideas, and then write about all those things. This multi-step process will require that the students be interested enough in their individual books to complete it, and that the students are actually capable of reading their books. Choice "b" allows students some choice, but ensures that the challenge level is appropriate. In Choice "a", more advanced students may find the process tedious if the books are too easy. Choice "c" suggests that students read books which are challenging, requiring additional comprehension work on top of that which is already assigned. The purpose of the project is to understand and synthesize information; selecting a difficult text may prove too much for some students. It is rarely a good idea to eliminate parameters whatsoever on book choice, because students could choose books which they are incapable of reading, or which would be too easy to challenge them.

39. C: Barron demonstrates the ability to read the words on a page, but struggles with several comprehension skills consistently. There is a pattern to Barron's issues: he has a hard time comprehending anything not stated literally in the text. Karishma may or may not have a hard time forming an opinion; we cannot tell as the prompt only says that she is uncomfortable speaking up in class, which seems to be a confidence problem rather than an academic one. Lynne appears to comprehend different genres of literature, which is a grade-level expectation, and it is common for students to have a bit more trouble with one particular genre. Sebastien is not unusual, as he is capable of intelligent contributions and comprehension, but primarily lacks interest. His is a problem of motivation rather than an academic struggle; he would possibly benefit from a wider text selection or a special project.

40. B: Cloze technique refers to the process of selecting a text to present to a student and deleting various words according to a pattern. Every fifth word has been omitted in this passage. The objective of a cloze-style assessment is to assess and increase reading comprehension. This type of assessment is unique in that there is no "correct" answer—students are only expected to use the context clues to fill in words that make sense in the blanks. If they have been able to create meaningful answers, then the exercise should be deemed a success. Choices "a" and "d" are not generally accepted forms of reading comprehension assessment. Choice "c" is an oft-used form of assessment which utilizes prepared questions and students' responses and should not be confused with the cloze-style technique.

41. A: There are differences in the way reading levels are assigned across research and history. These levels can apply to a variety of assessments, including reading fluency, comprehension, word identification and the like. However, it can be generally agreed upon that there are three broad reading levels: frustration, instructional, and independent. Frustration level indicates that the material is too difficult for the student and may create frustration or disappointment while reading. Frustration level typically refers to various assessment scores of below 40%. Instructional level refers to text that can be used for the improvement of reading skills, wherein a student can get about half of his answers correct, whether identifying words, answering questions, etc. Instructional level ranges from approximately 41% to 60%. Any score above an approximate 60% should be considered independent reading material for the student.

42. D: Teachers know that students are often expected to read works written long ago and whose relevance may not be immediately apparent. It is important that students have the information required to understand how the text was created. In Choice "d", students have the opportunity to learn about the socio-historical context in which the author created the piece. Armed with knowledge about the story's context, students can categorize and comprehend any of its aspects that would ordinarily be unclear. Students can also use this knowledge to find similarities and differences between aspects of their own lives and the context of the characters in the story. In choices "a"and "b," students are given the responsibility of determining what is important or unclear in the story. However, without understanding the work's context, students may not even be aware of the relevant information in the text, or may incorrectly interpret some events in the story. In Choice "c", the sole focus is on vocabulary, which may neglect other important characteristics of the writing.

43. A: In a longer text with chapter titles, these titles can give students an understanding of what the book might be about and allows it to be broken into regular increments. Creating questions that the students can answer during their reading will give them points at which they can stop and think about what they comprehend. In Choice "b", the students would be taught to focus primarily on the ending, which neglects the rest of the aspects of the text. Choices "c" and "d" could inappropriately influence the students' comprehension by causing them to rely on other people's opinions rather than on their own understanding.

44. B: There are many, many factors that affect reading comprehension in various proportions, depending on the student. Generally speaking, students must be able to recognize vocabulary, decode unfamiliar words, and monitor their own understanding in order to comprehend a given text. In Choice "a", all of these factors could affect comprehension; written language development and breakfast, however, are probably less important than the set of factors in Choice "b". In Choice "c", the factors seem to relate primarily to a student's understanding of the words in the text— vocabulary, sight words, and the ability to look up words. However, students must understand more than simply the words on the page; they must understand the relationships between the

words and the underlying meaning of the whole text. In Choice "d", classroom participation and performance in other subjects does not necessarily indicate or affect comprehension skills.

45. B: Comprehension is a process of creating meaning from that which a student reads, sees, hears, or experiences. The tools for comprehending are similar across genres. The teacher has specifically chosen a passage and wants the students to compare, not contrast, the pieces. Dickensian writing is not generally considered to be journalistic, as suggested in Choice "a". Choice "c" is correct—you can in fact compare even unlike things. However, Choice "b" provides a richer backdrop for showing students how to link that which they read in school to their own lives and use the same tools to comprehend and take meaning from whatever they read.

46. C: Reading for pleasure is an important part of building students' literacy for life. Often, the more parameters that are established around reading, the less students are apt to read for fun. By removing limitations and requirements on the experience of reading, teachers will increase the likelihood that students can enjoy it. Choice "a" does involve books which the students enjoyed, but would not increase the amount of time spent reading for pleasure, as the books have already been read. Choice "b" simply increases the amount of time spent reading for class, but may or may not be enjoyable for the students. Choice "d" establishes a plan for reading for fun, but does not ensure that the students will adhere to the timeline created. Choice "c" removes the limits on what the students can read and is inclusive of students who may not already like to read by allowing them to choose the type of material. Students also have a chance to discuss the different kinds of elements in texts that they enjoy and share them with the class.

47. A: Choice "b" creates opportunities for students to encounter words they might not read on a daily basis at school or while reading for pleasure. They are likely to employ context clues or dictionaries as a means of understanding the main ideas. Choices "c" and "d" are two different methods to expose students to new and unfamiliar words by hearing them in an instructional context and in conversation with adults. Both choices would create opportunities for indirect vocabulary building as means to understand larger ideas. Choice "a" extends the vocabulary assignment by adding harder words. This strategy would likely increase the number of words a student has learned; however, it would do so by direct instruction (words are directly assigned to be learned by students).

48. C: During the unit on imagery and figurative language, students will learn about how sensory experience can be translated into writing. In order to understand and apply these concepts, students will need an ever-increasing bank of descriptive words which they can identify and define. Choices "a," "b" and "d" would certainly be useful as supplements to this particular unit. However, Choice "c" most accurately addresses the question prompt in that it is an activity that directly increases relevant vocabulary skills. Word games engage students' interest, while building their knowledge of words they will encounter in their studies of imagery and figurative writing.

49. A: The text at hand contains several clues as to the meaning of this word, including the use of the words "peaceful" and "quiet" in the preceding sentence. Students may also recognize that Mom's requests for help with undesirable household chores interrupted Dad's peaceful, quiet 'reverie." Choice "a" is the specific method that would be most appropriate for determining the word's meaning; Choice "b" is a less reliable or systematic way of doing the same thing. Choice "c" would not be helpful in this case since "reverie" is not a word that can be decoded in a traditional manner. Choice "d" would not offer a realistic solution to this question since previewing and reviewing are more helpful in increasing comprehension of informative texts, rather than vocabulary words.

50. B: Inferential comprehension refers to a student's ability to understand ideas not explicitly contained in the text. By reading the paragraph, the student should ideally be able to understand that the girls knew they were getting out of helping with chores, because they grinned at one another conspiratorially and left immediately after gaining permission to do so. Mom also comments that she told everybody at breakfast that they'd need to help her out, which Dad has clearly forgotten. There are enough clues in the paragraph to help the reader understand what is happening without stating it in an obvious way. There are no clues to help the reader answer questions "a" or "c," In question Choice "d", the answer (peace and quiet) is stated explicitly, and would refer to literal comprehension instead of inferential comprehension.

51. D: When students read textual information for another subject, they are expected to pick out important words and concepts and retain them. By outlining the text, the student can keep track of the overall framework of information, as well as word definitions and main ideas. In Choice "a", the primary purpose for reading is likely entertainment. In Choice "b", a more appropriate reading comprehension strategy would not focus on key concepts at the expense of the literary style and tools. In Choice "c", it would be correct to analyze a persuasive essay for main ideas and supportive evidence, rather than an extended free-writing exercise.

52. C: The vocabulary list gives clues as to the type of text the students will be reading. Historical fiction is not likely to contain stories of deities or the supernatural, although the other vocabulary words might match. Poetry is not always considered as narrative text; nor would it necessarily explore culture or dualities (although those are possibilities). Drama, there again, is a possible match for this list, but does not match as well as Choice "c", mythology. Mythology encompasses many stories, typically ancient in origin, that explain and describe aspects of culture. Myths across cultures carry as many similarities as they do differences. Common in mythology are stories of duality, gods and goddesses, heroism, and more.

53. C: The goal of this exercise is to help students learn to interpret data in the form of a chart. This skill is vital to increasing overall comprehension skills and test-taking ability. However, we are not given much information regarding this chart other than types of hobbies and how many students in a particular group reported enjoying them. Therefore, we cannot make a judgment about Choice "a"—we do not know if some students reported enjoying more than one hobby, keeping us from answering that question accurately. Choice "b" offers students a chance to form personal opinions about a given topic, which is not the purpose of this exercise. Choice "d" would be more appropriate for building math skills while incorporating reading skills. Choice "c", however, requires students to analyze the types of hobbies, categorize them into physical exercise or artistic pursuits, and then answer the question.

54. B: Technology should not be relied upon to teach comprehension skills, but can be helpful in providing supplements to classroom instruction. In Choice "a", this particular practice can be very helpful for some students who have trouble recalling what is discussed in class. Choice "c" sets up a reward system to encourage students to finish their work but will not directly increase any specific skill. Choice "d" relies on students to pull comprehension-building information from articles, instead of providing them with direct instruction or explanation. Choice "b" provides interactive tools that will help students organize information that they have read, which is an important comprehension skill.

55. D: The key word in this question is "scaffolding," which refers to a practice of supporting and guiding learners with respect to a particular skill. Talking about reading is an important part of building literacy skills, but is rarely helpful without direct instructions on how to do it respectfully

and properly. In Choice "a", students are required to support a particular idea in a relatively high-stress format, in front of other students. Some students may struggle with this exercise while they are learning. Choice "b" removes the teacher or any type of guide from the discussion, which exempts students from direct instruction or scaffolding. Choice "c" may eliminate some students who are not confident speaking in front of large groups, and limits how much students can share at one time. Choice "d" gives students a safe, smaller group within which to discuss reading and also provides teacher moderation and discussion guides.

56. C: In this question, it is best to actually approach the exercise as the student would, reading through the choices and contemplating their relationships. Matching numbers 2 and 4 are easiest to do first because they include girls' names and can be matched with the lettered choices with female pronouns ("she"). Some of the choices could be categorized as facts or opinions, but not so consistently that Choice "a" would make sense. It would be impossible to assert accurately that these choices are main and supporting ideas without more information or sentences to prove this, as suggested in Choice "b". Choice "d" would also require more information to be considered a possible answer to this question. Choice "c" fits best, establishing a valid effect (letters) for each cause (numbers).

57. A: Mr. Garson's assignment is intended to expand his students' understanding of other people's points of view. Creative writing is a constructive process that requires many kinds of thought processes. In Choice "b", Mr. Garson would be undermining Kim's chance to think creatively and would constitute lowering his expectations of her due to the language barrier. In Choice "c", he cannot guarantee that Kim would choose a topic that would encourage her to think creatively about different perspectives. In Choice "d", collaborating with another English-language learner would not likely speed up the process of writing; it also may short-circuit her own creative thinking due to the influence of another person's thoughts. Choice "a" allows Kim to focus on the creative constructive process without the issues associated with writing in a new language. Kim will achieve the intended outcome of the assignment, saving translation and language issues to be dealt with separately with the guidance of a trained teacher.

58. D: The students in this scenario are only given the opportunity to memorize a specific set of words each week. However, they have not been given a chance to stretch their spelling skills through various styles of teaching and assignments. Therefore, their knowledge of spelling conventions and irregular spelling will be limited to their word lists. However, writing requires a more expansive spelling skill set and must be practiced in a variety of styles in order to solidify them. In order to build spelling skills in writing, students must have opportunities to practice their spelling while writing, perhaps by using words in original sentences, learning word groups, reviewing words before and after the weekly tests, etc.

59. B: Because writing is an ongoing developmental process, it is important to monitor students' development in various ways over time. During journal time, students can write freely without concern for being graded on various aspects of their work. This freedom will likely enhance their willingness to explore their ideas. This process allows the teacher to understand which rules of conventional writing have carried over into the students' long-term memories and skill sets. Ideally, students will continually add new writing skills to their free journaling, indicating that their writing instruction is improving their skills without the students needing to consciously apply them. Journaling also allows students to practice that which they have learned without paying undue attention to parameters for grading.

60. A: This letter is difficult to follow because it is not organized according to main ideas and supporting sentences. The letter also displays inconsistent capitalization and punctuation within the body. In Choice "b", the reference to writing style is vague and can be viewed subjectively. Teachers are responsible for teaching writing conventions; however, it is important to teach proper grammar without criticizing the student's specific ideas or style. In choices "c" and "d" references to misuse of active and passive voice are irrelevant to this particular writing passage.

61. C: Organization, punctuation, and capitalization are the primary issues with this piece of writing and the letters written by the class. While there are only a few spelling errors, it is always helpful to review commonly made mistakes, as well as discuss capitalization rules. However, the student in this case does not misuse passive or active verbs. Passive voice refers to the over-use of "to be" verbs and to sentences in which the subject is acted upon, most often including passive participles (i.e., verbs in the –ed form). For instance, a sentence stating that "he robbed a bank" is normally preferable to "the bank was robbed." Therefore, Choice "c" would not be as helpful as the other lesson choices in this case.

62. B: Writing is a complex, subjective process which will never be graded identically amongst teachers. The best teachers, however, know that students write more clearly and more accurately when they know that which is expected of them. In Choice "a", the inclusion of so many details may be confusing and cause the grading process to take too long. Choice "c" is certainly an important action to consider, but will probably not directly affect the students' writing skills. Choice "d" may communicate a certain point, but again, will not necessarily improve the students' skills; it will only affect the grading process. Choice "b" will engage the students actively in the writing process and in the building of skills. They will be able to analyze the rubric and determine how well they understand the assignment and whether or not they may need more practice or help in a particular area.

63. D: Writing is a skill that evolves over time because it is so complex and involves multiple skill sets. Because so many skills are important in writing, it is impossible to apply the same sequence to each new writer. Choice "a" is important for all writers, beginning to advanced, since writing, like reading, is a skill they will use across many contexts. Choice "b" gives students practice with the various aspects of the writing process that often prove difficult for new writers, especially when they are attempting to build content and write accurately at the same time. In Choice "c", students can diminish their fear or lack of motivation for writing because they will be able to explore it in a variety of ways. Choice "d", however, may create the problem of boredom for more advanced students and cause writing progress to be very slow for those still learning.

64. B: In the first sentence, the compound subject of the sentence is "each of the kids." This compound subject with a propositional phrase (of the kids) may trick students into thinking that the subject is plural, making the verb "love." But based on the singular subject, "each," the verb should be "loves." In the second sentence, the subject, "game," should change the verb to "is" instead of the plural "are." In the third sentence, the subject is compound with a prepositional phrase (in our class), but the verb should be singular, "enjoy." The punctuation suggested in Choice "a" and the word choice in Choice "c" is correct in the paragraph. There are no split infinitives.

65. B: Often, it helps writers to show their papers to a trusted friend or family member who is unfamiliar with the piece. A fresh set of eyes can identify errors that the student does not see while revising. Choice "a" creates unnecessary work for the student when only certain corrections need to be made. Choice "c" also requires a lot of work that may turn students off of the process of revision. Choice "d" describes most students' approach to revising their papers. There are, however, many

processes at work when creating written pieces and it is very difficult to develop and write your ideas without making mistakes.

66. D: In Choice "a", the teacher is providing remedial instruction or extra help, but is not sharpening the actual skills needed to revise. Many students can perform well on mechanics worksheets and exercises, but have trouble with the process of re-reading and revising. Choice "b" is not correct for the same reason. Choice "c" relies upon the students themselves to identify and correct others' grammar, which may not be consistent or accurate. The final choice helps students practice the re-reading and identification skills needed to revise a piece of writing.

67. A: Curriculum standards are important for determining when specific skills should be introduced and mastered. While most literacy skills evolve simultaneously, there is an applicable sequence that should guide teaching. Choices "b" through "d" are all general expectations for fifth-grade students. All students do not master every skill included in order to matriculate, but effort to expose them to each skill should be made. Choice "a" is a standard that students generally do not master until seventh or eighth grade, unless they are provided with specialized instruction at an earlier time and on a consistent basis.

68. A: In the writing process, the prewriting phase includes actions such as brainstorming, story mapping, and jotting down ideas. Most students need to organize their ideas before beginning to draft, or writing. It often helps students to organize their ideas with the use of drawings or diagrams instead of in a linear fashion. By requiring them to use pencil and paper in this phase of the writing process, teachers create an opportunity for students to use different tools to organize their ideas. Once the writing and publishing phases begin, it is appropriate to allow the use of word processors to that the students' work is legible for revision.

69. C: It is obvious when Mrs. Blaine first comments on Alex's report that he does well with literal comprehension and memory, but has trouble identifying and discussing his opinion about the book. Alex, like many students, is not confident in his ability to clearly state an idea and back it up with supporting evidence or ideas from what he has read. This is the skill she is suggesting he will need to use again and again. Alex has an opinion, that the book was "boring at first," but he "liked the way it ended." He knows how he feels about the book, but does not know how to explain his opinion in writing. Therefore, answer Choice "a" is inaccurate. Choices "b" and "c" are both likely to be necessary for Alex at some point, but are unlikely to be the most important skill Mrs. Blaine mentions.

70. A: Alex is having trouble expressing a logical argument in writing. However, he has an opinion about the book to get him started. By having him write each idea on separate items, Alex can use tangible objects to represent his thoughts. He can then move them around as he thinks through how they are related to one another. In this way, he can start to structure his thoughts with the help of visual aids, rather than attempting to do this abstractly. The remaining three choices might assist Alex with certain assignments, but will not give him concrete tools to help him organize his thoughts and write them in a clear, concise way.

71. A: Mr. Benton wants to use a clear-cut approach to writing, involving students in the process. As a teacher, Mr. Benton should know that there are six commonly agreed-upon writing traits: idea development, organization, voice, word choice, sentence fluency and conventions. These traits encompass the majority of writing skills that students will learn over the course of their studies. In Choice "a", not only does Mr. Benton provide students with this framework for thinking about writing, but helps them prioritize their needs in building their skills. The students can then work from the plan devised from that initial meeting. In choices "b" and "c", students are left primarily to

their own devices to build their writing skills. However, if most of the students are struggling with writing (as suggested in the question prompt), it would not be advisable to leave the writing instruction to the students themselves. Choice "d" provides faulty information--there are many types of writing that would not be written in the five-paragraph style or format.

72. B: Part of teaching older students is helping them give voice to what is happening in their lives and connecting that voice to what they are learning in class. In Choice "b", students not only have a voice, but can channel that voice into a particular type of writing. In this case, they will be writing journalistically. They also have a chance to turn their frustration into a positive activity that will give parents the information they would like to know. In Choice "a", the students do not build any particular writing skills, nor does the problem get solved for parents or students. In Choice "c", the students would have a chance to write about their feelings, but this does not eliminate the issue of parents wanting to know what is happening at school. Choice "d" only serves to make more work for the students, without building their writing skills.

73. D: The first two questions suggest that the primary focus of this exercise is word choice and vocabulary. The third question refers to the sound of the words chosen, and could also pertain to Choice "a", sentence fluency. The fourth question would work with choices "a," "c" or "d". But taken together, the questions point strongly to the concept of word choice. Choice "a", sentence fluency, refers to the way the words in sentences work together. Choice "b" refers to the way the students' ideas are developed in the paper. Choice "c" encompasses writing conventions such as punctuation, spacing, and capitalization.

74. B: In persuasive writing, the writer must introduce an opinion or statement about which he or she must provide supporting evidence. The paragraph or paper should start with the main idea and then segue into separate but related supporting details. In this writing sample, the student's ideas are written sequentially, as the student might think about them mentally. Introducing a visual aid to help him separate his primary idea and the ideas that give reasons for it may help him develop the piece into a longer, more logical argument. He already includes personal details and ideas that make the piece interesting to read, contrary to Choice "c". Choice "d" suggests that the student may have many grammatical and conventional corrections to make, which is not correct. While it is always important to encourage, as stated in Choice "a", Choice "b" would be the most direct, concrete way to assist this student in developing his skills.

75. D: When teachers talk to their students about writing, it is important to remember that young writers often leave out important details or information vital to its coherence. Students must learn to communicate clearly through writing and include all pertinent information. The teacher uses the metaphor of the alien from outer space to emphasize this point—an alien would have no prior knowledge that would aid comprehension, therefore the writer must be very thorough. This concept is important in all writing, but would be especially important in explaining to another person how to do something. In Choice "d", a student would choose a favorite activity, sport, or task and explain in a methodical way how to complete or participate in it. Neglecting any piece of information would make the piece irrelevant.

76. B: Many aspects of writing are difficult to teach directly. There are not as many specific exercises that show students how to write in their own voices without being overly colloquial or even incorrect. Students must always be working toward adhering to writing conventions, but also making that which they write personal and interesting. Part of "voice" is personal expression and making writing relevant to the intended audience. Often, the best way to show the students how to do this is to show them that which has already been done well and discuss why the writing is good.

The students can use this discussion to improve their own writing through emulation. Choice "a" suggests that personal opinions are always relevant to one's writing, which is not always the case, depending on the type of assignment. In Choice "c", students would be very limited should they only choose subjects with which they are familiar--they would rarely have a chance to grow. The final choice would encourage students to speak in someone else's voice, which would create variety, but would not grow their ability to speak as themselves in any relevant or interesting way.

77. A: Reading this excerpt, it becomes apparent that the student is using a limited writing vocabulary. The words "sweet" or "sweets" are used three times; "like" is used three times as well. The sentences feel very repetitive because many words are used again and again. Working with students to build their vocabulary is one of the most helpful ways to build writing skills. The more words in a student's repertoire, the more interesting and lively his writing will be. Despite the vocabulary deficit, the student's writing conventions and grammar are actually quite good in this excerpt. Choice "d" suggests that the student needs to stretch his writing skill by choosing more challenging topics, but we do not know from this piece whether or not the student is working at an appropriate level of challenge.

78. C: Choice "a" is misleading, as writing a letter is a specific format and kind of exercise; it is not typically considered a catch-all exercise for learning the five-step process or the six traits of writing. While every writing exercise can be a backdrop for these skills, Choice "a" is not the most accurate answer. If you read the question prompt carefully, you see that it is already acknowledged that this opportunity will be a good exercise for showing students how to write a letter well. Therefore, Choice "b" is redundant. Choice "d" is true; students should be careful of their writing conventions so that their writing is easier to read, yet Choice "c" is the skill than can be most directly applied when writing to students of another language and culture; the audience actually encompasses Choice "d", as students would determine in thinking about their French pen pals that they might have a hard time reading English, and that they should be cognizant of that fact.

79. B: By the eighth grade, students should begin to understand the purposes and effectiveness of various media. If the students have been learning about how to deconstruct media messages, they have likely been studying ideas about audience, point of view, and persuasive language. Assigning a project in which the students are guided to think through these concepts will solidify their understanding of how media messages are created. Each of the other answers, "a," "b" and "d" will likely be accomplished through the completion of this project. However, it is not likely that the teacher has designed such a specific kind of assignment in order to increase her students' real-life job skills, as not all of them will go into media-related fields described in Choice "a". Choice "c" assumes that technology will be used in the assignment, although it is possible for students to create the ads and essays without the use of computers or other technology. Choice "d" could be accomplished by any number of assignments and is less likely to be the primary intended outcome.

80. A: Inkblot images are often used to gain insight into an individual's thoughts. The teacher clearly understands that different people will interpret these images in various ways. She asks the students to write their questions down so that they will not be influenced by others' interpretations. While some visual symbols are universal, most images are not inherent as suggested in Choice "b". Choice "c" could possibly be true, but would be irrelevant to a group of sixth graders in most circumstances. Choice "d" supposes that students should confer with one another before forming their own opinions, which should not be a rule of thumb. By allowing students to interpret the messages individually and then share their perceptions, the teacher will demonstrate that the individual's point of view will affect his understanding of visual images.

81. D: Students typically enjoy watching film versions of literature, especially when the text is challenging to read. An important part of media consumption is building skills to deconstruct the embedded ideas and messages. The teacher in this scenario wants the students to think about how the structure and content of the film affects their understanding of a classic story. In choices "a" and "b", students are assigned to state their opinions about certain aspects of the film or play, but are not asked to critically analyze a specific message. Choice "c" simply creates a rather tedious assignment that will yield a rote list of examples. Choice "d" targets the unique setting of the film and encourages students to think about why the film's creators might have chosen to adapt the story in such a way, which is likely to suggest that the content of the story is relevant to people in any era or setting.

82. A: Mr. James is showing students the difference between a main idea (or concept) and its supporting evidence (or details). He has taken an element of a story and provided three details or character traits that provide proof of his claim. The organization of the graph helps students see the relationship between in the ideas, in addition to hearing it. This skill can be directly applied to either constructing meaning from a text or creating a well-planned paragraph. Choice "b" may not always be true, depending on the kind of questions asked. Choice "c" assumes that characters in texts can always be broken down into smaller components. Choice "d" refers to aspects of writing such as punctuation, grammar, spelling, etc.

83. B: Students are expected to have a variety of skills with respect to viewing, representing, and analyzing visual/media images by the time they enter high school. They should be able to understand visual imagery and how it affects or creates meaning. Students must also learn to deconstruct the messages they see and create their own for the purposes of communicating their own ideas. Choice "a" would, perhaps, be the goal of a consumerism or economics class, but is not the best choice for this scenario. This game would create understanding in students about different types of visual images, but they are not likely to be the same images used in their schoolwork at this juncture. Choice "d" is certainly true; the children will likely enjoy the game. However, Choice "b" most closely matches the educational requirements and standards laid out for students of this age.

84. D: Generally speaking, the following story elements take place in sequential order:
Exposition: refers to background information and actions in a story that describe the setting, characters, etc.
Rising action: events in the plot that lead up to the critical event or turning point
Climax: critical event, dramatic scene, or turning point in the story
Falling action: resulting events and actions following the conflict
Resolution: all actions and events are resolved and addressed
Teaching students about the plot elements they can find in most stories will help them develop many skills, including comparisons/contrasts, plot analysis, reading comprehension, etc.

85. B: Ancient Egypt provides a rich backdrop for a myriad of literacy skills. Students can develop their visual literacy skills in a number of ways, even using material and studies that date back thousands of years. In Choice "a", students are creating visual images with costume and dress, but no method for decoding those messages is stated in the answer choice. Drawing illustrations focuses on the same skill: creation of visual images, but no decoding or discussion of those images. In Choice "d", students could build their visual literacy skills if they were to discuss the visual images or representations in the film, but this activity is not included in the answer choice. In the correct answer, B), students are exposed to various representations and exhibits regarding the material in question and then have a chance to discuss and uncover meaning in what they have seen, with the guidance of the teachers.

86. A: If you read the question prompt carefully, you will notice that the question refers specifically to language skills. While Choice "c" is important and would likely result from the exercise, it does not signify a specific language skill. Students' motor skills are not likely to significantly improve over the course of one day, eliminating Choice "b". In Choice "d", the assumption that other individuals in the community would be able to interpret sign language is incorrect. But the seminar would indeed provide an opportunity for students to learn about how visual representations affect meaning. Using sign language allows them to hone listening and expression skills simultaneously, as well as to learn how to decode non-verbal expressions.

87. D: In literature and in media, storytellers often use the color red to symbolize a number of concepts: red can signal importance, danger, love, or simply draw the viewer or reader to the particular object in question. The question prompt tells you directly that the red objects signify that the main character is seeing a clue to solving the mystery. In essence, anything colored red represents, or symbolizes, a clue.

88. B: The primary purpose of visual aids is to extend or enhance meaning. Visuals can sometimes distract from the meaning of the presentation if used too much, as in Choice "a". Choice "c" could also create distractions in that students may be more likely to look at photos directly in front of them than pay attention to the student presenting. The final choice simply encourages students to read the information on screen, and will likely cause the presenting student to read aloud rather than communicate in his own words. Choice "b", however, utilizes the students' thought processes in determining where a visual might help enhance understanding, and requires them to use oral communication as well.

89. C: In teaching about this subject, students must be able to understand the intended meaning of a particular media image. To do this, they have to consider the image-creator's background, point of view, and anything else they might be able to determine from analyzing the image. Students need to be taught tools to dissect the barrage of images that they see on a daily basis. Choice "a" encompasses photos of real-life people and events. While these photos are valuable for many teaching purposes, it cannot be guaranteed that students would be able to apply their tools to current-day media analysis. Choice "b" is the choice least related to media influence in that it refers to a Social Studies text, likely created for didactic purposes. Choice "d" most likely refers to a cartoon found in the Funnies, created to entertain, rather than influence. The political cartoon in Choice "c" is the image most explicitly created to affect and influence public opinion by exaggerating personal traits and personalizing lofty issues.

90. C: Many factors affect the final outcome of a research paper or project, including the selection of sources, interpretation of source information, organization of ideas, and writing skills. The final project described in answer "a" is not always indicative of how efficiently a student has researched a topic because it is the end-result of many language processes at work. The outline mentioned in answer "b" would provide insight about the organization of ideas, but answer "c" would allow the instructor to assess the actual process of gathering and synthesizing sources of information.

91. A: One of the most important aspects of completing a research project is topic selection. A student must choose a topic that is appropriately narrow to avoid being overwhelmed by too much information. If the topic is too broad, the student will not be able to adequately research; if it is too narrow, he or she will get stuck. The student should also think critically about whether or not the topic can be researched. For instance, if a student chooses to study a current event, there may not be enough reliable information published yet to support a real research project. The teacher should play an active role in helping the student select a topic, especially on the student's first try.

92. A: The students tend to do well when they know they will be tested; this probably means that they only sit down to study when they are required to do so, unless they want to risk a poor test score. However, it is important for students to retain information each day and week, rather than cramming and memorizing for a test. By devoting a few minutes each day to preview or prepare students for what they will learn, they will begin to learn how to pay attention to the main ideas and salient details of the readings. By reviewing and summarizing, students can compare what they thought would be important during the preview to what they actually learned. The repetition will help the students retain the information from one day to the next.

93. B: If only the first graph was drawn, it may appear that the students were working simply on character analysis or even inferential comprehension. This first set of boxes creates a framework for analyzing and recording information about two specific characters and their personalities. However, taken with the second chart, it becomes apparent that the purpose of the first chart is to organize information in order to complete the second chart. The second chart requires students to think critically about how the two characters are the same and how they are different. This exercise most closely corresponds with Choice "b", comparing and contrasting, in the context of character traits. Choices "c" and "d" are certainly involved in this process, but are simply tools that are used in order to teach students how to compare and contrast

94. B: The question prompt states that the students' primary problems lie in homework: they are concerned about the volume of reading and ho to know what information is most relevant. Although Choice "d" is important and will help students, it will not improve their ability to deal with independent reading and assignments. Choice "c" will help students score more highly on tests, but will likely not improve their study skills. Choice "a" will simply encourage students to "cram' a lot of information for tests. Choice "b", however, teaching SQ3R, is a method by which students can study, internalize and sort through large amounts of information on an independent basis.

95. B: Writing a research paper is a learned skill that begins with proper topic selection. Students must learn to pick topics with guidance from their teachers that can be researched easily. They must be careful not to pick topics that are too broad or too narrow. In this scenario, students also need to pick a topic that can be found as the subject in a variety of sources, including newspapers, magazines, books, etc. Therefore, the topic should be well-known to most readers. Choice "a" is not likely to be found in these sources unless the Velasquez family is nationally, or at least locally, well-known. Choice "c" is probably not appropriate for the same reason. Choice "d" could be considered for an essay topic or another type of writing assignment, but may not be the best choice with respect to the variety of sources. Choice "b" offers a broad subject about which much will have been written.

96. D: The purpose of this kind of note-taking is, on one level, to help students distinguish between major ideas or concepts and the details that support or relate to them. This kind of note-taking also helps students understand how certain events and ideas influence one another. The most important benefit of this practice is that it helps the note-taker start to build meaning out of the information which they receive in class. Students often complain that they don't know how to pick out what will be on a test, or what is important, as they cannot possibly retain every sentence uttered in class. Students do best when they can pick out main ideas and organize their thinking around these concepts, learning details and supporting ideas as they go.

97. C: As is true with students and adults alike, we remember more information when we review it consistently over time. If a student takes meaningful and accurate notes, reviewing them periodically and consistently will help them retain the information and cut down on time spent

studying right before the test. This practice also helps the student identify any ideas or questions that need to be addressed before the test or paper is due. Choices "a" and "b" create the impression that a student will struggle if he does not record (in writing or via tape recorder) every word uttered in class. It is more important for students to learn how to create meaning and understand relationships between all of the facts, figures, and concepts introduced in class. Choice "d" would be very time-consuming and would not guarantee that students are choosing the most important ideas and information for use.

98. C: Allowing the students to practice these types of questions starts to open up their ability to show that which they know. Many students experience stress in the transition to various types of testing that do not provide answer choices in multiple choice form, or lack word banks. Choice "c" shows students how to approach these kinds of questions in a safe, un-graded way, and solidifies their thinking by discussing their attempts afterward. Choice "a" may assist with students' recall of information, but does not provide direct instruction on how to formulate answers. Choice "b" will give students time to approach the questions and revise their answers if necessary. For those students who experience more difficulty, however, it may not be as helpful as Choice "c". Choice "d" might also be helpful for any students who experience test anxiety or are taking a bit longer to understand the process, but will not scaffold their attempts as well as Choice "c".

99. C: In a piece of writing such as Sully's, there are two important things which he needs to do; namely, he must select the most important ideas and focus on those, rather than attempt to include every single idea he may have. Once he has done that, he additionally must include details or evidence to support those ideas. Choice "c" gives him a concrete way to identify the most important ideas and match them with appropriate and relevant evidence. Choices "a" and "b" require him to start over on a project, which is unnecessary. Choice "d" would cause him to create a very lengthy and too-detailed report without much focus.

100. B: Studying can be a mystifying experience for students as they begin to do it more frequently. Often, students do not know how to prepare properly for specific kinds of assignments, and direct instruction is helpful. In Choice "b", Mrs. Bray can identify why the students' preparation is not adequate for the examinations and help them understand alternative methods of preparation. In Choice "a", students may or may not improve their performance while taking more quizzes; in fact, their motivation and confidence may decrease if they continue to receive poor grades. Choice "c" contradicts the question prompt, as Mrs. Bray does not want to give the students too many ideas about what will be covered in the quiz; rather, she wants to improve their study skills. Choice "d" is less accurate and direct as a method for achieving her goals than is Choice "b", because parents do not always have good study skills or knowledge of the classroom.

Special Report: Additional Bonus Material

Due to our efforts to try to keep this book to a manageable length, we've created a link that will give you access to all of your additional bonus material.

Please visit http://www.mometrix.com/bonus948/ftcemidgreng to access the information.